D0483417

Asperger's Syndrome –
THAT EXPLAINS EVERYTHING

DISCARD

of related interest

Developing College Skills in Students with Autism and Asperger's Syndrome
Sarita Freedman
Foreword by Tony Attwood
ISBN 978 1 84310 917 4
eISBN 978 0 85700 292 1

A Practical Guide for Teachers of Students with an Autism Spectrum Disorder in Secondary Education
Debra Costley, Elaine Keane, Trevor Clark and Kathleen Lane
ISBN 978 1 84905 310 5
eISBN 978 0 85700 646 2

Helping Students Take Control of Everyday Executive Functions
The Attention Fix
Paula Moraine
ISBN 978 1 84905 884 1
eISBN 978 0 85700 576 2

Teaching Theory of Mind
A Curriculum for Children with High Functioning Autism, Asperger's Syndrome, and Related Social Challenges
Kirstina Ordetx
Foreword by Susan J. Moreno
ISBN 978 1 84905 897 1
eISBN 978 0 85700 623 3

Autism and Flexischooling
A Shared Classroom and Homeschooling Approach
Clare Lawrence
Foreword by Dr Luke Beardon
ISBN 978 1 84905 279 5
eISBN 978 0 85700 582 3

Asperger Syndrome in the Inclusive Classroom
Advice and Strategies for Teachers
Stacey W. Betts, Dion E. Betts and Lisa N. Gerber-Eckard
Foreword by Peter Riffle
ISBN 978 1 84310 840 5
eISBN 978 1 84642 591 2

Addressing the Unproductive Classroom Behaviours of Students with Special Needs
Steve Chinn
ISBN 978 1 84905 050 0
eISBN 978 0 85700 367 7

Asperger's Syndrome –
THAT EXPLAINS EVERYTHING
Strategies for Education, Life and Just About
Everything Else

Stephen Bradshaw

Foreword by Professor Francesca Happé

Jessica Kingsley *Publishers*
London and Philadelphia

Crown copyright material is reproduced with the permission of the
controller of HMSO and the Queen's Printer for Scotland.

First published in 2013
by Jessica Kingsley Publishers
116 Pentonville Road
London N1 9JB, UK
and
400 Market Street, Suite 400
Philadelphia, PA 19106, USA

www.jkp.com

Copyright © Stephen Bradshaw 2013
Foreword copyright © Professor Francesca Happé 2013

All rights reserved. No part of this publication may be reproduced in any material
form (including photocopying or storing it in any medium by electronic means and
whether or not transiently or incidentally to some other use of this publication)
without the written permission of the copyright owner except in accordance with the
provisions of the Copyright, Designs and Patents Act 1988 or under the terms of a
licence issued by the Copyright Licensing Agency Ltd, Saffron House, 6–10 Kirby
Street, London EC1N 8TS. Applications for the copyright owner's written permission
to reproduce any part of this publication should be addressed to the publisher.

Warning: The doing of an unauthorised act in relation to a copyright work
may result in both a civil claim for damages and criminal prosecution.

Library of Congress Cataloging in Publication Data
A CIP catalog record for this book is available from the Library of Congress

British Library Cataloguing in Publication Data
A CIP catalogue record for this book is available from the British Library

ISBN 978 1 84905 351 8
eISBN 978 0 85700 702 5

Printed and bound in Great Britain

To my children and their children,
for they are the future

CONTENTS

Part 4 Students' and Parents' Views – Perception of Reality

FOREWORD

When I was an undergraduate studying Psychology, I came across two books about autism in a second-hand bookshop in Brighton; they profoundly affected my future. The first was an account by the mother of a child with autism, perhaps one of the first published. The second was by the head teacher of a special school, explaining 'one way through' that had worked with his pupils with autism. In both books I found real-life examples that conveyed far more about autism Spectrum Conditions (ASC) than my undergraduate textbooks.

Many, many years later, when I was lucky enough to have turned my fascination for autism into a research career, I met Stephen Bradshaw. He invited me down to Farleigh College to tell me about his plans to start a specialist school for pupils with Asperger Syndrome. There I met Andy Cobley, the very gifted and insightful head teacher of North Hill House, with whom Stephen worked closely for many years. Their enthusiasm for the pupils they worked with, their humour and humanity, were instantly winning.

I agreed to bring together and chair a steering committee for the new school. I had no expertise in the area of education, so this was a great opportunity to collect the wisdom of a number of people working with children or adults with ASC whom I had had the privilege to meet over the years. Through our meetings I learnt a huge amount from this expert group, and from Stephen and Andy. For example, my original thought that North Hill House could act as a 'pit-stop' to tune up the young people's social skills and launch them back into mainstream school, was naive. As members of the steering committee rightly predicted, parents who had seen their children suffer and get excluded from the wrong schools, were so relieved and delighted to see them receive informed and appropriate education at North Hill House, they were loath to relinquish their place there.

On some matters, of course, Stephen and I agreed to differ, in the friendliest of ways. One example is the relationship between Asperger Syndrome and ASC; for me the research evidence is overwhelmingly in support of considering Asperger's one pattern among many possible manifestations of ASC. For Stephen, as he discusses in this book, Asperger remains a special and distinct condition. What we do not disagree about is the need for education that really values and appreciates the different ways of thinking that these pupils show; the need for respectful translation between the 'neurotypical' and 'Aspie' ways of seeing and doing things.

Like those two early autism books that so captured my imagination, in this book, Stephen gives many examples of the challenges, joys and puzzles of working with pupils with ASC, specifically those fitting the Asperger profile. Stephen too is careful to emphasise that what he describes is just one way through, among many possible successful approaches. It is a way full of insight and warmth, and I am sure readers will appreciate and learn from it.

Professor Francesca Happé
Professor of Cognitive Neuroscience
MRC Social, Genetic and Developmental Psychiatry Centre
Institute of Psychiatry (PO 80), King's College,
Denmark Hill, London SE5 8AF

ACKNOWLEDGEMENTS

I would like to acknowledge the following for their encouragement, support and suggestions. None more so than Emma Wickham who has painstakingly worked through every word of the manuscript until it flows, makes some sense and is complete. To Professor Francesca Happé who has been my hero, support and inspiration in working with children with Asperger's Syndrome and was instrumental in assisting the development of the ethos in the schools. I thank my wife Sarah and all five children who have continually been supportive and tolerant of my moods and long hours of talking incessantly about the subject of Asperger's Syndrome.

I am indebted to the professionals I have worked with over the years who have provided support and encouragement when things didn't go as well as expected, especially Dianne Zaccheo, Des Walsh, Andy Chiffers, Paul Bradshaw and Bridget Waller who all epitomise the qualities needed to work with children with Asperger's Syndrome. To one member of staff who has worked with me since 1994, June Wood, who has those special qualities of empathy, hard work and loyalty.

To the parents and children that entrusted me with their future and put their trust in me, I thank you. I especially thank those students and parents who contributed to the book and gave their honest appraisal of how the experience was for them.

Last word as usual has to go to my mother who at 86 still ensures I have a clean hanky and have eaten well, and has asked me on a weekly basis over the last three years, 'Have you finished that book yet?' Well, Mum – here it is.

Preface

Terminology

When talking about children in schools and colleges, I have used the terms 'student' and 'young people' if they are aged over 16. These terms also cover children, boys and girls, pupils, learners, clients and residents, which are used in different settings. I have also occasionally used the term 'kids', which is not meant as a derogatory term but one that will include children, young people, students and pupils. The use of the word as a term for human children was first recorded in 1599, while by the 1840s a more widespread usage within informal language had been established, with variations such as 'kiddo' appearing towards the end of the nineteenth century.

It is also important to mention that in this book the personal pronoun 'he' also encompasses 'she', and is not meant to focus on males with Asperger's Syndrome. As explained in Chapter 3, the Syndrome affects just as many females as it does males, although this may not be reflected in the numbers that are actually diagnosed. Similarly, when talking about the general population, the terms 'people' and 'individuals' are used to indicate both males and females.

The term Asperger's Syndrome is often referred to without the apostrophe or the 's'. There is no right or wrong format, but it was important when starting my first school that we had a consistent approach throughout. I insisted that the term was always written with an apostrophe and with capital letters. I also insisted that 'Asperger' was pronounced with a hard 'g' as in 'burger' rather than the soft 'g' of 'merge', again so we started out with a consistent approach.

Asperger's Syndrome is often abbreviated to 'AS', while Autistic Spectrum Disorder is abbreviated to 'ASD'. There is also a move to use the term 'condition' rather than 'disorder', referring to the spectrum as Autistic Spectrum Condition, 'ASC'. Again, there is no correct way, although the move to positive language can only be positive. There is a glossary of terms and abbreviations used at the end of the book.

Chronology 1996–2009

July 1996 Ravenscroft School for dyslexic Students closes.

Sept 1996 Farleigh College started with 40 students, of which 30 were diagnosed with SpLD (dyslexia) and ten with Asperger's Syndrome. The school was based on the Farleigh Castle site at Farleigh Hungerford, near Bath. This was a leased building with a five year lease. It had previously been the school site of Ravenscroft, a school for students with dyslexia of which I was also Headteacher.

Sept 1999 Farleigh College was oversubscribed – 56 students with 20 SpLD and 36 with Asperger's Syndrome. North Hill House started with five new students on the North Parade site in Frome. This was a new school for students with Asperger's Syndrome.

Sept 2000 Farleigh Further Education College started on the Farleigh Hungerford site with 14 students aged 16–20. This was to meet the needs of the students who had attended Farleigh College and had reached the age of 16 and were considering further education courses. The Further Education College also received referrals directly into the college of students who previously had attended neither Farleigh College nor North Hill House.

Sept 2000 Farleigh College: AS students moved to a new site at Newbury Manor, near Mells, Somerset. (Tried to purchase the Farleigh Hungerford site at the end of the lease – due September 2001 – but the owner sold it. It is now the headquarters of Bath Rugby Club.) As I was unable to purchase the Farleigh Hungerford site, I purchased a new building with ten acres of land nine miles away.

Sept 2001 Vacated the Farleigh Hungerford site – Farleigh further Education College moved to Frome. Due to the end of the lease.

Oct 2002 The Priory Group acquired the three establishments on four sites. The organisation had grown and it was seen that to join a larger group with all the infrastructure would be beneficial and there was a demand for similar types of school nationwide.

Sept 2003 North Hill House moved to Stoneleigh, a new converted office block with single ensuite bedrooms. Farleigh Further Education College moved into the vacated North Parade site. Stoneleigh was a larger purpose-built site across the road from North Parade in Frome.

Sept 2003 Farleigh Further Education Swindon opened in Swindon due to Farleigh Further Education Frome being oversubscribed.

Sept 2004 The Rookery opened; an adult service for adults with Asperger's Syndrome, Radstock, near Bath. To provide a pathway and transition for students into employment or higher education.

Sept 2006–09 As part of the Priory Group, I opened schools for Asperger's Syndrome in Surrey and a school for autism in Hampshire as well as adult services for autism to re-create the 'Farleigh model' in different geographical areas.

Jan 2008–July 2009 Considered the expansion of the schools into Europe, Middle East and Far East under the Priory name.

July 2009 I left the Priory Group which then had 24 schools, colleges and adult services. (In 2002 it had three educational establishments.)

Sept 2009 I joined the Options Group as Executive Chairman. The group had schools, colleges and adult services for individuals with autism.

INTRODUCTION AND BACKGROUND

CHAPTER 1

ASPERGER'S
SYNDROME – WEIRD
OR WONDERFUL?

I noticed when one of our young people went into the local
town that they would stand at the edge of the road next to the
zebra crossing and wait until a car was coming and then step
out in front of it. When I asked, 'Why do you do that? Why don't
you just cross when there are no cars coming?' He replied, 'I've
been told to cross the road only at the zebra crossing and if
there aren't any cars coming it doesn't work, it's only some
lines on the road.'

The general public perception of individuals with Asperger's
Syndrome (AS) is often one of individuals who are rude, isolated,
strange, whose emotional and social development has not kept pace
with their academic and physical development. They will be thought
of as taking things very literally and showing no emotion. They are
often described as academically bright but socially inept. They will
be seen as the computer 'nerd' or someone who focuses upon their
special interest to the exclusion of all else, no matter how bizarre that
special interest is. The press and film industry want to portray them
as isolated people with no friends but with a savant skill that makes
them exceptional, the crackers of codes or having the ability to retain
a large amount of factual knowledge. We will explore the role of
the media in creating this stereotype in Chapter 4. The perception

may also be of someone who is exceptional with numbers and has a photographic memory.

So are these stereotypes true? As with all stereotypes, they are generalisations but there are aspects that may be true. However, my own experience of individuals with Asperger's Syndrome is that everyone is in some way different from every other one – they are as individual and different as the rest of us. Two individuals with Asperger's Syndrome may have completely different profiles but both still have Asperger's Syndrome.

There are, however, traits that run through all individuals with the Syndrome. These include the inability to read social cues correctly or understand the complex rules that make up society; a high level of anxiety that may become debilitating and manifests itself in different ways; an interest that may become an obsession; and a desire to be part of the social world of ours and have friends, to be 'normal', but a distinct difficulty in social communication. Individuals with Asperger's Syndrome see the world differently to the average person, and will react in different, unexpected and even unusual ways to events and stimuli that most people would take in their stride; they will refer to the rest of us as 'neuro-typical'. I will explore a whole range of these differences in a later chapter, but it might be useful to discuss just a few here. Physically, those with Asperger's Syndrome will often have no clear distinctive features. They may, however, seem different to other children because of the way they walk, or because of certain mannerisms or gestures, often repetitive. It is often referred to as a 'hidden syndrome', so members of the public or people in authority cannot understand why they don't just 'get it' and think they are rude or abrupt.

They certainly will have rituals, superstitions and routines that they have to follow or it becomes difficult for them to function through the day. They often have a rigidity of thought that will not let them accept things but want to go back over incidents until they are resolved to their own satisfaction. 'Let it be' or 'get over it' is not an option. Their vocabulary is often extensive and will mask other difficulties or make them appear that they are operating at a much higher level than they actually are.

People with Asperger's Syndrome are less likely to be recognised as having a problem like autism, and are more likely to be labelled bad or ill. At one of the schools there was boy who I would describe as classic Asperger's Syndrome – would not give any eye contact, rarely spoke as he didn't see the benefit, was highly intelligent, would dance on the disco floor all night on his own – but because he had not been diagnosed felt he certainly didn't have Asperger's Syndrome. I will explore the difficulties with diagnosis in Chapter 3.

They are likely to behave in ways which are considered by others to be unaccountable, odd and/or unacceptable and will have complete 'meltdowns' caused by what we would regard as minor or insignificant factors, such as not following the same routine, unexpected change, different colours. They are likely to be conspicuous by their social immaturity, which may be accompanied by an innocent and trustful manner. It is when someone with Asperger's Syndrome is involved in social situations that other people begin to understand just how different they may be. It has been described as if you are at a Bulgarian cocktail party where you don't understand the language or the social rules and have no signposts to help you know how you should behave and what is expected of you.

For example, those with Asperger's Syndrome tend to take spoken words at their face value. This is because one trait of Asperger's Syndrome can be the lack of a highly developed imagination. Those with Asperger's Syndrome tend to be very logical in their thought processes. This can create humorous or confusing situations as you can imagine:

The sign on the local laundrette stated, 'When light goes out please remove all clothes.'

The toilet signs on 'theme' restaurants or pubs also creates confusion. How can someone with Asperger's Syndrome work out what the symbol on the toilet door means and whether it is supposed to be male or female? On a recent holiday to Spain I noticed that the toilet signs looked very similar with both individuals dressed in traditional Spanish smocks both appearing to have dresses on, but the men's sign had a discreet moustache. I was totally bewildered.

They will often have what appear to be highly developed verbal skills, but while they may have large vocabularies and perfect grammar, they frequently find it difficult to actually put the words together as part of a 'normal' conversation. They are challenged by such things as metaphors, sarcasm and irony, because of the inherent illogical nature of these. And they find non-verbal communications, which make up a huge part of normal, everyday conversations, very difficult to interpret.

They are usually very good at processes that involve logical thinking, in particular programming and using computers. They also tend to be very single-minded, in the sense that they will frequently develop an extreme interest or an obsession in a particular subject and learn everything they can about it. The real issue, though, is that they are likely to fixate on a very particular aspect of their chosen subject, to the exclusion of everything else about that subject – for example, someone with Asperger's Syndrome might claim to have an interest in a particular football team which may involve learning the players' dates of birth and how far they live from the ground, but they have never watched the team play or have no awareness of how they are performing in any particular season.

They will also be inclined to want to talk about their particular chosen topic at length, rather than engage in the ebb and flow of normal conversation and do not pick up any non-verbal cues from other people whilst talking about their 'special' subject. People with Asperger's Syndrome also frequently have problems with emotions. They are often incapable of understanding that people apart from themselves have emotions, which in a social situation can cause significant problems.

Individuals with Asperger's Syndrome can also suffer from heightened anxiety, particularly in social situations or situations where there are high levels of sensory input, such as public speaking, plays, speeches and fairground rides. I have worked with children with Asperger's Syndrome who were able to speak to a large audience but were very anxious about an individual interview. What's more, they seem to deal with this anxiety in different ways to the 'norm'. Reactions to anxiety can be extreme – including tantrums, aggression and self-harm – and are often difficult for those who have no experience of Asperger's Syndrome to understand or cope with. One individual described the level of anxiety as akin to standing at the top of a multi-storey office block on the edge looking down and having that feeling all of the time.

The effects of Asperger's Syndrome can range from the relatively mild through to the extreme, and those who have Asperger's Syndrome may also have other problems. The Syndrome can be debilitating, when individuals would rather stay at home within their comfort zone than try something they are unsure of. However, I would argue that the lives of all people with Asperger's Syndrome can be made immeasurably better if they are provided with the appropriate education and support from an early age.

Hans Asperger, when he first described the group of children who were later called 'Asperger's Syndrome', thought that it was a syndrome that only affected boys but later realised that it also affects girls. Even now the ratio of males to females that have been diagnosed is quoted at 4:1.

It is my experience that the real ratio may be much lower, but gender stereotypes seem to come into play. That is, if a boy is becoming anxious and his behaviour deteriorates and his work is affected then it is usually followed up with some assessment. As the boy grows and becomes physically challenging and his behaviour deteriorates to such an extent that he can no longer function in a school setting, the diagnosis will be one of the routes that is explored. On the other hand if the girl becomes withdrawn, anxious and ultimately depressed it is often regarded as 'teenage angst' and ignored. Or it is misdiagnosed as an eating disorder or an anxiety disorder.

This is a book about my own experiences in education and the wider field, how I had a passion to make a difference to people's lives, a passion and interest that grew out of working with individuals with Asperger's Syndrome. It is about how I developed that passion into a model, a way of working with individuals with Asperger's Syndrome, how I convinced other people to get passionate about this group and to encourage financial institutions to invest in developing schools and colleges to meet their needs. I started my first school in 1996 and am still opening schools with different groups today, as the world has changed and its understanding of this fascinating syndrome has grown.

I certainly made lots of mistakes: there was no 'model' or 'template'. Previously, schools had focused on teaching children with 'classic autism' and included students with Asperger's Syndrome amongst these rather than making separate provision for them. I did not have access to any funding and had to generate any capital myself before investing it into the schools. The result was far from perfect, but what follows is an account of those trials and tribulations.

Hopefully the book will inspire others to work with this group. It is certainly a book that I would have welcomed when I started, an account of what worked with some pupils and what didn't. Most importantly it includes accounts from the students who were those guinea pigs and not only survived but went on to be able to take part in society and contribute to it. It is their struggle and achievements, however large or small, that I want to celebrate. Let me explain how this all began: working with individuals with Asperger's Syndrome.

Chapter 2

How I 'Caught' Asperger's Syndrome

Of course, you can't catch Asperger's Syndrome, but when I started working with this fascinating group of individuals I became totally obsessive about wanting to find out more and more about how they viewed the world and what difficulties they had. I read every book with Asperger's Syndrome in the title (there weren't that many in 1994) and went to every course or lecture on the subject and, of course, bored my family and anyone else that would listen about what I had discovered. I had found my passion and where I wanted to 'make a difference'.

> On completing an assembly on 'tolerance' and the need to live together and be tolerant of others' beliefs in the wake of September 11, I was approached by one of our students. 'I really enjoyed that assembly, sir', he stated, 'and do agree with you that we should be more tolerant... I think that all intolerant people should be shot.'

2.1 The concept, dream and passion. Stage one: the dream

So where did my interest and passion about working with individuals with Asperger's Syndrome come from, you may ask. I suppose you have to go back to when I started teaching in the 1970s, or even to my school days.

I took the 11-plus and went to a local grammar school. My parents had great expectations of what I wanted to do or be. I had only one focus and that was to be able to play football. I did enjoy school, but discovered that I could get away with doing the minimum and was able to focus on sport for most of my time. At the end of the first year all pupils were graded into streams for the rest of their time at school, so I made sure my end-of-year examination results placed me in the 'B' set, so I would not be an 'A' stream student with a high work ethic and high expectations, but not be in the lower streams and be dragged into the disruptive groups.

Life was getting easier towards the end of the sixties; the world was changing and becoming more tolerant of differences. Youth for the first time, through music, sport and influencing politics, seemed to gain a voice and the world was beginning to listen, or so we thought. I was very focused and single-minded in what I wanted to do and what I wanted to achieve – most people referred to it as a 'stubborn streak'. But I always wanted to work with children and always had an interest in others that see the world in a different way and wanted to make a difference.

I qualified from teachers' training college in Physical Education and Geography with a keen interest in children with Special Needs. I suppose we all have a soft spot for the underdog and have this desire to help where we can. My philosophy in education was developing, my football team had just fallen from grace and been relegated to Division Two for the first time in its history, the fading euphoria of the 1960s gave way to the problems of the 1970s: miners' strikes, three-day weeks and an education system that was still stuck in the previous century.

However, I had a real interest and desire to work with disadvantaged youngsters to understand their difficulties and see if there wasn't another way of working with them. At that time I was discouraged from going directly into a special school as soon as I had qualified as I would need to complete my probation year and special schools were not regarded as proper schools. They were seen as schools where the care model came first and education second. The cynics called it 'contain and entertain'. Even then I saw education in its complete form as a therapy and a way to increase self-confidence and self-esteem, lack of which held many children back.

Physical Education and Outdoor Pursuits offered an opportunity for young people to excel in areas that they hadn't failed at in the past and opportunity to get out of the classroom and for them to increase their self-confidence by learning new skills. The number of students who found the classroom environment stifling and oppressive yet excelled in the outdoors was many, and this shaped my view of teaching and how to deliver the curriculum.

I came from a generation where the pedagogic model was to deliver information to pupils sitting in rows and ask them to regurgitate this knowledge at the right time in examination conditions. There was no understanding of different learning styles or teaching styles. Many teachers prepared and taught a syllabus for one year and then repeated that year 'ad infinitum'.

After 18 months in a mainstream comprehensive school I was keen to 'cut my teeth' in a school for boys with behavioural difficulties who had also fallen foul of the law. These children had rejected the classroom, often had some learning difficulties or at least had missed out huge chunks of educational time, and also had a problem with accepting boundaries and discipline being imposed upon them. The school leaving age had just risen to 16 and children felt they were trapped in a system that didn't fit their own desires and aspirations, so they opted out. I was keen to develop a relationship with this group of youngsters, to engage them in activities where they didn't think or feel they were learning and the skills became relevant.

For the next eighteen years I served my apprenticeship in both independent and local authority special schools for children with behavioural difficulties as a teacher, curriculum coordinator, Head of Care and Deputy Headteacher. Many of these children who were diagnosed with 'Emotional and Behavioural Difficulties' also had a co-morbidity of learning difficulties, autism and attention deficit. But the philosophy then was, and in some areas still is, to develop programmes and models that focused on the behaviour exhibited rather than the causes of that behaviour and try and change that behaviour through behaviour modification. This always seemed to work initially with young people when they regarded the external rewards worth having, but unless they internalised these controls the change was short-lived. I have seen similar parallels with programmes developed for children with autism.

I then developed a thirst to understand more about this different condition. I did some research to see whether they were diagnosed differently and what the Local Authority did with them in terms of education. I was also keen to broaden my knowledge base to complement the experience I had gained by working with these unique children. I took an Open University degree in Social Science and Criminology, then a Master's degree in Educational Management, before studying for a Bachelor of Philosophy degree in autism.

I achieved my first headship in 1991 in a Local Authority school for children with Emotional and Behavioural Difficulties. It was evident that many of the pupils had learning difficulties and a few of them saw the world from a different perspective. These children I now know to have had Asperger's Syndrome.

It was evident that they didn't exist as a separate group and were either included as 'Behaviourally Difficult' or on the 'Spectrum', referring to the Autistic Spectrum.

2.2 Turning the dream into reality. Stage two: the reality

In 1994 I moved to an independent school for pupils with dyslexia as Headteacher and the group of youngsters that I felt could be described as having AS was even more significant in this school. I was keen to see if I could develop a different way of working with this particular group.

This opportunity arose when the owner of the school suddenly announced that she was going to close the school and move to France. I was asked if I would like to buy the school, something I had never considered. I had always worked for other people, happily receiving a salary and having a mortgage. The thought of running my own school and business and working for myself was exciting and scary. I got my accountant to have a look at the commercial side of the school and was advised that it was losing money and the likelihood of making it a success was slim. As usual I ignored all sensible advice and sought a bank loan to finance the purchase. Initially this proved more difficult that I thought, and approached every bank within 200 miles unsuccessfully.

I thought my business plan was sound and wondered why anyone was questioning my sanity. I wanted to set up a school for youngsters with Asperger's Syndrome, which was a condition that the world had only just accepted and very few had heard of. In business terms, there was no market, no group of students, no demand, and no Local Authority with this type of student seeking placement. I was a teacher with a great deal of experience, though very little of it with this group, and had to train a staff group in a model that no one had heard of. I had no business background although I'd always made money for other people at school and been able to market the school really well. I had no comparable price point in terms of fees so most of the learning process took place whilst doing the job. There were no other schools to learn from and no track record, so how could I fail!

I eventually found a bank some 250 miles away that would back me, but I had to have a charge on my house and raise 20 per cent of the loan in cash. So if this failed then I would have no house and no career and a debt to repay. I did have a couple of things going for me: I am not afraid of hard work, have never been a quitter and had a belief in what I was doing. I was fascinated by this group of young people and was certain that it would work.

I then applied to the Department for Education (I'll use the generic term as the government changed the name of the department as often as the government changed) for registration to start a school for 40 students with Asperger's Syndrome and was told that they did not exist as a separate group of young people. You have to remember that in 1996 this was very new and little-used term. The DSM (Diagnostic Statistical Manual) had only included the diagnosis of Asperger's Syndrome for the first time in 1995 in DSM-IV, and the British Psychological Society also only started using the term in 1995. But the DfE allowed me to have five students with Asperger's Syndrome out of a population of 40, with the other students having Specific Learning Difficulties (dyslexia). I then started the school with 35 pupils: 5 with AS and 30 with SpLD. This was Farleigh College, the first school in the country, and so far as I am aware the first globally, specifically set up to meet the needs of children and young people with Asperger's Syndrome. I did later learn that Hans Asperger had set up his own school to work with this type of children but unfortunately it was bombed at the end of the Second World War by the allies.

I became fascinated by Asperger's Syndrome. Indeed, obsessed with it – ironic, given that the condition itself usually involves compulsive and obsessive behaviour. As an aside, the more you learn about Asperger's Syndrome, the more you tend to see traits of it in yourself and in many of those around you.

I read every article which featured Asperger's Syndrome, went to every conference where it was mentioned and talked incessantly to colleagues about this unique group of people. As I previously stated I took a degree in autism – the thirst for knowledge was insatiable. However, the time when I really started to learn was when I started to try to look at the world through the eyes of someone with Asperger's Syndrome.

Once you start to do this then you actually begin to comprehend the difficulties these individuals have with 'our' world and with its complex and often bizarre social rules and differences.

As a teacher, it became obvious that the education system has been set up to support and to perpetuate these social roles and differences. I began trying to identify what had happened to these youngsters with Asperger's Syndrome in an educational sense up to that point, and how a better educational system might be created to help them develop to their fullest potential.

It became clear that at that time, the mid-1990s, no-one saw Asperger's Syndrome children as being different from any other group of children with Special Education Needs.

I believed differently. I saw, and still see, autism and Asperger's Syndrome as two completely separate syndromes, although clearly with potential overlaps. This debate continues today and with DSM-V and the discussion of whether to include AS into Autistic Spectrum Disorders (ASD) the debate will continue for a few years yet. Labels are important in terms of resources but it is more important that the young person's needs are met and the provision is appropriate.

After a year, the DfE made its first inspection of the College, and promptly gave us the go-ahead to take in 12 pupils with Asperger's Syndrome. While this was a step in the right direction, I was not convinced that the integration of two groups with such clearly defined separate needs was the way forward.

The model I was hoping to develop with both groups is that they would develop their understanding of each other. The pupils with Asperger's Syndrome would develop and practise their social skills with the pupils with dyslexia and the dyslexic pupils would develop different learning strategies from the other group. This was not the case, however. For the first time in their life the pupils with dyslexia had a group that had lower self-confidence and were more vulnerable, so the pupils with Asperger's Syndrome became victims and the social skills were not learnt by osmosis but needed to be taught and practised in a safe environment in a structured way over and over again. I therefore had to think again and develop a school within a school. The group of students with Asperger's Syndrome needed to start with individual tuition and single bedrooms that were ensuite, which had not been the norm in special schools previously. I then went about designing a separate residential unit, improved the staffing to 1:1 and set up a bespoke classroom programme. The learning process had commenced, but it was also evident that each student was completely different so had to have a completely individual programme yet have access to the National Curriculum and external examinations. I made some obvious mistakes, thinking that vulnerable children with Asperger's Syndrome would not be able to cope with large groups such as assemblies or in the dining room and thus we allowed the students to be taught individually and eat separately. I quickly learnt that in order to develop social skills and strategies of survival and independence then all the students had to be exposed to what was, after all, a normal occurrence, of meeting other people in small and larger groups. So the programmes would have a gradual approach to 'normality' or what I assumed was the norm. At least our students would be exposed to eating in a McDonald's restaurant and going to a sporting or musical occasion, in other words giving them choice.

Farleigh College grew quickly and became oversubscribed with pupils with Asperger's Syndrome. The choices I then faced were:

- to continue as before

- to convert Farleigh College to taking only pupils with Asperger's Syndrome

- to set up another, completely new, school.

I decided to launch a new school, called North Hill House, which was the original name of the building, just for students with Asperger's (although I did later make Farleigh College a school purely for Asperger's Syndrome). As far as I knew then, and as far as I know today, this was the first time that anyone had ever taken the decision to set up a school purely for pupils with Asperger's Syndrome from scratch.

It was both an exciting and a terrifying experience. I had no model on which to base a school, just my experience of working with these youngsters over the last six or seven years (and with pupils with Special Educational Needs for the last 27 years). I did, though, have an excellent staff team that has grown and developed through the birth of Farleigh and lived through the pain and thrills of working with a complete new group of students.

Over the next five years the schools 'grew like topsy', ending up with three educational establishments on four freehold sites.

From the outset, I had clear ideas on what would not work. However, I was far less certain about what would work. To help me, I brought in leading experts, notably Dr Francesca Happé, who gave me huge amounts of invaluable advice. Dr Happé created a steering committee with some eminent practitioners and researchers: Prof. Pat Howlin, Pam Yates, Dr Peter Carpenter, Brian Evans from the National Autism Society (NAS) and Julia Cooke, an experienced ex-special school Headteacher.

I also approached the University at Bath, who were advertising a Teacher Company Scheme with a grant from the Department of Trade and Industry. The purpose of the scheme was to link in the academics of the universities with industrial companies so that they would benefit from each other's skills by placing academics from the university into the production process of the company. When I first applied I was told that 'educational establishments' were not industrial companies. I then had to explain that I thought they were: we had a raw material, a product that we were hoping to produce and had to be commercial. I also created a company name, Aspergers.co, that would not only have schools in but in future years would be able also to provide advice and consultancy to others. Aspergers.co was accepted into the scheme and became the first educational company to join. The purpose of the pilot scheme was to develop and produce an e-learning programme for the staff at the school that could be accredited by the university. I appointed a project leader and worked closely through a pilot scheme to develop the e-learning programme in working with children with Asperger's Syndrome. The university used the model for more of its courses, developing certificate, diploma and degree level courses that were first piloted at the school.

The training of the staff would be crucial within a new school and essential to get right for a new group of students. From the start, I wanted to create a school and an educational programme that would be flexible enough to respond to the individual needs of the students and also to the latest research. At the same time, it had to be structured enough to provide the students with the solid framework that they needed – Asperger's Syndrome children (and adults) are very logical, and respond well to structure.

Many of the students with Asperger's Syndrome had previously been placed either in mainstream schools, schools for behavioural difficulties, Speech and Language units or in schools for pupils with autism. There was a feeling that the child with Asperger's Syndrome just didn't fit into any school, which given the nature of the Syndrome was hardly surprising.

This was not just Local Education Authority thinking – many educational experts felt that the number of pupils with Asperger's Syndrome did not warrant any separate provision. Other professionals did not necessarily accept a diagnosis of Asperger's, preferring other labels.

However, I have to admit that at that time I was very naïve in my approach to and my knowledge of Asperger's Syndrome. Obviously, I was aware of the literature describing it, having adopted the works of Frith, Happé and Attwood as my bibles, and I had done some basic Inset (In-service Education and Training) work with the staff group.

The vision I had was the creation of an establishment which was able to meet the needs of students with Asperger's Syndrome by offering a 'wrap-around' approach. What I mean by 'wrap-around' approach is that everything is focused on the child to lower their anxiety; it is structured and predictable. The focus is purely to lower the child's anxiety and engage with the child. If the child wants to sit on the floor to do his or her mathematics and use a red pencil then this approach is acceptable, though it may be challenged if the child is still doing that after a year. Once the child is engaged and the anxiety lowered then the individual programme is negotiated. The programme will then have 'negotiated and non-negotiated' aspects to it; this I will explore in more detail later in the book. The proposed school had to be able to be flexible enough to meet individual needs, whatever they might be. At the same time, structure and routine would be necessary to reduce anxiety levels, and change had to be kept to a minimum.

It was also important that I kept abreast of any new research in AS and that I ensured that the structures and working practices could adopt valuable new ideas – if they benefited the students.

More than that, I wanted to be able to influence research as well as respond to it, so providing a link between practice and theoretical research. The link I had developed with Dr Francesca Happé and her PhD students at the Maudsley Hospital in London allowed research links to be forged between her department and the school.

The main thrust of my vision for the new school was attention to detail. I believed that if we could get the little things in place, then the large things would follow.

It was at this point that I tentatively started to share my ideas with other individuals who were involved in research on Asperger's Syndrome or who were working with people who had it. I gathered as much information as I could about youngsters with Asperger's Syndrome and about how people were working with them and the theories about how best to educate them.

At that time there was very little specifically on Asperger's Syndrome – most of the research and practical work was directed at autism and the autistic. A few schools had considered taking these children, and when I talked to others I was often told, 'Oh yes, we've one of those', but that hardly qualified those schools to present themselves as catering for Asperger's Syndrome, although many claimed they did.

I visited as many schools as was possible; but, given that none of them had been set up from scratch to solely accommodate pupils with Asperger's Syndrome, my visits and my other research did not provide me with much to work with.

I was going to have to develop and codify my own ideas, then put them into practice and learn by trial and error. It was exciting and scary – and I was certainly opening myself up to being shot down.

I decided that I had to start with the physical aspects of the school. I wanted a building that was within reach of Farleigh College and that was also on the edge of a town. A position on the outskirts of a community was important because I wanted the opportunity for students to be involved in the life of the community and to be able to practise their social skills in real situations. I did not want them to be isolated.

The building had to be large enough to provide living accommodation for up to 30 pupils and with suitable classrooms, but not too large to appear impersonal, intimidating or institutional. Commercially it also had to work. I was not supported by anyone with capital; any borrowing was to be done from the banks. I had not discovered the world of venture capital or private equity at this time. I felt then that the optimum size for a school with students with Asperger's Syndrome was between 30 and 40, but that there must also be the opportunity to break groups down to allow individual and small-group work to take place.

The ideal building would be an attractive one, in order to impress prospective Local Education Authorities (LEAs) and parents, yet one that was functional.

Quite a tall order – I had no idea whether such a building actually existed.

After some 18 months and a great deal of house-hunting, I saw North Hill House advertised for sale in the newspaper. I immediately realised that the building and location were ideal for our project.

North Hill House, which is in Frome, Somerset, and about 11 miles away from Bath, had been the headquarters of the huge dairy company, Dairy Crest; previously it had been the council offices. My first impressions were that it was great, although I quickly discovered that, as an office building, it did not have many bathrooms or medical rooms.

What it was, though, was a building that had been set up to receive information from all the company's factories and channel it into a central computer system. The access, server and wiring were all in place, with 40 phone lines coming into the building and three phone points in every room. That meant we would easily be able to have a sophisticated computer system up and running from day one – perfect for a student body which is almost without exception obsessed with computers, and perfect for the staff who would be teaching them.

In December 1998, I heard that our bid had been accepted. The next step was planning permission. A major issue was the question of how the residents of Frome would react to the idea of having a school for pupils with Asperger's Syndrome on their doorstep.

Explaining what Asperger's Syndrome was to the planners and residents was not easy. However, I was able to reassure all concerned that children with Asperger's Syndrome were well behaved youngsters who happen to see the world in a different way to the rest of us, who are vulnerable and anxious and who should be given the opportunity to reach their full potential in a secure environment. I ignored that they may become agitated and aggressive at times and focused on the positives.

I was also able to point out the positive effects that our proposed school would have on Frome, including creating a number of new jobs and bringing parents and families of students to the town.

Well, I got the 'change of use' planning permission. The dream – and all the risks it involved, financial and otherwise – was fast developing into a reality.

I had the building and permission to turn it into a school. It was April 1999. By September 1999, I wanted to have everything in place to open the school, including staff, pupils and a building that was fit for purpose. The time-scale was extremely tight.

Fortunately the previous occupants had carried out a great deal of work and the building was in excellent condition. An architect was employed and I set to work on the internal designs.

I felt that it was also important that we met various other regulatory bodies – the Department for Education, the Social Services Department, the Fire Department and the Environmental Health Agency. I decided to invite all these agencies to the site before we made any plans or alterations. Fortunately, I already had a good relationship with these groups and I was able to ask them for advice before starting any work.

Finally, it was time to put my ideas into practice.

2.3 Getting it right – the environment influencing behaviour. Stage three: the school design

I was keen to ensure that the rooms were bright and colourful. They should meet the required size for inspection purposes but still provide a pleasant learning environment. At the start of the project, I also believed that all our bedrooms should be single rooms, due to the difficulty that pupils with Asperger's Syndrome have with issues such as sharing, settling at night and developing friendships.

The issue of bedrooms, however, is an excellent example of how you must always be ready to modify your approach when dealing with pupils with Asperger's Syndrome.

I had planning permission to convert all the rooms I planned to use as bedrooms into singles, but the work was to take two years. That meant that when the first potential pupil looked around the school, while we were still working on converting the building, most of the bedrooms were still doubles.

He reacted extremely positively to the idea of sharing a double room, saying that he had never had a friend to share with. So I shelved the idea of changing all the rooms to singles and decided to leave some as doubles.

I believe that it was vitally important that we got the school environment right from the start. Fortunately, my wife is an interior designer. At very little cost, she was commissioned to design and decorate the internal aspects of the school.

She spent a great deal of time speaking to professionals who work with pupils with Asperger's Syndrome and also talking to both youngsters and adults with Asperger's Syndrome about their preferences, their thoughts and opinions about possible design and colour schemes.

The whole school had to be a coherent visual experience, which supported and underlined the ethos and the work being carried out with the pupils. I was also keen to ensure that the environment was a calming influence, aesthetically pleasing but functional, too.

The results were stunning. Each room had its own individual colour scheme and individual theme. No longer did the magnolia colour scheme exist that is used to decorate our schools and public buildings making the maintenance easy and swift. What was evident when pupils looked around the school was how pleased they were to see that the bedrooms were all different from each other and also from the rooms in the rest of the school.

It was important that each pupil's bedroom was 'special' to them, that they felt it was theirs, and that they were comfortable with it. They were encouraged to bring items from home to personalise them, which usually meant special blankets, duvet covers or cuddly toys.

Obviously, the furniture was chosen to be hard-wearing and functional as well as aesthetically pleasing. But it was also important, when designing double bedrooms, that there were two sets of everything – wardrobes, lockers, chairs, tables, everything.

It is vitally important that pupils with Asperger's Syndrome who are sharing bedrooms are given their own space and their own furniture. Children with Asperger's Syndrome have issues with sharing facilities with others.

So in each shared bedroom, each student had their own notice board, which held copies of their individual timetables, their strategies for coping and visual prompts and reminders.

Moving beyond bedrooms, the physical aspects of the wider school were equally vitally important.

Years of experience of educating children with Asperger's Syndrome in a residential environment had taught me a number of things. For example, water and Asperger's Syndrome can often be alien to each other, and they may have to be coaxed to come together. Hygienic toilets and bathrooms were essential. Bathrooms, toilets and showers had to have floor coverings that were welded to the walls, so there was no opportunity for water to go anywhere else than where it should.

While some degree of privacy is vital for AS youngsters, in designing the bathrooms for the new school I saw it as vital that private bathrooms remained accessible to staff and did not become rooms in which pupils could barricade themselves. This was resolved by having all doors on double hinges so that they could be opened both ways if necessary and able to be unlocked by the staff in case of emergency.

Children with Asperger's Syndrome are often inveterate tinkerers, and there is always a danger that they might fiddle with or take apart anything they can get their hands on. That means that temperature regulators for showers have to be in separate rooms, to ensure that pupils cannot scald themselves or others by changing the settings. Similarly, toilets need cisterns that are boxed away from prying eyes or fingers.

Classrooms had to be designed in such a way as to allow for both different teaching styles and different learning styles. It was important that students could be taught individually but have an opportunity to work with one other student and also in a larger group. Access to computers for youngsters with Asperger's Syndrome is vital not only as a learning aid but as part of lowering their anxiety. It was going to be essential to give students access without it feeding an obsession – in other words the computer was to be used to assist and not hinder learning.

The classrooms would have to feature individual booths so that we could follow some of the principles of the TEACCH programme (TEACCH – Treatment and Education of autistic and related

Communication handicapped CHildren – is an educational system first created at the University of North Carolina in 1966). They would also have to have a computer workstation for each child, as well as tables that could be set out singly, in pairs and in groups, as and when required.

Rooms assigned for teaching obviously needed to be big enough to cope with class sizes of up to six students but had to offer flexible use of space, including the possibilities for 'distraction-free' areas to be created when needed.

There would need to be equipment that facilitated the visual presentation of instructional material. Interactive white boards were just being introduced into the educational environment and it was essential that these were a part of the resource available to the teacher.

The rooms needed to be bright, airy, warm, accessible and colourful as well as near to the toilets and not difficult to find. There needed to be rooms available for withdrawal and for use by the therapists employed by the school. Rooms were required for meetings and reviews. All this had to comply with the Department for Education and Employment's guidelines for designing a special school as well as the care standards of the social services.

It was also essential that I clearly understood how the students moved around the building, how they got from their bedroom to the lounge, or from their classroom to the dining room or playground. We spent a great deal of time producing flow diagrams to highlight how students got from A to B and who they were likely to meet and where the 'hot spots' were during the day. The corridors were areas where confrontations occurred and students became highly anxious about their ability to navigate a building without meeting students who were likely to hinder their journey. I did discover that there was a natural flow to many buildings and an optimum size for corridors: too wide and students went from wall to wall, too narrow and they bumped into everyone coming the opposite direction. Enough room to pass people coming the other way was ideal, two metres in width if possible. This just highlighted the level of detailed planning that was required to be put into their learning programmes.

I now had the building. The next step was to recruit staff members who would be just as committed and dedicated, and who would be able to share the vision. Given the fact that the staff had to be fully trained and up to speed with the ethos of our new schools before the first students arrived, it was a race against the clock.

It was my intention to provide flexible timetables and programme content, but structured for the individual. I wanted to monitor and 'trouble-shoot' individual problems as seen from the perspective of the individual.

This became the 'template' for developing schools for students with Asperger's Syndrome and I used it through developing and setting up all the Priory schools and latterly within the Options Group and with a new school run by Piscari that I have helped design and set up in Cambridge.

I decided that it was important to get all the systems in place and the staff trained before admitting too many students. Consequently, although we were oversubscribed with referrals, I kept the numbers down to five students in the first six months and 11 in the next 12 months. This didn't make the work any easier but did allow the staff team to develop individual programmes for the students.

At that time the Department for Education would not register a school until it had five students and the Local Authorities would not send students to a school unless it had been registered and thus inspected. I was able to talk to the Local Authorities that used Farleigh College and explain what I was doing setting up a new provision and fortunately I was able to persuade five Local Authorities to place children under the proviso that we would obtain registration and approval within the first 12 months.

This we achieved.

2.4 Reaching more students. Stage four: growth

At the same time, I was being approached by parents to consider extending the age limit for our students at Farleigh College past 18. At that time, although children were able to stay at Farleigh College and North Hill House until they were 18, it was anticipated that they would return to the home area for further education at 16. I was keen that all the excellent work we had started in these schools was not undone by any available unsuitable provision at 16.

I then started to consider how to develop a post-16 service. The funding at that time, 1999, was from the Further Education Funding Council (FEFC). Once again I looked for a suitable building within the town that could provide the residential base for a group of students. I already had strong links with the local large FE College in Trowbridge, and they allowed me to purchase individual courses for the students and rented me a group of three classrooms that would provide a base within the college for the prospective students. I approached the FEFC who agreed to inspect our premises and look through the documentation and the model we were proposing.

The inspection went well and I was told that we could start at the beginning of September 2000. However, the setting up of the sixth form college became extremely complicated, mainly due to the lack of clarity of its funder. The registration and funding came from a central government agency, the FEFC (Further Education Funding Council), which later became the LSC (Learning Skills Council), and is now the YPLA (Young Person's Learning Agency). They did not have a clear mandate for special needs nor were they supportive of 'new' colleges. It certainly was not easy to negotiate with them or work out what their aims were. So once again there was a need clearly identified, and we were willing to meet that need for young people over the age of 16, but the registration and funding were extremely confusing.

Suffice to say, despite numerous difficulties I eventually got funding and the college started, though it did take six months to work through this and we had already accepted a group of students that we were working with. The college started as Farleigh Further Education College at the beginning of September 2000 with 14 students, again the first college designed specifically for students with Asperger's Syndrome.

Despite this difficult start the college has been oversubscribed each year it has been open. Farleigh Further Education College Frome now has over 75 students on six residential sites working with three mainstream Further Education Colleges. The demand for places meant I was able to open another new college in Swindon under the same name.

2.5 Making the project sustainable. Stage 5: consolidation

Farleigh Education Group by 2002 had three separate educational establishments on four different freehold sites catering for over 80 students and was growing year on year. I was still managing the group from a converted garage. I was attracting the interests of healthcare companies that were backed by private equity. The organisation was growing; commercially it was doing well but expanding at such a rate that the debt was expanding with every new venture. I had a decision to make, either to reduce the debt by bringing in a business partner and creating a 'central office' support facility or to join another group that shared the same ideals and passion. At this time I was approached by a number of healthcare groups that were interested in the schools becoming part of their group. Previously schools groups had not been seen as good business models and there was no track record of other groups or individual schools joining healthcare groups.

Farleigh Education Group joined the Priory Group in October 2002. Priory had become involved superficially in special education, having three schools with pupils with behavioural difficulties that were struggling to develop a cohesive approach. The Farleigh schools doubled the size of the education segment overnight and I joined the Priory as Managing Director of Priory Education Service with the brief to grow the education business. This basically allowed me to develop three segments within the education division, one for Behavioural, Emotional and Social Difficulties (BESD), one for autism (ASD) and one for Asperger's Syndrome (AS). Over the next five years I grew the educational division from six schools to 24 schools, either by opening new schools or by acquiring schools within the three segments. Priory grew to become the largest special education group in the country, and the educational division was becoming its largest part. I was also able to provide a transition from the FE Colleges that I had set up into adult services, providing clear pathways for students into adulthood or employment opportunities. In 2007 I was also asked to look at the possibility of taking the Priory Education name into special education overseas. This was an exciting opportunity but unfortunately coincided with the world economic downturn and the reluctance of companies to invest in new projects. I left the Priory Group in July 2009, at a time when the education segment was still growing and opening new schools and developing new services. However, I felt it was time for a new challenge and wanted to see if I could do the same with other groups.

In September 2009 I was asked to join another education group, this time as Executive Chairman of the Options Group. It had lost its way somewhat, having had a clear vision from its owner and built some excellent schools and colleges, but unfortunately had not thought of how to market and fill these schools. Thus the amount of debt in the business was difficult to repay. The shareholders thought it had tremendous potential and would back a new management team. This was another challenge I would relish. In the last two years the group has started to flourish both operationally and commercially. It now has a clear purpose and strategy and although the majority of schools are for classic autism it will be no surprise to hear that they are moving into High Functioning Autism (HFA) and Asperger's Syndrome (AS).

I also run my own consultancy company, Aspergers.co, and I have been asked numerous times to provide advice and support either for firms that would like to open or purchase schools or for groups that had opened schools and then found themselves in difficulties. One such group was Piscari, who owned a pre-prep and special school in Cambridge. They had opened the special school but were not sure whether it should be for children with ASD or AS and had admitted their first pupil within the first month. Unfortunately they didn't admit any more children and the Local Authorities were unclear what types of children the school was catering for.

I set about using the template that I had first used for North Hill House, redefining the purpose and structure of the school, changing the management team and working closely with Local Authorities to meet their needs and the needs of the students being referred to the school. It was important that it followed the same model and developments as before.

The school took 20 students in the following year, registered to take residential pupils and increased the registration with the Department for Education. The relationship with the Local Authorities improved to such an extent that students were directly referred from the Authority whereas before they had been referred via the parent. Commercially the school was also sustainable. The owners now feel confident that they can grow the school from this point on, though only time will tell.

I feel it is important to share the trials and tribulations that I and the team went through to establish the number of schools we did. The learning process was at times painful and there was a little bit of 'trial and error', but if this book assists one parent or one member of staff to understand that others have struggled like they are doing and that it is a difficult job but very rewarding, then the purpose of the book will have been met.

CHAPTER 3

WHAT IS ASPERGER'S SYNDROME?

3.1 What do different people think Asperger's Syndrome is?

We can all see different characteristics of Asperger's Syndrome in ourselves. The following of routines for most of us reinforces staying in our comfort zones. However, coming out of those routines and comfort zones for us will not create levels of anxiety that are debilitating, unlike the individuals with Asperger's Syndrome. Lorna Wing stated:

> All the features that characterise Asperger's Syndrome can be found in varying degrees in the normal population. (Wing 1996, p.32)

Hans Asperger (1944, p.74) had previously stated:

> We are convinced, then, that autistic people have their place in the organism of the social community. They fulfil their role well, perhaps better than anyone else could, and we are talking of people who as children had the greatest difficulties and caused untold worries to their care-givers.

As I stated in Chapter 1, perhaps the greatest difficulty with understanding Asperger's Syndrome, in my experience, is that every person with Asperger's Syndrome is in some way different from every other person with Asperger's Syndrome, even if there appears to be a common thread of a distinct difficulty in social communication and heightened levels of anxiety. When one attempts to describe Asperger's Syndrome it is only the tip that is described, as each individual is different and may not have any traits that another person with Asperger's has. The analogy that I often use is the Indian spice tray, which will contain all the spices we use to cook our curries. They may be coriander, cumin, garam masala, turmeric, saffron, cardamom pods, tarragon, mace, cloves, cinnamon, fenugreek, mustard seeds, salt, peppercorn, chillies, ginger, fennel, lemon grass, the list is endless. We use what spices we think will give us a certain taste and strength of flavour. We all recognise the dish and that it is a curry, but we can also recognise the tastes of different ones. We also sub-categorise curries into different types, whether they are Rogan Josh, Tandoori, Korma or whatever. Each curry will be different depending upon the combination of spices we use, but we do not use all the spices in any one, nor in the same amounts. We change these depending upon the outcome we intend. The analogy with individuals with Asperger's Syndrome is that each individual with Asperger's will have different symptoms, characteristics of differing strengths, and although there are common themes each one is individual.

So what is Asperger's Syndrome, which the Americans often refer to as Asperger's Disorder? Asperger's Syndrome is a developmental disorder which affects how people who have it perceive the world around them, how their brains and nervous systems process information and how they relate to other people. In practical terms, someone with Asperger's Syndrome will often find it a challenge to function in general society for a number of reasons.

However, with the right education and support, many people with Asperger's Syndrome can meet and beat that challenge.

> People with autism desperately need guides to instruct and educate them so they will survive in the social jungle. (Grandin 1996, p.95)

The effects of Asperger's Syndrome can range from the relatively mild through to the extreme, and those who have the Syndrome may also have other problems. However, I would argue that the lives of all people with Asperger's Syndrome can be made immeasurably better if they are provided with the appropriate education and support from an early age.

Asperger's Syndrome existed before Hans Asperger first described it – indeed, it has almost certainly existed for as long as mankind itself. Some experts have speculated that many famous people throughout history may have had the condition – including George Orwell, Albert Einstein, Isaac Newton, Jane Austen, Vincent van Gogh and many others. There is considerable argument about any list of historic figures who might have had Asperger's Syndrome, and it is difficult at present to imagine how it might be proved or disproved.

However, there are many famous people alive today who reportedly have Asperger's Syndrome or who have said openly that they believe they have it. Some include Bobby Fisher, Bob Dylan, Robin Williams, Bill Gates, Daryl Hanna and Gary Numan.

It has been argued that in the past, before our modern-day obsession with labelling people began, people with Asperger's Syndrome would have been regarded as odd or eccentric, but would not have faced the same stigma that they do today. Indeed, their peculiar abilities may often have been welcomed. For example, research suggests that Asperger's Syndrome runs in families, and that in families where members have Asperger's Syndrome there are higher than average numbers of individuals with highly developed mathematical or engineering skills.

I knew I was different from my high school peers. I just couldn't work out what I was doing wrong. (Grandin 1996, p.179)

Temple Grandin also goes on to describe that she believes many discoveries and inventions would not have happened if it were not for the autistic mind.

This highlights that people with Asperger's Syndrome can play a useful role in society, and may at times make phenomenal contributions to it. Simply having Asperger's Syndrome does not stop people from learning and developing their knowledge and skills, although it does make the whole educational process more complicated to navigate.

Granted, some of those I have worked with will never be able to take their place in the wider world of work. But many will, so long as they have the understanding and support of those around them. Some will in fact go on to make remarkable contributions, not simply finishing school, but going to university and getting degrees and even doctorates before embarking on successful and fulfilling careers, as is shown later in Chapter 10 by the responses from individuals who have been through the schools.

Asperger's Syndrome is often classified as a form of autism, or on the Autistic Spectrum. This classification is partly because the two disorders share some common symptoms, partly because they appear to have some kind of genetic link and partly through an accident of history: they were first described within a year of each other, and in both of those first scholarly articles, variants of the word autism were used.

Many experts, however, including myself, actually believe Asperger's Syndrome is a completely separate disorder, which may have some common causes, but which is very definitely not the same as 'classic' autism.

From the educational point of view, I would always view autism and Asperger's Syndrome as completely separate, although it is clear that there is some overlap between them. As I have stated before, perhaps the greatest difficulty with understanding Asperger's Syndrome, in my experience, is that every person with Asperger's Syndrome is in some way different from every other person with Asperger's Syndrome.

Recent studies using techniques such as MRI scanners (Magnetic Resonance Imaging), which allow scientists to examine brain activity, seem to support the idea that Asperger's Syndrome is not a form of autism. When scientists have asked autistic people and those classified as having Asperger's Syndrome to perform a range of tasks, it appears that the Asperger's Syndrome subjects will use different parts of the brain to process information compared with those with autism.

The situation is further complicated, however, by the fact that Asperger's Syndrome and autism seem to have some sort of common genetic link. Both appear to run in families, and it is not uncommon for a family tree that includes one or more individuals with Asperger's Syndrome to also have individuals with autism, and vice versa.

In some cases, I believe that it is possible for someone to have both Asperger's Syndrome and autism; I would certainly argue that I have come across a number of students of whom this is true.

The question of whether Asperger's Syndrome is a sub-set of autism or a different but related condition is one which many experts are constantly arguing over. But then, the whole issue of what is autism, what causes it and whether a whole range of developmental disorders should be put under the heading of autism or not is perplexing many in the field.

3.2 Brief history of autism and Asperger's Syndrome

Leo Kanner and Hans Asperger were both Austrian physicians who wrote their papers within a year of each other, Kanner in 1943 and Asperger in 1944. So why was there such a delay in the English-speaking world accepting this syndrome? Probably one of main reasons was that Leo Kanner moved to America and wrote his paper in English in 1943 and Hans Asperger was living in Austria and writing in German in 1944. Writing in German at the end of the Second World War would not have been very popular and only when the paper was translated into English did anyone start to discuss the findings.

As a result, to the English-speaking world, the term Asperger's Syndrome is a relatively new one. Indeed, it was not until the late 1990s that the UK authorities actually finally accepted that it existed.

Asperger was born on a farm in Hausbrunn just outside Vienna on 18 February 1906 and he died on 21 October 1980. He was the elder of two sons and may have had the Syndrome himself – he had difficulty finding friends and was considered a lonely, remote child. He was talented in language; in particular he was interested in the Austrian poet Franz Grillparzer, whose poetry he would frequently quote to his uninterested classmates. He also liked to quote himself and often referred to himself from a third-person perspective.

Asperger studied medicine in Vienna and practised at the University Children's Hospital there. He became a doctor in 1932 and married in 1935, having five children. He continued to study children suffering from the problem and write about them until his death in 1980. Asperger died before his identification of this pattern of behaviour became widely recognised. The first person to use the term Asperger's Syndrome was the eminent British psychiatrist and researcher Lorna Wing. Her paper, 'Asperger's Syndrome: A clinical account' was published in 1981 and challenged the previously accepted model of autism presented by Leo Kanner. Asperger's papers were only translated into English in 1989, one of which appeared in Uta Frith's (1991) book. Unlike Kanner, Hans Asperger's findings were ignored in the English-speaking world in his lifetime.

Near the end of the Second World War Asperger opened a school for children with autistic psychopathy, with Sister Victorine Zak. The school was bombed towards the end of the war, Sister Victorine was killed, the school destroyed and much of Asperger's early work was lost. So maybe we were not the first school to open for children with Asperger's Syndrome.

Indeed, when I first put forward the idea of developing an educational programme designed to help children with Asperger's Syndrome realise their full potential, the educational authorities claimed there were no children with Asperger's Syndrome in the UK. Having already had considerable experience of running a school for children with learning difficulties and developmental problems, I knew differently. Ironically, however, the official attitude – that Asperger's Syndrome did not exist – made it much easier for us to set up our first school specialising in educating Asperger's Syndrome children.

As mentioned, one of the reasons it has taken so long for the English-speaking world to accept the idea of Asperger's Syndrome is the fact that he was writing for a scholarly journal published in what was then the Greater German Reich, towards the end of the Second World War. Asperger's original paper was published in the *Archiv fur Psychiatrie und Nervenkrankheiten* (*The Archives of Psychiatry and Nervous Diseases*) with the title, in the original German, of 'Die Aunstisehen Psychopathen im Kindesalter', which translates into English as 'Autistic Psychopathy in Childhood'.

Unfortunately for Asperger, a further complication was that, a year earlier, as already noted, eminent child psychiatrist Leo Kanner described what we would now recognise as 'classic' autism in a paper entitled 'Autistic Disturbances of Affective Contact'.

Like Asperger, Kanner had also been born in Austria, but had moved to the United States of America in 1924. By the time he wrote his paper, he was Associate Professor of Psychiatry at Johns Hopkins University in Baltimore, Maryland. Kanner was writing in English and lived in the United States and he was already a highly respected child psychiatrist. Asperger was writing in German, at a time when Germany (which had annexed Austria in 1938) was very obviously losing the Second World War.

It is unsurprising that Kanner's vision of autism became the dominant one and that when Asperger's work was eventually translated into English in the 1980s, Asperger's Syndrome should be considered a sub-set of Kanner's autism. The debate continues today whether it is part of the autistic spectrum or not.

Incidentally, Asperger did not borrow the word autism from Kanner, and probably, given the war, did not even see Kanner's paper. The term 'autism' had actually been first used in 1908 by the Swiss psychiatrist, Dr Eugen Bleuler, to describe what he saw as the key symptom of schizophrenia. Bleuler took the word autism from the Greek word 'autos', which means the self. He used it to describe the way in which schizophrenic patients lost contact with reality and appeared to turn in on themselves. At the time he published his paper, he had been working as a paediatrician for some 12 years.

Asperger's paper described unusual behaviour and abilities in a number of young boys. The behavioural issues included problems with empathy and with forming friendships, a tendency to intense and even obsessive focus on particular interests, clumsiness and difficulty understanding the give and take of normal conversations.

Asperger believed that many of the boys he identified as having these problems actually had special skills, and postulated that they would use these special skills in adulthood. He first thought that it only affected boys and described it as the 'ultimate in maleness'.

It is unfortunate that Asperger and Kanner should have been writing about apparently similar and potentially related developmental disorders at much the same time, and that both should have chosen to use words derived from the Greek 'autos'.

As a direct consequence, Asperger's insights into the group of children he had identified were ignored by the world at large for nearly 40 years, with awful consequences for many of the children with what we now call Asperger's Syndrome.

Kanner's paper, written in 1943, described the behaviour of 11 children; of one he writes:

He seems to be self-satisfied. He has no apparent affection when petted. He does not observe the fact that anyone comes or goes, and never seems glad to see his father or mother or any playmate. He seems to almost draw into his shell and live within himself. (p.217)

Kanner used the word 'autism' which previously had been used in reference to schizophrenia. In the early years autism was often referred to as 'childhood schizophrenia'. Kanner goes onto say:

The children's aloneness from the beginning of life makes it difficult to attribute the whole picture exclusively to the type of early parental relations with our patients... We must, then assume that these children have come into the world with innate inability to form the usual biological provided affective contact with people. (p.250)

Asperger probably was not aware of the papers of Ewa Ssucharewa, a Russian neurologist whose works were brought to people's attention by Sula Wolff in 1995. Ssucharewa in 1926 talked about a condition that she referred to as 'schizoid personality of childhood' (p.235). When reading both Asperger's paper and Ssucharewa's on schizoid personality disorder it is obvious they are talking about the same thing.

The understanding of autism took a turn for the worse in the 1960s when Dr Bruno Bettelheim, an Austrian-born art historian, became director of the Orthogenic School, a home for disturbed children associated with the University of Chicago. Bettelheim's theory was that children became autistic because of cold and emotionally distant mothers, women he referred to as 'refrigerator mothers' rather than seeing autism as the neurological condition it is, a stigma that has not totally disappeared. Many parents, especially mothers, do blame themselves for doing or not doing something at a critical stage. Bettelheim's book was published in 1967, called *The Empty Fortress: Infantile Autism and the Birth of Self.*

Previously Rimland had discredited Bettleheim's book *Infantile Autism: The Syndrome and Its Implications for a Neural Theory of Behavior* in 1964, where he stressed the plausibility of a biological base for autism. This turned our understanding towards autism being a neurological disorder that is biologically based and has nothing to do with parenting style. Rimland insisted: 'autism is a biological disorder, not an emotional illness. Refuse psychotherapy, psychoanalysis and intensive counselling. These approaches are useless' (cited in Gazella 1994, p.34).

Dr Ole Ivar Lovaas was a psychology professor at the University of California who developed an approach to younger children with autism that placed the implementation of treatment in the child's own home with the child being the centre of the therapy focus. The children made significant progress initially on these programmes. He was one of the fathers of Applied Behavioural Analysis.

There are many models designed for working with children with classic autism: TEACCH (Treatment and Education of Autistic and related Communication handicapped CHildren), Lovaas, Daily Life Therapy, Son Rise programme, ABA (Applied Behavioural Analysis) and many, many more. Each one of these programmes claims they do something the others are unable to achieve and that it is better than the others. I would not criticise any of these programmes nor say that one is any better than the others. It is a matter of personal choice and what works for one child may not necessarily work for another child. I would never advocate just one programme exclusively as they all have their strengths and weaknesses. Most of the models listed above also state that youngsters with Asperger's Syndrome should be included, although they tend to be a little restrictive and repetitive, and there is very little I have come across specifically for young people with Asperger's Syndrome. The model that this book will outline hopefully takes the best from the different programmes, but it is more an explanation of what worked and what did not and the young people's and parents' views of what worked.

3.3 Definitions of autism and Asperger's Syndrome

The debate continues over the diagnosis of Asperger's Syndrome. The UK National Autistic Society itself seems to be uncertain about whether Asperger's Syndrome is a form of autism or not. On the page on its website dealing with Asperger's Syndrome, it categorically states at one point:

> Asperger syndrome is a form of autism. (NAS website, *What is Asperger syndrome?*, p.1)

However, only a few paragraphs later, it says:

> While there are similarities with autism, people with Asperger syndrome have fewer problems with speaking and are often of average, or above average, intelligence. They do not usually have the accompanying learning disabilities associated with autism, but they may have specific learning difficulties. (p.1)

The World Health Organisation (WHO) has established a system for classifying diseases, called the International Classification of Diseases or ICD. The latest edition, ICD-10, Version 2007, categorises Asperger's Syndrome as one of a number of Pervasive Developmental Disorders. It gives PDDs the classification code F84, and defines 'AS' by the difficulties with social interaction and communication as well as repetitive interests and activities which pervades all situations.

Classic autism is defined as a PDD that manifests itself before the age of three, and has abnormal functioning in reciprocal social interaction, communication and stereotyped behaviour. They also list other features as being common, phobias, sleeping and eating disorders and aggressive behaviour.

Paraphrasing the WHO definition of Asperger's Syndrome, they go on to explain that it is a disorder of uncertain nosological validity which has the same abnormalities in social interaction that typify autism. It goes on to say that these abnormalities are likely to persist into adolescence.

Nosology, by the way, is the branch of medicine that deals with how diseases are classified. So what the WHO definition says, right at the outset, is that WHO's experts cannot be absolutely sure that Asperger's Syndrome exists as a separate condition from autism.

I, on the other hand, am sure: it does exist, it is separate from autism, and if children who have Asperger's Syndrome are to be allowed to develop fully, then they need to be taught in the right way.

The United States has its own classification of mental diseases, The Diagnostic and Statistical Manual of Mental Disorders (DSM), which is published by the American Psychiatric Association.

Paraphrasing DSM-IV, it defines Asperger's Syndrome as:

- An impairment in social interaction by two of:
  - non-verbal behaviours such as eye-to-eye gaze, facial expression, body postures and gestures
  - a failure to develop peer relationships
  - a lack of sharing enjoyment, interests or achievements with other people
  - a lack of social or emotional reciprocity.

- Having restricted repetitive and stereotyped patterns of behaviour, interests and activities.

- Having encompassing preoccupation with one or more stereotyped and restricted patterns of interest.

- Having an inflexible adherence to specific, non-functional routines or rituals.

- Having repetitive motor mannerisms.

- Having a persistent preoccupation with parts of objects.

- Impairment in social, occupational or other important areas of functioning.

- No clinically significant general delay in language.

- No clinically significant delay in cognitive development.

There is general agreement, though, that the biggest difference between autism and Asperger's Syndrome is that Asperger's Syndrome people tend to be of average to high intelligence and learn language skills at the same time as the 'normal' population. autistic people tend to be of lower intelligence, and are usually late in learning language skills.

Experts in autism and other developmental disorders of childhood tend to bring together a number of different problems under the heading of the Autistic Spectrum or Autistic Spectrum Disorders.

The three most common problems placed within this Autistic Spectrum are autism, Asperger's Syndrome and Pervasive Developmental Disorder – Not Otherwise Specified (PDD-NOS). This last is something of a catch-all term: it covers cases where an individual exhibits some but not all of the 'classic' symptoms of autism or another PDD, such as Asperger's Syndrome.

The boundaries between these problems are unclear, and as a result the professional literature is full of other labels as well. In addition to Autistic Spectrum Disorder, Asperger's Syndrome can also be referred to as 'mild autism', 'High Functioning Autism (HFA)' or 'Semantic Pragmatic Disorder'.

There is also still considerable confusion about the difference between Attention Deficit Hyperactive Disorder (ADHD) and Asperger's Syndrome.

Although the situation is better today than it was in 1994, when I first began working with children with Asperger's Syndrome, there can still be a great deal of misdiagnosis. Even where Asperger's Syndrome has been correctly diagnosed, there can be considerable misunderstanding about what it actually entails and how people with the disorder can best be educated.

Back in 1994, Asperger's Syndrome was still a new diagnosis – or rather, one that had been newly accepted by the English-speaking medical profession and educators. At that time, many professionals felt that the numbers of pupils with Asperger's Syndrome did not justify the creation of separate schools or units within schools for them. The situation was further complicated by the large number of different labels being used (and to an extent still being used today) – 'mild autism', 'part of the autistic spectrum disorder', 'Pervasive Development Disorder (PDD)', 'Pervasive Development Disorder – Not Otherwise Specified (PDD-NOS)', 'High Functioning Autism' (HFA) and 'Semantic Pragmatic Disorder'.

As discussed above, there was also a great deal of confusion about the difference between Attention Deficit Hyperactive Disorder (ADHD) and Asperger's Syndrome and thus a great deal of misdiagnosis.

This confusion is likely to continue. The proposed DSM-V and no doubt ICD-11 are recommending that Asperger's Syndrome should no longer exist as a separate syndrome but be incorporated into Autistic Spectrum Disorder (ASD) as AS is very similar in outcomes to HFA (High Functioning Autism), which again is ill-defined. I do not propose to get into a discussion about whether Asperger's Syndrome should be part of the Spectrum or not. Suffice to say that dyslexia has existed for a number of years as a diagnosis and understanding of the condition still does not appear in DSM-IV and the debate regarding diagnosis of syndromes will continue as there is no definitive test to define Asperger's Syndrome. Professionals will often state, 'it feels like Asperger's Syndrome', and then spend a large amount of time trying to prove or disprove what they first thought.

The proposed guidelines for DSM-V diagnosis, which is not yet published and is still being debated, for ASD which is proposed to include Asperger's Syndrome are:

Must meet criteria 1, 2, and 3:

1. Clinically significant, persistent deficits in social communication and interactions, as manifest by all of the following:

   a. Marked deficits in nonverbal and verbal communication used for social interaction

   b. Lack of social reciprocity

   c. Failure to develop and maintain peer relationships appropriate to developmental level.

2. Restricted, repetitive patterns of behavior, interests, and activities, as manifested by at least TWO of the following:

a. Stereotyped motor or verbal behaviors, or unusual sensory behaviors

b. Excessive adherence to routines and ritualised patterns of behavior

c. Restricted, fixated interests.

3. Symptoms must be present in early childhood (but may not become fully manifest until social demands exceed limited capacities).

So the deliberations and disagreements continue.

Finally, my experience suggests in this country that there has always been a great reluctance to diagnose individuals as having Asperger's Syndrome for fear of being contradicted later by other professionals, or being wrong. What then happens is that psychologists, teachers and psychiatrists all end up using phrases like 'Asperger's tendencies', 'exhibits Asperger's traits', 'could be on the Spectrum' or 'partially Asperger's'. It is like describing someone as 'partially pregnant' – not very helpful at all, as surely we all have 'Asperger's tendencies' that are part our makeup.

Many within the medical and educational establishment justify this reluctance by claiming that 'labels don't help' or 'children should not be stigmatised by being labelled'.

The truth, I feel, is that the real motive is the belief that by avoiding categorising people as having Asperger's Syndrome, the establishment can avoid the extra financial commitment which would be entailed by having to devote funds to looking after and educating such children.

The argument about whether to label or not, and whether segregated provision is the way forward, is something I will return to later in this book.

The labelling theory is one that has been discussed long and hard, and it is significant that before DSM-IV in 1995 a diagnosis of Asperger's Syndrome was extremely rare. When it was included in DSM-IV it gave rise to psychiatrists and psychologists using the term and diagnosing many more children. The diagnosis itself is fraught with difficulty, as it is a syndrome that is diagnosed on the basis of the individual's behaviour and interaction and understanding of social situations. This is a subjective judgement and can only be made by seeing the individual in a social setting. However, we all behave differently in social settings and then it becomes a factor of severity or whether the behaviour is debilitating. There is also the question of whether 'language delay' has to be present as part of Asperger's Syndrome. As a result 'Asperger's Syndrome' is often used loosely with little agreement: for example, Williams *et al.* (2008) in a survey of 466 professionals reporting on 348 relevant cases, showed that 44 per cent of children given Asperger's, PDD-NOS, atypical autism or 'other ASD' labels actually fulfilled the criteria for Autistic Disorder (overall agreement between clinician's and DSM-IV criteria).

There has always been concern about labelling and how difficult it is to get some labels and how easy it is to get others and how these labels 'stick'. This is clearly demonstrated in the David Rosenhan experiment outlined from his paper 'On Being Sane in Insane Places' (1973) in *The Psychopath Test* (Ronson 2011):

He co-opted seven friends, none of whom had ever had any psychiatric problems. They gave themselves pseudonyms and fake occupations and then, all at once, they traveled across America, each to a different mental hospital. As Rosenhan later wrote:
They were located in five different states on the East and West coasts. Some were old and shabby, some were quite new. Some had good staff-patient ratios, others were quite understaffed. Only one was a strict private hospital. All of the others were supported by state or federal funds or, in one instance, by university funds.
At an agreed time, each of them told the duty psychiatrist that they were hearing a voice in their head that said the words 'empty', 'hollow' and 'thud'. That was the only lie they would be allowed to tell. Otherwise they had to behave completely normally.
All eight were immediately diagnosed as insane and admitted into the hospitals. Seven were told they had schizophrenia; one, manic depression.
Rosenhan had expected the experiment would last a couple of days. That's what he'd told his family: that they shouldn't worry and he'd see them in a couple of days. The hospital didn't let him out for two months.
In fact, they refused to let any of the eight out, for an average of nineteen days each, even though they all acted completely normally from the moment they were admitted. When staff asked

them how they were feeling, they said they were feeling fine. They were all given powerful antipsychotic drugs.

Each was told that he would have to get out by his own devices, essentially by convincing the staff that he was sane. Simply telling the staff they were sane wasn't going to cut it. Once labeled schizophrenic the pseudopatient was stuck with that label.

There was only one way out. They had to agree with the psychiatrists that they were insane and then pretend to get better.

When Rosenhan reported the experiment, there was pandemonium. He was accused of trickery. He and his friends had faked mental illness! You can't blame a psychiatrist for misdiagnosing someone who presented himself with fake symptoms! One mental hospital challenged Rosenhan to send some more fakes, guaranteeing they'd spot them this time. Rosenhan agreed, and after a month, the hospital proudly announced they had discovered forty-one fakes. Rosenhan then revealed he'd sent no one to the hospital. (pp.246–247)

The experiment was a disaster for American psychiatry and their self-esteem was very low. This experiment encouraged the development of the DSM booklet which was then an attempt to remove human judgement from psychiatry.

But, whatever the reasons behind the reluctance to label children as having Asperger's Syndrome, back in 1994 it was clear to us that the majority of students with Asperger's Syndrome – whether diagnosed or not – were either in mainstream schools or in schools for children with other Special Educational Needs. Chris Gillberg (2002), in *A Guide to Asperger Syndrome*, feels, and I agree with him, that a diagnosis of Asperger's Syndrome cannot be made before the child is five and usually not until well into school age. There is often confusion with other diagnoses, including autism.

The system, frankly, was failing children with Asperger's Syndrome.

3.4 How prevalent is Asperger's Syndrome?

So how large is this group that is difficult to diagnose and doesn't exist as a separate group? The prevalence rates for Autistic Spectrum Disorder are taken from the NAS website and summarised in Table 3.1. These figures are derived from a paper by Lorna Wing and David Potter which was originally published for the Autism99 Internet conference.

The earliest criteria, suggested by Leo Kanner, were very narrow. The current standard classification systems (ICD-10 and DSM-IV) are much wider, even for the sub-group of 'Childhood Autism' (or 'Autistic Disorder' in DSM-IV).

Thus, the earliest epidemiological studies used Kanner's very narrow criteria and found the often-quoted prevalence rate of 4 to 5 in 10,000 children. Later studies have used wider criteria, so it would be inappropriate to calculate a mean prevalence based on results from the earliest and the later studies.

Table 3.1 Estimated prevalence rates of Autistic Spectrum Disorders in the UK	
People with learning disabilities (IQ under 70)	Approximate rates per 10,000
Kanner syndrome	5
Other spectrum disorders	15
Total	20
People with average or high ability (IQ 70 or above)	
Asperger's syndrome	36
Other spectrum disorders	35
Total	71
Possible total prevalence rate of all Autistic Spectrum Disorders	91

Until such research has been carried out and published, the NAS response to the question is based on two epidemiological studies of prevalence. The first was by Lorna Wing and Judith Gould involving a cohort of children born between 1956 and 1970 in the former London Borough of Camberwell (Wing and Gould 1979). This looked at children virtually all of whom had IQ levels below 70. The second study focused on the children with IQs of 70 or above and was conducted in Gothenburg (Ehlers and Gillberg 1993). This study looked for Asperger's Syndrome and High Functioning autism.

In order to give an estimate of overall prevalence, the NAS combined the rates from Camberwell (20 per 10,000) with those from Gothenberg (35 per 10,000 or 71 per 10,000 if all those with social impairment were included).

As described above, combining the results of these two studies gave an overall prevalence rate for the whole autistic spectrum, including those with the most subtle manifestations, of 91 per 10,000 – nearly 1 per cent of the general population.

We do not know if the prevalence of Autistic Spectrum Disorders or of one or more sub-groups has risen or is still rising. There is evidence both for and against. Anecdotally there does seem to have been a rise in the numbers of people diagnosed with autism and with Asperger's Syndrome. However, the 'other' category which would take in all other difficulties and syndromes appears to have dropped.

3.5 Sub-types of Asperger's Syndrome

There is much debate surrounding where Asperger's Syndrome sits and whether it is part of the Autistic Spectrum. There are certainly a lot of similarities with High Functioning Autism, but is it the same thing? The 'Asperger' label has proven popular and acceptable over the last few years and has widened the recognition and understanding of autism with the added combination of good language and intelligence.

Diagnosis of Asperger's Syndrome is usually later than that of autism, seven years according to Deisinger (2012) while Ramsay *et al.* (2005) think 11 years. The term Asperger's Syndrome is now being used quite loosely with little agreement, as was highlighted by the Williams *et al.* 2008 survey of 466 professionals reporting on 348 relevant cases which showed that 44 per cent of children that were given Asperger, PDD-NOS, atypical Autism or 'other ASD' labels actually fulfilled criteria for Autistic Disorder (according to DSM-IV). So the debate will continue.

Or does Asperger's Syndrome even exist at all? There is a school of thought that we all have Asperger's Syndrome – just at different levels of severity. We can all quote different patterns of behaviour, whether it is lining up our cutlery before we eat or having to do things in a certain sequence once we wake up in the morning. Maybe we will check a dozen times to make sure we have our keys with us. Do we have Asperger's Syndrome or are we just creatures of habit? The main difference with individuals with Asperger's Syndrome is that these routines may have to be followed or they are unable to function on that particular day. These routines can become debilitating. We all have routines and interests, but when do interests become obsessions? Many people have an interest in sport or an activity, which can take a large percentage of their time, but does this make it an obsession? I suppose the general rule of thumb is whether you are unable to function without these routines or interests and they alter your behaviour and affect others around you.

The debate about what is Asperger's Syndrome and where does it fit with other syndromes will continue for some time yet. This in my opinion is not as important as whether we can socially and educationally provide an environment that will assist individuals to develop survival skills and meet their needs. What could be useful is to describe the different sub-types of Asperger's Syndrome that I have come across in working with children and adults with Asperger's Syndrome because this may assist in the understanding and the different programmes I will explain later in the book.

The diagnosis of individuals is an effective way of describing a group, but working with a group under that diagnosis poses many other different problems. As I have previously stated, although they may have the same 'label' they remain very distinctively individual, which does seem contradictory and difficult for parents and teachers to comprehend.

For example, if we are to consider a medical problem, say chicken pox, we know what symptoms to expect: a rash, itchy skin, high temperature, headache, loss of appetite, general feeling of being unwell and then spots emerging all over the body. We know it normally occurs in children and is contagious, we know what the expected recovery time is and how it will manifest itself. If we transpose the analogy to Asperger's Syndrome then we struggle – we are aware of a common bond but we are also acutely aware of the differences between them.

There is a great deal of overlap with the other syndromes and conditions and many of these will co-exist with Asperger's Syndrome: Pervasive Development Disorder (PDD), Pervasive Development Disorder – Not Otherwise Specified (PDD-NOS), High Functioning Autism (HFA), Semantic Pragmatic Disorder, Fragile X Syndrome, Attention Deficit Disorder (ADD), Attention Deficit Hyperactive Disorder (ADHD), Obsessive Compulsive Disorder (OCD), Autism. It is often felt that these are all part of a spectrum of needs covered by Autistic Spectrum Disorder (ASD), a phrase coined by Lorna Wing.

The children who attend our specialist school may all have a label of Asperger's Syndrome, and thus come under that umbrella, but be very distinctly individual. Without this specific label they would not have received the resources through the Statement of Special Educational Needs. This is a very difficult concept for parents and professionals, who often say, 'Oh, he can't have Asperger's Syndrome because he has an imagination' (or because he is sociable, or because he has a girlfriend). In our experience the individuals with Asperger's Syndrome have a collective label with some common themes yet can have totally separate and individual needs requiring completely different approaches. I also find parents telling us that students respond completely differently at home to the way they do at school. Many of the students cope better in small groups or with individual withdrawal. This may allow the student to focus on the task in hand but part of the purpose of school is to be able to work with others, and it is in interaction with others that the youngster with Asperger's Syndrome has most difficulty. So it is important to be able to re-integrate the students back into larger groups and to focus on skills such as sharing, a collaborative approach, turn-taking and understanding others' point of view. In school, students need to be able to work and live together, which is a difficult enough task for young people without being further complicated with Asperger's Syndrome. All these students require individual space and time to manage their anxiety yet be able to communicate and socialise with others in the school. The students in school are grouped together depending upon their social mix, that is, their ability to get on and their tolerance of others, along with their chronological age which is a set criterion in schools. This helps us to begin to define the different groups clearly and maybe also the sub-groups we find within Asperger's Syndrome. Here we define five different sub-groups, labelled from A to E. It is certainly not the case that these are the only groups and they are clearly defined, but it is worth noting these groupings within school. Note also that Gillberg (2002, p.41) describes just three groupings:

There are probably at least three major 'types' of presentation in Asperger syndrome: the withdrawn-autistic, active-odd and passive-friendly. These three variants were first described by Wing (1996) in adults with autism.

Group A: Dominant and aware

This group appear more socially aware than any other of the groups; they are dominant 'street-wise', appearing to be socially normal though displaying challenging behaviour. Although this group appear confident, they are also vulnerable and have areas of misunderstanding. Also, because they think they are safe, this leaves them as vulnerable as the other groups.

Example: This manifests in manipulation of other children, typically those of the more susceptible sub-groups. They will want to be part of the street culture and have 'mates'. They will perform tasks, often risky or illegal, just to gain kudos within the group. They are often the ones that are caught doing wrongdoing yet 'set up' by the others. Ironically, in the wider forum of the community, these students are most at risk as they perceive better the more undesirable pastimes of emerging town youths such as shop-lifting, swearing, spitting or drug-culture interest as a passport to credibility and acceptability. They often become the 'fall guys' for the more socially aware groups in towns and cities. They are often unaware of the risks until it is too late.

Group B: Rigid but unaware

This group are often highly intelligent with a rigidity of thought and routine who are prone to behavioural and violent outbursts prompted by Asperger's Syndrome rather than a conduct disorder, unaware of what others may think of them.

Example: One boy refused to get up and start morning routines each Wednesday at the start of the Autumn term. This reoccurred on several occasions, stopping the boy getting to school as the situation escalated. The staff couldn't understand what the problem was until they finally worked out that in the previous term he had been allowed a lay-in on Wednesdays as a treat and that although the academic year had moved on, for him the year only changed in January. This was carefully explained in great depth and reinforced in black and white; the situation quickly resolved itself when explained.

Group C: Rigid but aware

This group are highly intelligent; they are more flexible in routines but will have certain areas where they are rigid in their behaviour. They can have tantrums and become violent if challenged. They have their own understanding of fairness. If things are promised to be done then this must be carried through. They have no remorse or guilt.

Example: By carefully involving the Local Authority, home and school, one boy's request to travel a considerable distance to home every weekend was planned. One particular weekend was not part of the plan so the student staying at school turned to particularly difficult, abusive and disruptive behaviour. This resulted in additional sanctions that the boy blamed the staff for. He additionally stated that as he wasn't going home he couldn't see the point of behaving as the situation couldn't get any worse.

Group D: Sensitive, gullible, unaware

This group are not especially academic and are socially inept, having one-dimensional social interactions. They can also be unpopular, non-violent, sensitive and gullible, easily taken advantage of. They will not have behavioural outbursts but will retreat into their shells, they are very vulnerable individuals. They can be taught responses to situations but are unaware of the subtleties required in making the correct response.

Example: The student greeted everybody he met in exactly the same way and repeated his greeting on every occasion throughout the day whenever he met someone. This is a common problem with students and relatively easily resolved through teaching alternative greetings and strategies. However, the problem remains to an extent, as it is very difficult to teach every eventuality. I recall one boy using his taught greeting strategy. 'Hello Mr Bradshaw, did you have a nice holiday?' asked the boy cheerily. 'No, I'm afraid I didn't, my wife's mother died on Christmas Day,' I replied. 'Good,' said the boy and happily went on his way oblivious to his faux pas, as this was his rehearsed greeting.

Group E: Sensitive, gullible, aware

This group are very sensitive, highly anxious, dependent upon their parents and with separation anxiety. They often have good social skills and are 'likeable', and they find adult reprimand difficult. This group are poor at reading others' 'non-verbal' signals, are gullible and prone to being bullied.

Example: A pupil was generally anxious and had little concept of the way of the world, believing only the real concrete examples before him. He also was very attached to his mother who he constantly worried about, and always thought something bad would happen to her. On one occasion in the past these thoughts were confirmed when she was involved in an accident. He then needed constant reassurance that she was all right when he couldn't see her. It being a residential school, a careful timetable of phone call opportunities was drawn up. If a call was late by a few minutes his anxiety would increase and he would constantly seek the reassurance of the adult staff around him. On one occasion there was need to call her during the day and when she didn't answer he was beside himself. He had no concept that she could have gone out; he perceived her only as being at home ready to confirm her status to him over the phone. This easily made him the target of other boys who would only have to insinuate there was a disaster near his home-town, believable or not (he was unable to discriminate), and he would be inconsolable.

The difficulty comes when you start then to sub-divide these groups – you end up back with every individual with Asperger's Syndrome being in a separate group. The further difficulty with looking at sub-groups within the group of students with Asperger's Syndrome is the confusion brought about by co-morbidity. Asperger's Syndrome, like most syndromes, is rarely found in a pure form but will often co-exist with other difficulties, most commonly dyslexia, ADHD, Obsessive Compulsive Disorder, epilepsy, bipolarity and occasionally autism. The other point is that individuals with Asperger's Syndrome will change through age and develop their own sub-group. There is no cure for Asperger's Syndrome, although I have met a number of educators that think there is and we should be looking for that magical formula or potion first. However, individuals can develop strategies that will assist and allow them to contribute to society and, importantly, make sense of the social rules that form our society.

3.6 Does Asperger's Syndrome actually exist at all?

This may seem like a strange question to pose in a book about working with kids with Asperger's Syndrome but with all the debate around DSM-IV and V, I think it is worth exploring the labelling issue. If it is true, as Lorna Wing states, that all the features that characterise Asperger's Syndrome can be found in varying degrees in the normal population, then surely we are looking at just degrees and extremes of behaviour and not something that is different.

The publishing of DSM-IV was a revelation. It had 886 pages and listed every known mental disorder, currently 374. Reading through it is like looking up symptoms on the Internet – you think you have got everything. I certainly have three or four disorders and my children think I qualify for many more! Following its publication, in which Asperger's Syndrome was included, there was a significant increase in the levels of diagnosis.

Jon Ronson in his book *The Psychopath Test* (2011, p.33) outlines some of the extreme examples:

> For example 'Frotteurism' is described as being 'the rubbing against a non-consenting person in a public transportation vehicle while usually fantasising an exclusive caring relationship with the victim'. Most acts of frottage occur when a person is aged 12–15 after which there is a gradual decline in frequency.

L. J. Davis of Harpers Magazine reviewing the DSM once wrote:

> It may well be that the frotteurist is a helpless victim in the clutches of his obsession, but it's equally possible that he's simply a bored creep looking for a cheap thrill.

Another example Jon Ronson states is Rhinotillexomania, nose-picking, which you would regard as something all children at times experiment with. Rhinotillexomania, however, is not just common or garden nose-picking, but incessant picking of the nose until the facial bones are exposed.

So does DSM describe normal behaviour that is taken to extremes? Is it just the severity and debilitating aspect of the condition that warrants inclusion in DSM?

Does that mean we all have Asperger's Syndrome, just some of us more than others, or is the analogy like pregnancy, that is, you can't be partially pregnant. We all certainly have our routines that we adhere to; we are certainly creatures of habit. I certainly will line up my knife and fork before eating, will follow the same routine every morning – and just ask my family how my behaviour changes in an airport terminal! The point is that these routines, if changed, do not stop me or most of us from functioning adequately.

We do like to classify, label and group everything in our lives and this gives us an identity – a belonging and joint values in the groups we aspire to be part of. However, most of this is through choice. I object when someone wants to put me into a group that I feel I don't belong to.

Chris Gillberg (2002, p.100) felt:

The single most important intervention when it comes to improving the quality of life of individuals with Asperger syndrome and their families is the attempt to change people's attitudes, both as regards the specific problems and their nature and the people affected. Such a change of attitude cannot take place without a proper diagnosis.

So is labelling a good thing? Is it over-zealous or important? Labels change over time: some become obsolete and some are regarded as inappropriate ways of describing, such as terms like 'idiot', imbecile and sub-normal which were used to describe children and adults of lower cognitive ability. Some countries still use terms that would be found offensive in the UK, terms such as 'mental retardation'.

One of the students at school who had a particularly difficult home life stated:

The day I got my diagnosis was the best day of my life. It was the day my mum stopped locking me in the cupboard.

So how does Asperger's Syndrome manifest itself and what can be done to assist in overcoming the debilitating process?

When I looked at the cohort of the students at the schools, from time to time I was able to see which group (A to E) the individual was in and how some of them had moved from one group to another as they developed social skills. There is always the argument that every individual with Asperger's Syndrome is different and should be treated and educated individually, which in many ways is true, but the difficulty for individuals with Asperger's Syndrome comes in social interaction. This was the main reason I decided to develop a school just for pupils with Asperger's Syndrome to assist them with this interaction rather just hope they would 'get it' through maturity or 'osmosis'.

SOCIAL CARE

CHAPTER 4

HOW DOES ASPERGER'S SYNDROME PRESENT?

It is important to know what Asperger's Syndrome is, but it is more important to know how it manifests itself and what to expect when working with individuals with it. As Temple Grandin (2006) says:

I am different not less. (p.120)

It is important to realise that Asperger's Syndrome is defined by a set of behaviours rather than a physical or cognitive disability. It is a cognitive difference or style rather than a disorder. It is something that cannot be cured and the individual will always have it and have to live with the consequences, but can develop strategies that allow them to cope with the pressures of life.

I had to learn to live with my mind and body and be at peace and stop trying to run away. It's a fight for my life, but now I've started to beat it and the good days are beginning to outnumber the bad, that is what makes it all worthwhile. When the world comes alive and you again begin to experience all the things you've been missing, life can be amazing, truly. There are no difficulties too big to overcome. I believe you can achieve anything. (Heidi, ex-student, Farleigh)

What is interesting is that many of the young people who have gone through the schools learn to cope with their Asperger's Syndrome so well they think they no longer have it. Often their associated difficulties become more and more prominent and they feel that is what they are left with.

So to revisit the main clinical features we need to consider how two eminent professionals in the field see these features manifesting themselves. Lorna Wing (Delfos *et al.* 2005, p.368) described the main clinical features of Asperger's Syndrome as:

- lack of empathy

- naïve, inappropriate, one-sided interaction

- little or no ability to form friendships

- pedantic, repetitive speech

- poor non-verbal communication

- intense absorption in certain subjects

- clumsy and ill coordinated movements and odd postures.

It is important to reiterate that not every individual with Asperger's Syndrome will have all the traits, and two individuals can have a completely different set of traits.

Chris Gillberg in his 1991 diagnostic criteria considers the following impairments:

1. Social impairment

2. Narrow interest

3. Compulsive need for introducing routines and interests

4. Speech and language difficulties

5. Non-verbal communication problems

6. Motor clumsiness.

It is confusing to have a number of different diagnoses and DSM-IV had another definition in 1995, as did ICD-10 in 1993. Thus there was not total agreement on the diagnosis of Asperger's Syndrome but it was often a preferred diagnosis over autism, which people felt had a 'pessimistic' ring to it.

Once again, these descriptors seem to be very clinical and you may be asking how they manifest themselves. What follows is some of the features associated with Asperger's Syndrome. It is not an exhaustive list and not every individual with Asperger's Syndrome will have all of these features, but they certainly will have some of them.

They are often not interested in team games/activities and will focus on more individual pursuits, such as chess and trampolining. Going to the gym is an anathema to them. The whole process of getting changed and showering in front of others and then joining in physical contact sports is something they will avoid.

Collecting unusual items such as toe nails, Marmite jar labels, dead insects and then categorising them by date are often associated with individuals with Asperger's Syndrome. (Do train spotters have to be Asperger's Syndrome by definition?)

> Very narrow interest patterns are often very conspicuous during the school years, and may develop into a major problem. Most of the time it is not the interest content that is problematic, but rather the way in which the child gets absorbed in the interest. It is important to distinguish between having a hobby/interest on the one hand and the kind of obsessive pursuit of narrow interest which is the rule in Asperger Syndrome on the other. (Gillberg 2002, p.32)

They will often have an aversion to certain things: physical touch, water, physical exercise, textures of clothes, buttons. They may also like certain clothes, materials and styles. It is often difficult for parents to understand a young child who doesn't seek out adults for a cuddle or finds some clothing rough on their skin.

When they are free to play in a playground they will often be isolated and playing on their own. They will find their own space or go into a classroom or the library or attach themselves to a teacher, or want to spend time on the computer in their 'virtual' world where they have friends.

They will have little or no empathy or no understanding of another person's feelings. This makes it then difficult for them to say sorry or understand they have offended someone:

> What's the point of saying sorry? It's only a word and doesn't change anything at all. (Former student at North Hill House)

> When asking one mother what they wanted from their child, she replied that she wanted them to say they loved her. On asking the student if he loved his mother and whether he ever told her, he said, 'Oh yes, and I have told her.' When then

asked when he had told her, he replied, 'Oh, about five years ago!' There was no understanding of the other person's needs or that you needed to reaffirm some things.

They will have difficulty recognising their own emotions or those of others. It is not that individuals with Asperger's don't have emotions, it is that at times they often cannot recognise the different emotions and do not relate the physical changes to what has previously occurred. There is little 'cause and effect' linkage:

Why would someone cry at the story of the 'snowman'? It's only a snowman and was always going to melt! (Former student at Farleigh College)

When discussing emotional relationships:

Unfortunately, it is difficult for my mother and other highly emotional people to understand that people with autism think differently. For her it is like dealing with somebody from another planet. I relate better to scientists and engineers, who are less motivated by emotions. (Grandin 1996, p.92)

They need a lot of reassurance and coaxing, especially when things go wrong.

Often their 'walk' or 'gait' is different and they can be clumsy or totally unaware that they are invading other people's personal space:

One student developed an extended gait that resembled a dressage horse, as if they were unaware of where the floor was, similar to using the stairs in the dark searching for the extra step at the top or the bottom of the staircase.

Their musical tastes will often try to be trendy and cool but they fail in understanding what the latest musical trend is:

It was not unusual for students to carry their 'cuddly toy' and their Pokémon cards, yet they would listen to the rap music at the same time, because it had swear words in and they thought that was 'cool'.

Their dress is often as an older adult, trousers pulled up high above the waist, bow ties, colours that don't match, looking like the 'little professor', cute at five years old but 'uncool' at 16:

> There seemed to be a direct correlation between the height of the trousers and the level of Asperger's Syndrome that was evident in individuals. This often carried on into adulthood.

There appears often to be a 'little professor' in their speech, very factual and distinctive speech pattern, often pedantic, and they will correct any factual inaccuracies with others. Their conversations are often based around their 'personal interest'. When starting to talk as a toddler they will often start with complete sentences. Their verbal skills are often in advance of their cognitive understanding, which leads to people thinking they are functioning at a higher level than they actually are. They also have difficulty in seeing other people's views or accepting them:

> One student for his 'speaking and listening' examination at GCSE played out a game of chess between Hitler and Churchill, including all the idiosyncrasies and accents. Another would recount the football scores that had been on the radio and rarely make a mistake.

They have little understanding of social rules, status or levels of acceptance, and will often make statements that are rude or inappropriate without realising. They will only seek out those in authority, preferring to go straight to the top, or wanting support from those academically superior than others:

> One student only wanted staff with a professional degree to support him. It didn't matter what degree, just so long as they had one.

> One student when introduced to a Director of Education as Dr so and so replied, 'Oh, I thought your name was Margaret.'

Their disco dancing is often distinctive, not related to anyone else and not related to the music. They will often spend the whole night on the disco floor dancing on their own:

The end-of-term disco was always a fascinating spectacle of group dynamics, with the disco floor being full of students but no one actually dancing with each other and often not in beat with the music. Usually when a 'poor' record comes on, at a disco the dance floor will empty. At the school disco the floor would always be full. There was no 'last dance situation' of making sure you ended up with a partner.

They will mix up the rules regarding public and private. In other words activities that are acceptable only in private, for example, getting undressed, will often be performed in public:

One student when purchasing some clothing at Marks and Spencer would try the items on without going to the changing rooms.

Another student who had always been told to take his trousers and underpants off when going to the toilet would do the same at a public urinal.

Eye contact is often avoided or used inappropriately, thus they will often either avoid eye contact or stare at people. This may be why many individuals with Asperger's Syndrome seem to prefer computer chat rooms to face-to-face conversations, there being no eye contact or understanding of body language required:

I did ask one student if they would look at me. Their response was, 'Why do I need to look at you – I know you're there!'

They will often expect you to know their thoughts and experiences and start a conversation in the middle of a sentence, expecting you to know what they are thinking and thus talking about:

Sometimes it would take a few minutes to try and understand what the individual was referring to, yet the expectation was that you knew what they were thinking.

They will often take things literally, which can prove difficult or amusing. For example:

A label on the side of a 'push up' roll-on deodorant said, 'push up bottom'.

'Pick your brain', 'Pull your leg', 'Take a seat', 'Raining cats and dogs', will all be taken literally.

In assemblies the students could 'stand up' and 'sit down' but struggled when told to 'sit up'. You would have to say, 'Straighten your backs and push your bottom back into the chair.'

They would also struggle with metaphors, thinking that they were just a lie: 'She was the apple of his eye', 'I laughed my socks off' or 'I've had a pig of a day' were just considered untrue.

They will not like change and become anxious when change occurs, not understanding why the anticipated routine has gone. Their behaviour often reflects their anxiety levels. This can vary from coping with everything that happens to a complete 'meltdown'.

They will often have a photographic memory for factual things, and sometimes collect statistics and information on various topics:

One student could recite the whole train timetable for the Great Western Railway, where trains started, which stations they went through, which they stopped at and where their destination was. They could also give you the times of trains each day. But ask them to tell you how to use the tube or how to get across London and they were incapable of doing so, as they had no interest in that information. So the collection of useless information is something that many individuals with Asperger's Syndrome excel in.

They may have routines that must be completed before 'moving on', for example, lining up their cars before leaving the bedroom in the morning:

Admittedly one might speculate that autistic children's routines are an attempt to reduce the anxiety they feel when they are faced with apparent unpredictability of other people's actions. (Baron-Cohen 1989, p.579)

They may have difficulty with sensory issues and be incapable of cutting out any background noise. They often will make their own noises and movements. Anxiety levels may rise in noisy, crowded or bright places:

One student would attempt to 'drown out' background noise by humming loudly, which in turn would upset other students as they focused on the background noise.

Another student explained when he was asked about making 'eye contact' that if he looked at me he could not hear me as he could only do one thing at a time.

Another student explained that he could not listen to a member of staff because they sounded like a bird screaming for its life as it was caught in a device being killed. Her voice was far too high for his ears.

Overly sensitive skin can also be a big problem. Washing my hair and dressing to go to Church were two things I hated as a child… But shampooing actually hurt my scalp. It was as if the fingers rubbing my head had sewing thimbles on them.

When I was little, loud noises were also a problem, often feeling like a dentist's drill hitting a nerve. They actually caused pain. I was scared to death of balloons popping, because the sound was like an eruption in my ear. Minor noises that most people can tune out drove me to distraction. (Grandin 1996, pp.66–67)

Their interests often develop into obsessions:

So when does an 'interest' become an obsession? Probably the defining step is when the interest has to be focused on to the detriment of all other activities and the individual cannot function without the interest.

They will be desperate to have friends but may not have the social skills to be able to develop levels of friendship:

This is probably why social network sites like Facebook are so popular; individuals are able to 'invite' others to become their friends. These are usually acquaintances and there seems to be a desire to show how popular you are as an individual by how many friends you have on Facebook. This is ideal for the individual with Asperger's Syndrome who struggles to understand the concept of friendship.

They will be unable to read non-verbal cues and body language and thus often misread situations:

This is so difficult in social situations and the start of relationships where the body language and cues are intentionally confusing and it becomes a 'game' of 'will you won't you' before anyone will commit themselves.

They can dominate conversations – speak loudly, non-stop:

Often individuals will be unaware in conversations that they are dominating them or speaking loudly, non-stop or on subjects that are of no interest to the others involved in the conversation. They may also have an aversion to the telephone which often has unexpected questions or situations that they struggle to understand.

They have to follow rules/instructions at all costs – such as structure, boundaries, expectations and timetables:

It is essential that there is 'scaffolding' to the day. This will give them clarity and structure, but you need to understand that this may mean that these rules/instructions are followed at all costs and there is little thought about whether they may vary in time and with differing circumstances.

Individuals with Asperger's Syndrome also have difficulty in telling lies as this requires complex emotions and deception. They will tell the truth as they see it: their perception is reality. This at times can cause major problems when they come into conflict with authority figures such as Headteachers or the police:

autistic people tend to have difficulty lying because of the complex emotions involved in deception… Lying is very anxiety-provoking because it requires rapid interpretations of subtle social cues to determine whether the other person is really being deceived. (Grandin 1996, p.135)

4.1 The media's view

As is often the case with stereotypes, they are created or developed by the media and have a modicum of reality. This is also true of individuals with Asperger's Syndrome, whether they are the 'loner', 'computer nerd', 'genius' or cracker of mathematical codes. 'Asperger's Syndrome' in the tabloid press is often used synonymously with criminal activity that shows no empathy or understanding of the seriousness of the crime or what is wrong with a particular behaviour. Cases recently reported in the press are often associated with hacking into computer systems such as the American Military or some mullti-national company or using their computer skills to point out failings in the system. Individuals with Asperger's Syndrome are no more likely to commit criminal acts than any other members of the community but will be described as having 'superpowers' and capable of becoming major terrorists just because they are loners and see the world in a different way.

In films there is also a tendency to use stereotypes or to describe extreme behaviour traits of individuals with Asperger's Syndrome. Dustin Hoffman in 'Rain Man' did a lot of good in raising public awareness of autism. But it also created a belief that every individual with autism had 'savant' skills. It is true that there are more people with Asperger's Syndrome or autism that have savant skills than in the general public but it does not mean that every one has a savant skill. There seems to be a belief in Hollywood that to be certain of getting an Oscar you need to play someone with a disability, such as in 'Rain Man' or 'The King's Speech'.

When I started the schools the term Asperger's Syndrome was rarely used by professionals, never mind the media. Now it is in many of their story lines. There have been a couple of excellent novels specifically about individuals with Asperger's Syndrome, notably Mark Haddon's *The Curious Incident of the Dog in the Night-Time* and Jodi Picoult's *House Rules*, both excellent portrayals and the authors got the characteristics and their research totally accurate. However, the students at school did not like the characterisation of the individuals with Asperger's Syndrome as they felt it highlighted all the difficulties with the Syndrome in one person, which would be very unusual.

Then you start asking, 'Are individuals with no apparent empathy and capable of horrendous crimes individuals who have Asperger's Syndrome?' Does Kevin in Lionel Shriver's novel *We Need to Talk About Kevin*, who has no remorse after killing a group of students from his school, have Asperger's Syndrome?

There have also been a number of films that included an individual with Asperger's Syndrome or High Functioning Autism, including the excellent 'Temple Grandin' starring Claire Danes, which is the account of Temple's life. Asperger's Syndrome has attracted its fair share of labels to describe it: 'geek', 'weird', 'strange', 'freak' and 'uncool' – the media tend to reinforce the stereotype.

There are, though, some films where the subject is dealt with sympathetically. 'Mozart and the Whale', a film about two individuals with Asperger's Syndrome starring Josh Hartnett and Radha Mitchell, showed many aspects of Asperger's Syndrome in a positive light. 'Mary and Max', an excellent animation about a man with Asperger's Syndrome and his young pen friend, is funny and tragic, which sums up Asperger's Syndrome in the media. One does have to remember that the main purpose of films is to entertain and not inform, but the subject does seem to have been dealt with at times quite sensitively.

The difficulty with stereotypes is exactly that – they are stereotypical, based on some facts, but fit few individuals and make generic assumptions. Many of the students that go through the schools to university will no longer use the label or explain to more than a few friends that they have Asperger's Syndrome for fear that they will be labelled as 'different' or 'weird', so once again the label is both a help and a hindrance. I think it is far too easy to say that individuals with Asperger's Syndrome do not have any empathy therefore are capable of committing horrendous crimes or that individuals that commit those types of crimes had Asperger's Syndrome.

4.2 Co-morbidity – what is often linked with Asperger's Syndrome?

It is not unusual for individuals with Asperger's Syndrome to also have another syndrome or disorder. When another syndrome appears alongside this it is called co-morbidity. It is like having flu and pneumonia. When this occurs with individuals with Asperger's Syndrome it is often difficult to tell if it is an extension of the Asperger's Syndrome or another completely new syndrome. For example, many individuals with Asperger's Syndrome are clumsy but do they have dyspraxia? It is all a matter of severity, and whether the other difficulty sometimes disappears or takes over completely. It is difficult to see where one syndrome finishes and another one begins, which is why Lorna Wing adopted the term 'Autistic Spectrum' which would encompass a range of difficulties. Attention Deficit Disorder (ADD), Deficits in Attention, Motor Control and Perception (DAMP) and probably reading disorder would be part of that spectrum. Asperger's Syndrome is often seen with Conduct Disorder, Obsessive Compulsive Disorder, Epilepsy, Tourette's Syndrome (TS), Anxiety Disorder, Depression, Schizophrenia, Bipolar Disorder, Psychosis and Elective Mutism.

The anxiety disorders, Depression and Bipolar, seem to be part of many Asperger's profiles yet can co-exist, as can the genetic disorders of Fragile X, Williams Syndrome and Down's Syndrome. The behavioural disorders of Behavioural Emotional Social Difficulties (BESD), Oppositional Defiant Disorder (ODD), and Pathological Avoidance Deficit (PAD) are rarer but do occur. The language difficulties of Dyslexia and Hyperlexia also often are co-morbid with Asperger's Syndrome. I have also known a student at school who had Asperger's Syndrome and autism. Autism and Asperger's Syndrome were initially confused with schizophrenia and sometimes referred to as 'Childhood schizophrenia'. It is now more likely to be considered that some symptoms will appear alongside Asperger's Syndrome. It is important that these symptoms are fully examined and the restricted stereotyped repertoire of interests and activities and social impairments that characterise Asperger's Syndrome are not mistaken for psychotic illness.

We do have to remember when working with young people with Asperger's Syndrome that they are also adolescents and bring their own level of angst, stroppiness and deviance. The art is to work out which behaviours are due to the difficulties with Asperger's Syndrome and which are because they are going through adolescence.

4.3 Medication – the pharmaceutical model

It is important to realise that some of the co-morbid syndromes can be treated in different ways. When I first started working with students with Special Educational Needs (SEN), different models were delivered by different organisations: the treatment model was delivered by the health department, the social care model by the social services, the therapeutic model by therapists and the educational model by schools. Rarely were these models combined; rather, they competed with each other.

It is clear that no one model is more successful than any other, or that anything should be taken in isolation. The best model is surely the one that meets all the needs of the individual rather than a 'bolt-on' service.

There was an aversion to using any form of medication within schools as it was felt that children were being 'controlled by drugs'. However, it is clear to me that there is a part for medication to play in the life of an individual with Asperger's Syndrome, and with associated conditions such as epilepsy and bipolar it can save lives:

> Taking the medication is like adjusting the idle adjustment screw on an old-fashioned automobile engine. Before I took Tofranil, my 'engine' was racing all the time, doing so many revolutions per minute that it was tearing itself up. Now my nervous system is running at 55 mph instead of 200 mph, as it used to. (Grandin 1996, p.115)

It is also important that medication is used appropriately and as part of an integrated programme that is overseen by the appropriate profession. I have come across children on quite high doses who were assessed some time ago, and the prescription has just been repeated without anyone seeing, monitoring and reviewing the child on a regular basis. There have also been quite a few cases of misdiagnosis of Asperger's Syndrome where medication has been prescribed and not evaluated over time. So it does need to be part of a clear plan that is carefully monitored. It is part of an integrated programme and not the only component or the substitute:

> The proper use of medications is part of a good autism program, but it is not a substitute for the proper educational or social program. Medication can reduce anxiety, but it will not inspire a person the way a good teacher can. (Grandin 1996, p.119)

There is no one specific pharmacological treatment for Asperger's Syndrome. However, there are treatments available for the depression, anxiety, OCD, social phobia, attention deficits and mood swings which can accompany Asperger's Syndrome. These treatments are not Syndrome-specific but rather targeted at various symptoms. Medication can be effective in combination with other forms of treatment in assisting with anxiety disorders, depression, inattention and aggression. Risperidone and Olanzapine have been shown to reduce the associated symptoms of Asperger's Syndrome. Risperidone can reduce repetitive and self-injury behaviour, aggressive outbursts and impulsivity, and improve stereotypical patterns of behaviour. The Selective Serotonin Reuptake Inhibitors (SSRIs) have been effective in treating restricted and repetitive interests and behaviours.

It is important that medication is overseen and prescribed by a consultant who knows the individual and can work closely with the staff team at the school. The other main issue is the side-effects which are often masked by the individual's Asperger's Syndrome. Abnormalities in metabolism and cardiac conditions and type 2 diabetes have been raised with these types of medication. Although there have been no clinical trials, many consultants feel that SSRIs may contribute to reduce depression and compulsive behaviour associated with Asperger's Syndrome. However, SSRIs can lead to an increase in impulsivity and sleep disturbance. Weight gain is another side-effect of Risperidone. Obviously, sedative side-effects will make concentration difficult within the classroom.

Tricyclic medication also appears to have a marked effect on obsessive-compulsive symptoms and is helpful in the case of severe depression, but again there are side-effects to these drugs.

Neuroleptics are also helpful in reducing levels of aggression but have side-effects of drowsiness and weight gain so cannot be used for any length of time. Anti-epileptic medication, barbiturates and benzodiazepine are obviously useful for epilepsy and Asperger's Syndrome but can cause side-effects of hyperactivity, aggression and cognitive blunting. Lithium is used in the treatment of bipolar.

It is worth repeating that there is no medication that will treat the core symptoms of Asperger's Syndrome and I am certainly not advocating the use of medication to assist in its treatment. The pharmaceutical model should be used in conjunction with the therapy, the educational and the social model in working with individuals with Asperger's Syndrome. However, medication has proved successful if used to treat co-morbid difficulties if monitored closely and as part of a multi-disciplinary programme. It is important that anyone working with youngsters using medication as part of their programme are aware of the side-effects. The use of medication can be very positive but it can also create as many issues as it solves.

4.4 Gender differences

Hans Asperger first thought that Asperger's Syndrome only affected males and that females could not have the Syndrome. He did later change his mind but there is still a view that it is predominantly a male preserve. This view may be partly due to the way Asperger's Syndrome manifests itself differently. In my own experience Asperger's Syndrome in boys is often defined by their challenging behaviour, which may be physically challenging. The different view they have of the world makes it difficult to fit in with their peer group. Girls with Asperger's Syndrome will often be withdrawn, individually focused, moody and socially inept but rarely physically challenging. These highlighted gender stereotypes will shape the need for diagnosis; the boys are often referred to psychologists or psychiatrists for an explanation of their behaviour traits. The girl's symptoms are often regarded as 'teenage angst' and diagnosis is slow to be made:

> Some girls appear to have few or even no interests. They are often generally characterised by negativism and a tendency to say 'No' to just about everything. Some of these are similar to the children described by Elisabeth Newson (Newson and Newson 1983), and whom she refers to as 'pathological demand avoiders'.
>
> Sometimes there are two or three interests at the same time, but rarely more than that. The interest may come and go, even though a proportion will stick with their first 'and only' interest throughout life. Even when the interests change, the style in which they are adhered to rarely does. Again it has to be said that it is not the interest in itself, but rather the character of the person's relationship to the interest, that is the problem.
>
> (Gillberg 2002, p.33)

To reflect how Asperger's Syndrome manifests itself it is important to remember that it is a cognitive style that is defined by a set of behaviours rather than a physical or cognitive disability. Though there still is not a single agreed diagnosis there is some consensus of the types of behaviour which an individual with Asperger's Syndrome will exhibit.

All too often energy is spent on trying to decide whether or not an individual has Asperger's Syndrome when it would be far better to spend the time and energy identifying the individual's needs and how those needs can be met. Unfortunately the label still means resources, and without it resources often don't follow. The label is the beginning of the process, not the end. Far too often professionals will diagnose Asperger's Syndrome without going on to what that means and how those issues can be supported.

The individual with Asperger's Syndrome may look and act differently from others, but they are desperate to be part of this social world of ours. The misunderstandings of the teenage years appear to get magnified to a level where they become debilitating for the individual.

Asperger's Syndrome rarely comes in a 'pure' form and a co-morbidity with OCD, ADHD or bipolar is very common. Sometimes the AS is not picked up for some years, as some professionals assume you cannot have more than one syndrome or difficulty.

Chapter 5

'I'm Not Anxious, Just Worried'

Anxiety and Asperger's Syndrome

But one thing I must add is that I could have all the support in the world and still never get over my problems. The support we all need more than anything is the support and love within us and that's not meant to be a cliché. (Ex-student from Farleigh)

One of the common threads is that nearly all individuals with Asperger's Syndrome seem to have a heightened level of anxiety which can manifest itself in different ways. This can result in aggressive behaviour which is often described as complete 'meltdown' where the individual is likely to scream and shout and is unable to be calmed down by anyone or anything. At the other end of the behaviour spectrum they can be withdrawn or depressed and in extreme cases suicidal.

Anxiety is such a significant part of individuals with Asperger's Syndrome that it is important when working with them to consider it at all times. However, it is worth mentioning how anxiety appears to take over an individual's life and how they are incapable of functioning at all.

What helps to lower the level of anxiety is events being predictable, knowing what is going to happen, the same thing occurring over and over again. This may be the routine of events, the same food, the same mode of transport or the same groups and people in the same setting. Change one of those factors and it will raise the level of anxiety for the individual. For example, one day I was walking down a corridor carrying a saw and passed by one of the students, I said 'Morning' to which he replied 'Morning, Rob' – Rob was the school carpenter and looked nothing like me.

Individuals with Asperger's Syndrome would like each day to be the same. 'Groundhog Day' would be ideal, but unfortunately life is not a repetition of every day – there will always be change and things will just happen. We even have phrases to explain this: 'sod's law', 'what will be will be' or 'shit happens'. The difficulty when working with individuals with Asperger's Syndrome is that events that usually create a rise in anxiety in ourselves do not always do so with individuals with Asperger's Syndrome, and events that you may regard as 'normal' can create great anxiety. For example, most students at the school had a strict routine to follow in the morning, not only for things to happen at certain times but bathrooms and showers had to be available at that time, thus having ensuite bathrooms alleviated the problem of the room not being available. If they were not able to follow this routine then it was sometimes impossible for them to function in school during that day. If they were able to follow their routine then their anxiety was lowered, which allowed them to function. Many individuals developed their own anxiety-lowering strategies, which could be fiddling with a piece of cotton, singing a song in their head or out loud, watching something over and over again, flapping of the hands or saying the same word over and over again. This often happened when the anxiety had started to rise and they were attempting to regain control.

One student was excellent at public speaking and went on to work for the social services in his local area, but would get very anxious about speaking to people individually. By contrast, most of us would initially be concerned about addressing a large group and comfortable about speaking to an individual. Another would worry about his mother and whether she had been in an accident or was still alive; to assist him we would set up phone calls home throughout the day. This worked well when his mother remembered to be available but once when she was not available then his anxiety went totally off the scale and he was inconsolable as he feared the worst.

The individual with Asperger's Syndrome will, with help, develop strategies to assist with keeping the anxiety under control. This may be by lining up a set of toys or pens or repeating an action over and over again. Or they may have a favourite DVD or scene from a DVD that they watch constantly, which will allow them to relax. This is similar to young children who carry their favourite toy or piece of material or watch the same TV programme or DVD. This practice with young people with Asperger's Syndrome would often continue into adolescence. If the student used these strategies to lower their anxieties then it would be important that these continue and not be initially challenged by the school as being unacceptable or age-inappropriate.

When interviewing new students and their parents before admitting them to the school, I would explain that our philosophy was a 'wrap-around school'; this will be explored fully in Chapter 9.

If this process was not followed then often the student was unlikely to function at all. This process would take anything from a few weeks to a few months. One student stated that in his case it took four years before he was able to start to work, but then he achieved the highest mark in the country in two A level subjects. Parents and educational professions often worry that students with Asperger's Syndrome are 'missing out' and being 'left behind', yet it is more important to get the relationship and the anxiety in order, as without this, they will not make significant progress.

We had one student who would only eat cheese-flavoured Quavers at 9.00 pm. If this didn't happen then the likelihood of him not going to sleep at all that night was very real. Some staff thought that initially this was just pampering to him and he should not get his own way, but this was part of his programme and after 12 months we were able to start to move away from this rigidity, though still in very small steps.

This always meant that every activity had to be carefully planned and the attention to detail was crucial. Normally, if a student is going on any trip then it would be expected that they would be told about the purpose of the trip, where they are going and maybe the time they are leaving. A student with Asperger's Syndrome, however, needs another level of detail. They must know when they are going to leave, the precise time, who is taking them, what they are travelling in, where they will be sitting in the vehicle, which other children will be in the vehicle, how long it will take them to get there, if there are any stops, what is the activity they will be doing when they get there, what time they are due to return, what clothes they should wear, how much money they will have, what they will eat and where they will eat it. Nothing must be left to chance. If the planning is not this thorough then the likelihood of an incident or their anxiety levels rising is real.

Once when transporting the students home at the end of term we had agreed to meet parents at one of the service stations on the M4. The students were told that we would be there at 11.30 am, but unfortunately the motorway was congested and the journey took longer than expected. The staff failed to pass this information onto the students and at 11.30 am one of the students tried to exit the moving vehicle as he presumed that his parents were waiting and they had arrived at the destination.

As previously stated, some individuals develop their own strategies to calm themselves, such as reciting a phrase or a song over and over again or moving in a particular way, but many will just 'switch off' from the world or go into a 'meltdown'. 'Meltdowns' are when the individual loses total control and may become violent or distressed. I will discuss strategies to deal with these situations in Chapter 9 on classroom management.

The way in which individuals with Asperger's Syndrome take their place in the world is very different from that of 'neuro-typical' individuals. The world is made up of physical parts but it is our interaction in a social setting and our experience of different situations that allow us to function in certain ways. Heightened levels of anxiety are caused in a number of different ways. Normally the symptoms of anxiety are clear and obvious: raised heart rate, sweating, 'butterflies in the stomach', restlessness, etc. We usually also understand what the causes of these physical symptoms are. The social environment for a child with Asperger's Syndrome is very different to this, and equally, anxiety manifestation can be very different. Individuals with Asperger's Syndrome appear to manifest anxiety in some non-conforming social situations and have been observed to fail to manifest anxiety in other situations.

This manifestation of anxiety appears difficult to account for using the current theories of autism, yet the confusing picture might well be due to, or confused by, a deficit or difference in selective attention. Eysenck (1992) discusses anomalies he found in the selective attention of high anxiety trait subjects. Amongst the situations in which Asperger's Syndrome individuals appear to manifest anxiety or fear in different ways to the normal population are public presentations, plays, speeches and major fairground rides. This difference was succinctly stated by Temple Grandin (Bogdashina 2003), who has Asperger's Syndrome and has given an insight into the world of the Syndrome through her numerous books:

> Various stimuli, insignificant to most people, created a full blown stress reaction in me. When the telephone rang or when I checked the mail, I'd have a 'stage fright' nerve attack. What if I didn't get any mail – or what if I did and it was something bad? The ring of a telephone set off the same reaction – panic. (Bogdashina 2003, p.54)

In addition, children with Asperger's Syndrome are obsessive by nature; they may pursue interests which are beyond socially acceptable or normally accepted boundaries. It was not unusual for a student to focus on a bizarre topic, for example, the life of the fruit fly and its reproductive cycle, to the exclusion of all other subjects. Examples of obsessions might be a need to sit in certain places for particular activities; certainly at mealtimes it was essential to maintain the same seating positions so as to keep resulting anxiety at minimal levels. Common obsessions are food hygiene, food colour, arrangement of food on a plate, eating in a certain order, even only eating the same type of food every meal. Once again the 'special interests' or obsessions are a way that the individual creates order, routine and sameness and thus lowers their anxiety – they are in their 'comfort zone' where life is predictable and they are in control. One of the aims of the school was to broaden these interests and obsessions – not remove them but give the student different experiences that would assist them to cope with levels of change.

One of the students had never eaten anything hot for his meal as he believed all of the hot food would join up inside him and burn him. Eventually when he was with a group cooking hot dogs over a campfire he was intrigued and curious about the food. He decided to ask if he could try some to be part of the group, let it cool and ate it. He enjoyed the experience and was surprised that the food did not burn him. He then went on to try every new food he saw. Eventually tiring of long periods of food cooling, his hunger took over, and he ate food normally.

Another child only ever ate pasta and cheese for every meal. This became a real problem when faced with the prospect of a night walk and barbeque, and, not wishing to be left out, and a little hungry, the obsession was broken by voluntarily eating a cheese burger.

Individuals with tactile sensitivity are not uncommon, with a desire to stay clean or equally an aversion to soap, water, shampoo or teeth brushing. An obsession could be all-involving, a single purpose and focus to life, to the exclusion of all other things. This is a really difficult area: who should make the decision that a specific interest or an obsession is not good for the individual or that it should be time-limited? As adults we make those decisions about children all the time, but what happens when the individual becomes an adult – are they then able to make those decisions and feed their own interest or obsession?

One student tried to exclude himself from school by using violence, in order to be sent home. It transpired that at home his computer, linked to the Internet, was his sole focus; he was allowed to surf for an unlimited time, and saw absolutely no reason why this could not occupy his every waking moment. He would even fall asleep with the Internet still connected. He had no concept of the consequences of his action or any interest in what the future would hold beyond each moment when he was connected to the net.

As the time approached for him to return to school after holidays or breaks, his anxiety levels would heighten at the dawning realisation that he was to be bounded by different rules. This would cause him to 'kick off' in a tirade of challenging behaviour.

Computers, smartphones and electronic games and devices were favourite companions of our students with Asperger's Syndrome. It was as if machines that were predictable and showed no emotions were much easier to relate to than people, so lowered anxiety when needing to communicate.

Anxiety is partly borne out of anticipation; the individual starts to consider 'what if' and predicts the resulting effect. General anxiety, too, is prevalent in Asperger's Syndrome. It is both touching and shocking to understand the depth and intensity of anxieties:

One student was clearly anxious and it took us a great deal of time to list his areas of concern. We then went through them all point-by-point. His concerns seemed minor: about another boy's reaction to him, about a journey he was due to make at the weekend. We went through all of the difficulties. Then I asked him if he felt better, and he said he did as we had talked about a lot of things that had worried him. 'Anything else?' I asked. 'Yes,' he said. 'When will I die, is my Mum all right, when will she die, what will happen when my parents die, are they all right now? How do I know they are all right now? I'm very worried about that...'

This was his normal level of anxiety. He could not distance himself from these nagging feelings, and he was certainly not unique within the school. Another student with similar worries additionally was concerned that bombs might explode in his town when he wasn't there, or that his parents could be in an accident. He would consider every negative possibility, and was inconsolable until he was able to speak with his parents. This highlights another aspect of Asperger's Syndrome: an inability to believe anything but what can immediately be seen, touched or heard. Once again, another massive source of anxiety.

5.1 Anxiety and social interaction

Reality to an autistic person is a confusing interacting mass of events, people, places, sounds and sights. There seems to be no clear boundaries, order or meaning to anything. A large part of my life is spent just trying to work out the pattern behind everything. Set routines, times, particular routes and rituals all help to get order into unbearable chaotic life. (Volkmar *et al.* 2005, p.324)

When Kanner (1943) and Asperger (1944) almost simultaneously described a group of children who appeared engrossed in their own worlds it was the beginning of in-depth investigations into the intricacies of the human mind in its interaction with others. This research continues today. People with Asperger's Syndrome can be viewed as out of harmony with their social environments. As a result, they constantly feel this as conflict that in turn manifests in the form of anxiety. Asperger's Syndrome individuals are astute, yet confused people. They have the cognitive ability to function at least equally with, and often above, their peers, yet are thrown by the intracies of social communication. The world in which we live is governed by cultural and social rules which are implicit within our social interactions, and they form the hidden code of communication.

Amongst these key facets of communication are personal space, body language, facial clues and gestures. These all underpin our everyday communication and are frequently more powerful than the spoken word.

We operate in and out of communicative modes, switching and changing emotions, intonation, humour, expression, etc.; all the subtleties of interaction within an invisible, unwritten, synchronous, mutual agreement. We adjust our interactions depending upon so many factors: the social environment, job interview or party, theatre audience or intimate restaurant. We are affected by the way we believe others in the interaction are reacting to us; we constantly appraise other people's perception of us, and then readjust ourselves within the context of the interaction. We even dress to project a personality or adjust people's thinking of us. 'Power dressing' to exert control, 'street cool' to impress mates at school, designer clothes to indicate individuality and wealth, pop cultural clothes to indicate our tastes and interests. All these additional elements are aspects that make or break situations before speech even begins, and are often misunderstood by individuals with Asperger's Syndrome:

'Define "cool"', I asked Emily my then teenage daughter (who is now married with children of her own). After some thought she retorted, 'I can't, Dad. All I know is I'm cool, and you're not...'

A student who was desperate to be part of the 'social scene' in the local town and wanted to get himself a girlfriend would spend a lot of time in the town centre, 'hanging out':

One Saturday he returned from a shopping trip to the local market in tears. When asked what was wrong, he explained that the market stall holder had sold him a pair of sunglasses for £10 claiming that if he was wearing these then he would get himself a girlfriend in a matter of minutes, guaranteed.

He bought the sunglasses and all day visited the local coffee shops and all the places the young people 'hung out' but alas he was unsuccessful in his search for a girlfriend.

He could not understand why the market stall holder was able to tell lies and get away with it.

Faced with this intuitive knowledge in other young adults around him, what chance has the student with Asperger's Syndrome of understanding the rules of social engagement, how to dress, react, say, stand, walk? Training and taking them through situations, offering strategies, and role-play can all help, but equally have pitfalls.

One of the students asked for a script of how he should talk to other young people at a youth club. It is extremely difficult to give someone an actual 'script' as all we say and the way we act depends upon the situation, the people, the conversation, how friendly they are, often depending upon the first word they say. No wonder individuals get it wrong. How many of us read the signals wrong as teenagers and ended up admitting we got it wrong?

One of the students had returned from the local youth club having had his face slapped by one of the local girls that attended that club.

When I asked him what happened, he said, 'She just slapped my face.'

'So exactly what did you say?'

'I just said that she looked good.'

'Is that exactly what you said?'

'Almost.'

'Tell me exactly what you said.'

'I said, "you've got a great pair of tits", then she slapped me.'

I then tried to explain that it was rude and inappropriate and people don't want to be told that.

'But she did have a great pair. Would it have been better if I had said breasts?' he replied.

This highlights the difficulties young people have of making sense and joining into social interactions without falling foul at the first hurdle. It also highlights the drawback of global strategies and admirably indicates the huge difficulties in helping children to manage social introductions.

Our approach to an interaction is dependent on our desired outcome, and how we exert influence on those engaged in conversation. Consider the different situations of trying to impress the boss at work and buying a car in a showroom. Each demand interaction and the ability to read, interpret and react to the other people. This complex web of social interaction, governed by rules, awareness of others and social niceties are alien to most children with Asperger's Syndrome. Frequently we see students who have a single way of interacting, irrespective of the situation. Consider these examples:

We were visited by an HMI school inspector; on entering the room a child said, 'Who are you then?'

Another of our students, on holiday in Greece, was on a guided tour of an ancient site. Seemingly bored he shuffled from room to room. 'These are paintings of the 12th century,' said the guide. 'No they're not,' piped up the young person, 'they are Byzantine,' and he stated the name of the artist. 'You're right,' replied the guide who then continued to refer to the boy prior to each introduction to a new artefact.

School assemblies, a difficult area for children, can be peppered with corrections, questions and answers to the rhetorical questions of assembly talks.

These are not situations in which a student is 'letting us down' or behaving badly, it is simply they are unaware of the often constricting social rules within which we operate every day. They will often say what I am thinking but am unable to say due to politeness or social convention. Given the absolute critical importance of mastering socialisation and the massive deficit students with Asperger's Syndrome experience, it is not surprising that their general anxiety increases. They know the 'game of social life' is being played every minute of the day, and know they need to understand it in order to gain the benefits they see in playing it for the people around them, yet, despite being aware there is a strict set of rules, they cannot be made aware of the intricacies of each individual rule, and therefore are ill-equipped to join in.

Donna Williams in her autobiography confirmed this feeling of anxiety borne out of growing uncertainty about the surrounding world:

The more I became aware of the world around me, the more I became afraid. (Williams 1992, p.11)

Unlike individuals with autism, those with Asperger's Syndrome are extremely effective in the use of verbal language yet due to their lack of understanding of the rules of interaction they frequently fail in social communication. This is one of the cruel paradoxes of Asperger's Syndrome. They understand that social interaction is underpinned by complex, fluid and subtle rules, guidelines and niceties, succinctly described as 'social chess' by Humphrey (1984),yet they are unable to perceive and understand them and thus function at best awkwardly, and at worst become totally withdrawn in the company of others. As a result they may live in a world of introversion and conflict. They desperately want to be part of the world in which they live – the most common request of young people with Asperger's Syndrome is to have a friend, yet they are ill-equipped to be accepted by their peers.

Once again, what does work is explaining social situations and rules to individuals with Asperger's Syndrome when you know they are going to experience something new. Whether this is an interview, a trip to the local shop, a meal in a restaurant or independent travel home, it is important to practise these social situations in the safe environment of the school. Carol Gray's social stories are excellent for helping the individual to practise the situation before experiencing it in a different environment. What doesn't work is the 'sink or swim' method of throwing the student into new situations and seeing what will happen. This often puts the student further back in their development than they were and they will associate the environments with failure. For example, if a student has had a bad experience at school with bullying they will associate bullying with every school and will not want to go into an environment with bad memories.

To give an example, when a student was due to go for an interview, college or work experience, this would be practised at school over and over. The introduction was scripted: how to look the person in the eye, offer your hand in a handshake and say 'Pleased to meet you, I'm John Smith' and make sure that you don't invade their personal space. The handshake should be firm but not too firm; you should then wait to be offered a seat and then sit down. You should sit in the chair with your back straight and comfortable but not sloppy, with both your feet on the ground, and rest your hands on your knees. The answers to the question should be not too short or too long and not offer any more unless asked to do so. Don't speak about your special interest and if you don't understand the question ask them to repeat it. Concentrate on the questioner and not on any other noises in the room or outside. At the end of the interview say 'Thank you for your time' and ensure that you come over as positive and keen, but not too keen. It is essential that this is practised but is not too rigid that one change from the script will throw the student. It is also important that the interviewer is also briefed with a positive spin of the student's strengths and weaknesses.

It is difficult to plan for every social situation but the more planning and rehearsal that can take place then the better the chances of success.

It is also good to discuss areas that are 'taboo', helping students to understand there are areas in life that they should not comment upon as they are a social minefield: people's clothes, people's hair, toileting, sexual habits, criticism of adults. Opinions of other people should be thought and not said, and the truth should be told with sensitivity. When expressing opinions about religion or politics they should consider who they are speaking to and what the other person's views might be. Although these are very difficult areas for the individual with Asperger's Syndrome to understand, they can be taught.

The more prepared for situations students are, then the lower the anxiety should be when they come across them in the future.

5.2 Anxiety and obsession

I love to copy, create and order things. I loved our set of encyclopaedias. They had letters and numbers on the side, and I was always checking to make sure that they were in order or putting them that way. I was making order out of chaos. Searching for categories then did not stop with the encyclopaedias. I would read the telephone directory, counting the number of times 'Brown' was listed, or counting the number of variations on a particular name, or the rarity of others. I was exploring the concept of consistency. It may have seemed that my world was upside down, but I was looking to get a grip on consistency. The constant change of most things never seemed to give me any chance to prepare myself for them. Because of this I found pleasure and comfort in doing the same things over and over. (Williams 1992, pp.38–39)

- Obsession or interests?

- What are the dangers of obsession?

- Are they normal?

- When does an interest become an obsession?

These are questions we frequently pose about individuals with Asperger's Syndrome. Almost without exception the young people I have met have some form of deep interest, termed 'an enthusiasm' by Temple Grandin. These enthusiasms typically involve a comprehensive knowledge within a very narrow field. Sometimes the interest can border on the bizarre, but perhaps this reflects the ability of the child with Asperger's Syndrome to focus on extreme detail:

One child who visited the school spent a great deal of the time staring out of the window that overlooked the car park. Wishing to make some introduction in an attempt to find common ground about which we could converse, I said to the child, 'You like cars then?' 'No,' his mother replied, 'he likes exhaust pipes.' It further transpired that so detailed was the child's knowledge of his interest that he was able to spot the type of car by looking at and listening to the sound of the exhaust.

It is important to realise and accept that often the obsession has grown to give the individual a 'comfort zone' – an area where they feel empowered by having more knowledge and understanding of a particular subject. This is part of lowering their anxiety and coping with the world. Repetition and safe areas are used at times of stress to regain control.

Part of trying to get individuals more socially aware was to try and move their interests and obsessions into broader or more socially acceptable fields. For example, the particular young person described above is now in his late twenties and is still obsessed, no longer with exhaust pipes but he has broadened it to cars, although he is still able to recognise the make of car from the sound of its exhaust. This is a far more acceptable obsession, especially among young men. These types of interest are not unusual. I have met young people who have 'spotted' and 'collected' details of objects from numbers on lamp-posts through to every detail about a specific make of car. Equally, countless people in society have these same traits. On a recent visit to Wembley Stadium I noticed people 'coach-spotting': gathering and collecting details about bus coaches. Anthropologists are grateful to countless historical organisations that collect details about historic eras and re-enact them. The examples of enthusiasms within society are innumerable.

In addition, I have noted, again almost without exception, that most individuals with Asperger's Syndrome are interested in and often extremely competent in the use of computers. Many of the young people are very interested in simulation and strategy games in which they are able to set and control the virtual environment in extremely predictable ways. This appears very comforting, although frequently obsessive. They appear to see the computer as a means of playing games that isolate them from the outside world; but perhaps more importantly they are able to control the minutiae of the virtual worlds in which they play. They are frequently very knowledgeable about computers and many revel in the numbers and statistics that define the world of information communication technology.

Part of the programme at the schools was to offer a very varied week with highly structured evening activities; sometimes this would be using the computers for games play. However, at home, the young person can frequently push the limits of use beyond those seen as acceptable by parents. Once again the individual seeks to exert control at home and demands longer and longer on the computer. One young person spent an entire weekend on the Internet, day and night, finally falling asleep exhausted, his computer still online.

The Internet can become obsessive for many individuals, but is particularly attractive for the individual with Asperger's Syndrome. It offers them access to details and facts about interests and enthusiasms; it gives access to tiny details seen as critical by the individual. It allows them to feel they are on a level 'playing field' with others. They are able to 'explore and live' within virtual worlds on the net, even able to create ideal personas for themselves for 'communicating' effectively within chat rooms. The Internet is a powerful tool, but is highly attractive and addictive:

One parent installed cheap unlimited access to the Internet at home during the holidays for their son who was unable to break from its use. He used the computer literally day and night; his sole focus when he left his computer was to consider the best ways of upgrading it. He used control, poor behaviour and tantrums at home to get these upgrades that in turn stoked his obsession. Finally, he returned reluctantly to school, but remained depressed and unhappy because his use of the Internet was severely curtailed by the everyday activities of school. He could not understand why he needed to be at school and couldn't just stay at home and use the Internet. 'It has everything I need,' he said.

This young man, who is now studying for a BSc in Computer Science, when asked about his experience at the school some ten years previously, stated that:

The main issues were the poor Internet controls, lack of Internet to the bedroom. In this day and age, all people need access to these technologies 24/7 and I was in the pre-Smartphone era where I couldn't use it on demand.

In this case, and it is by no means isolated, the enthusiasm is destructively obsessive, and it begins to radically affect the way in which a young person functions. Perhaps this is the definition of the difference between obsession and an interest or 'enthusiasm'.

Another child, again totally obsessed by the computer, would frequently forget to go to the toilet whilst playing a game and would soil himself.

There have been numerous reports of individuals with Asperger's Syndrome who have 'hacked' into protected government computer databases, then later fall foul of the law when trying to explain that they just did it to show it was possible. Some individuals who may or may not have been diagnosed with Asperger's Syndrome have developed computer systems that have changed the world, and created some of the biggest valued companies on the planet, from their obsession with computers.

Some obsessions can be destructive to the chances a young person has to socially integrate and succeed in normal social settings, whilst others will be regarded by society as quirky, eccentric perhaps, but largely harmless. It is when the interest becomes a blockage for the effective socialisation for the young person that we need to examine it in closer detail. Does an exhaustive knowledge of Star Trek, tropical fish, Jaguar cars, really affect everyday living? Then again we always smile when we hear comments from school reports, Gary Lineker being told that 'you can't earn a living from playing football' or Bill Bailey being told 'he is becoming a bit of a comedian, which won't help him when he is looking for a job'. It is only when socialisation patterns are radically detrimentally disrupted or altered to accommodate interests that alarm bells should ring.

I believe we all have elements of interests within us. I have played football and supported the same football team since watching my first game at the age of six; all of my children have been introduced to the same team as part of their initiation and are now as keen as I am. For many years, travelling to home matches took me 20 minutes or a short bus ride; now the journey takes over three hours each way, and I still rarely miss a match. To listen to avid golfers speaking together effectively excludes most people from the conversation: they use the 'language of golf' and many spend as much time as possible on the course. Golf as a sport is intrinsically linked to a dress code, a social scene and a sport that can occupy swathes of a day. It is typical of an interest or enthusiasm. However, what we understand as individuals is that there are extremes of our interests.

I would argue that we are aware of when we spend too much time with our interest and when it begins to dominate our lives. We have an awareness of how our life may be altered by a growing interest and either look to curtail it or to incorporate it into our lives in order to minimally affect those around us. Thus, returning to our golf analogy, the golfer may reduce the number of times he plays, or go out earlier in the day. The 'normal' enthusiast may want to spend every waking moment with their interest but knows this is neither practical nor socially acceptable to their immediate family. They consider how their immediate circle of friends may feel and internally control their enthusiasm. This 'sliding scale' of awareness of others balanced with the desire to practise the interest or enthusiasm is severely compromised in children with Asperger's Syndrome. Their interest is totally consuming; it means they will forsake sleep, food, washing to continue involvement in the interest.

It does seem as if there are socially acceptable obsessions and some of these are age and/or gender related. Many young boys are obsessed with tractors and diggers and later move to trains and planes; girls can be obsessed with horses from a very young age. Later in life males seem to have obsessions with sport, especially football, golf, Formula One, cars, drinking and sex. Adult females are often obsessed with horses (still), fashion, texting, handbags, shoes, wine and talking to friends.

Thus, obsessions and interests need to be considered in terms of the effect on the socialisation of the individual; whether the interest is a potential blockage to acceptance into the wider society. One adult with High Functioning Autism documented their particular interest in seeing and 'playing' with sticky saliva; however, equally they realised that whilst this gave them pleasure and lowered their anxiety this was far from the case for those around them. This is an extreme example of enthusiams acting as blockage for social integration. In the same way, some food fads are likely to compromise social situations.

It is debatable whether interests and obsessions are commenced to lower the anxiety of the individual with Asperger Syndrome. They are, however, certainly a significant part of their profile and whilst engaged in these activities the individual is in their 'comfort zone' and as such anxiety is lowered and under control.

5.3 Anxiety and ritual

If the link between obsession and anxiety is tenuous, what is certain is that the link to rituals is crucial to keeping their anxiety under control:

> One child I met needed to line up his toys in the morning before leaving for school, and if this wasn't done, he would be unable to function due to heightened anxiety.

Rituals take many forms. If we honestly analyse our own behaviour, most of us would admit to some kind of rituals in our lives. They are often heightened at times of anxiety, stress and pressure. How many colleagues have we seen who have to untwist the curly telephone handset cable, or straighten cutlery, coasters or items in front of themselves on desks and at meetings? How many of us check the door on leaving the house more than once to ensure the door is locked, knowing that it must be locked? Perhaps more importantly, how many of us could leave for a holiday away if we didn't go through our ritual of over-checking the front door to ensure it is locked? How would we feel? Our sole preoccupation on holiday would be asking ourselves if the front door was locked, and we would be unlikely to get past that thought. Not surprising then, that the young person who lined up his toys on the window sill was unable to function at school if this ritual wasn't completed before leaving for school.

This ritual is linked to a feeling of impending events, and we feel that by undertaking a ritual we are ensuring the event will not occur. Even if we know the ritual will have no effect at all, we will continue it, just in case. Consider sportsmen, footballers who know that wearing a particular shirt, item of clothing or leaving a changing room in a certain order will have no effect on the game, but they are unable to enter the field of play with confidence unless they undertake these rituals. They are mentally 'in limbo', filled with raised anxiety if the ritual is not completed, and, arguably, will be unable to function so effectively unless they have completed the ritual first.

How can we expect young people with Asperger's Syndrome to function if we make no allowances for these rituals? If anxiety is raised, the ritual becomes more important, and thus anxiety in turn spirals out of control. What we need to consider as adults working with the young people is what harm may be behind the ritual. Firstly we must consider if the ritual is harmful personally to the young person. Secondly we must undertake a 'social risk assessment': what will be the effect on others if this ritual is witnessed? Will the child be socially compromised, stigmatised, even bullied for their behaviour? In these cases we must look to modify, reduce and remove the behaviours through a variety of approaches. In some cases this will be impossible and we may seek to replace the ritual with something more discreet or socially acceptable, in order that the anxiety is reduced as a consequence.

5.4 Anxiety manifestation

So how does the anxiety manifest itself and how does this differ from levels of anxiety that we all experience? As explained previously, this manifestation can range from being withdrawn, depressive and, in the extreme, suicide or aggressive and violent behaviour outbursts towards others. I have also come across young people who were capable of inducing vomiting or emptying their bowels at times of heightened anxiety.

It is useful to label the emotions so young people can associate the physical change that is happening with what causes it and what it is called. It is not that individuals with Asperger's Syndrome do not feel any emotion; it is often that they do not associate the physical change with any reason. Most individuals with Asperger's Syndrome find it difficult to be empathetic and cannot put themselves in other people's shoes, so it is pointless asking them how would they feel as they will often answer 'Don't know'. Nor could they describe the 'type of day' they were having. A useful strategy is to ask them to describe what kind of a day one of their fellow students had; they then seem more than capable and willing to impart that information.

When I first considered developing a school for students with Asperger's Syndrome I felt that all those areas that would create extra stress and anxiety should be avoided. So I started thinking that having no morning assemblies would be a positive move, thus avoiding any large gathering of crowds. Similarly, the eating facility should also be small and intimate. It was soon obvious that this was the wrong approach. Students needed access to larger groups and dining rooms; it was not realistic to think they could always avoid crowds. Such areas are noisy, bright and crowded but they should not be avoided.

These meeting places became an integral part of their social learning and development. The staff sat with the students in assemblies and eventually the students took part in their own assemblies, using them as a forum to express their own views within a structured format. The dining room became the most important social setting for conversation, turn-taking, sharing and understanding how much revolves around eating and what a social focus it is and the only way they were going to 'learn' and practise those social skills was with members of staff eating with them:

> Human beings normally live in constant interaction with their environment, and react to it continually. However, 'autists' have severely disturbed and considerably limited interaction. The autist is only himself and is not an active member of a greater organism which he is influenced by and which he influences constantly. (Asperger 1944, cited in Frith 1991, p.38)

When Asperger talked about 'autists' he was of course referring to the group he was studying and later we called Asperger's Syndrome. This may consist of disassociated behaviours and events, for which calm and comfort can only be gained from actions and situations conforming to narrow, predefined expectations without social awareness or understanding. The individual rarely has an understanding of why such comfort is derived. A notable exception is Temple Grandin, a professor in the University of Illinois who has High Functioning autism, possibly Asperger's Syndrome, and has used her lifelong obsession with cattle as a basis for a highly successful international career. (She designs highly complex cattle-holding pens that humanely move animals based on her belief of how the animals feel.) In order to combat her anxiety and craving for pressure without the proximity of human interaction, Grandin designed a 'squeeze box' designed to give comfort through pressure. She claimed that the squeeze machine had a calming effect on her nervous system (Grandin 1992).

This is a radical solution to anxiety but it clearly demonstrates that anxiety manifestation and treatment in Asperger's Syndrome are clearly not anchored in a 'normal social context'. This is further demonstrated by Grandin's belief that the squeeze machine could be adopted widely in the field of Asperger's Syndrome 'treatment' – a concept we find difficult to comprehend.

Grandin (1992), who found that spinning children in chairs reduced anxiety, has documented evidence of pressure and anxiety to assuage anxiety in autism. This has also been observed by other workers (Schopler, Mesibov and Kunce 1998) who have witnessed the calm autism sufferers have felt following normally 'fearsome and exhilarating' energetic fairground rides. Perhaps this is why the students benefited greatly from early morning physical activities before breakfast, and then continuously timetabled physical activities throughout the day.

Awareness and tolerance of our social world are formed from repetition and organisation of expected events irrespective of a social understanding of why anything happens. Therefore anxiety is caused by any break, big or small, from the confined anticipated structure the child has learnt to adopt as normal.

Anxiety is often manifested as actions or behaviours that mask the frustration or fear of change. This is because anxiety states are normally associated and structured within a 'normal' contextual framework of social interactions. This is not a framework common to people with Asperger's Syndrome.

One of the students had no anxiety or concern when reading, or performing, in front of large audiences; whole-school assemblies and parent gatherings for instance. When asked about his lack of anxiety he failed to understand what it was he should be anxious about. The same reaction was noted in at least three other students with Asperger's Syndrome. The paradoxical nature of his anxiety was demonstrated by 'trigger words'. These words were associated with negative events that occurred when out with other students, words including 'shopping trolley' and 'donkey'. In fact his anxiety was triggered by any word that fellow students had found would gain a reaction. Despite enormous efforts over many months he was unable to understand that his fellow students continued to say the words solely because of the reaction the tormentors got. He was unable to ignore them; he was clearly incapable of changing his comprehension of others' mind states.

The words then became entrenched in a 'black list' in which any reference to them in normal day-to-day conversation or teaching by anyone was perceived to be part of a structured global attack on him. Posters on walls or reading books all served to heighten his anxiety. This is because he was unable to separate the objectives of the tormentors from the innocent references of friends and teachers, and irrespective of context he perceived the words were used indiscriminately to cause him stress and discomfort. What made progress difficult was that despite lucid and rational discussion between him and his counsellor, often including role-play and social interpretation, in which he would appear to comprehend situations and readily assimilate concepts, he was in reality 'blinkered', and was unable to adjust his understanding. His understanding appeared to be fixed. The changing of understanding is key to progress with students with Asperger's Syndrome and can only be achieved through long periods of intense sensitive work:

> Children with autism are postulated to have no sensory impairment but do have a central cognitive deficit in their capacity for mind reading. The task then in teaching them to mind-read, may be considerably harder than teaching a blind child to read since changing understanding is involved. (Howlin, Baron-Cohen and Hadwin 1999, p.12)

Taunting initially involved using a trigger word in the context of bullying. When the context changed, the subject was unable to override the original intention (anxiety, distress, bullying) in favour of an internally constructed one, namely that the context in which the trigger word was then used was innocent and appropriate.

People with Asperger's Syndrome are easily bullied, and make obvious victims due to their inability to be socially accepted. It is fascinating that there appears a lack of anxiety in what we would normally consider as stressful situations, the assembly for example, contrasted with stress and anxiety connected to beliefs we would find as incomprehensible. Perhaps this is best explained by the Theory of Mind which hypothesises that autistic children are unable to de-centre and think about the way other people may be thinking or responding, to people, events, objects or places. To have a functioning Theory of Mind is to be able to understand and predict the behaviours of others by holding independent states of mind for self and others in a range of scenarios, which may be real or imaginary.

The orders of Theory of Mind, and the ability to perceive levels of others' thinking about you, clearly underline the complexities for people with Asperger's Syndrome in understanding others in a range of situations. Clearly this lack of comprehension could be a catalyst for anxiety in some situations, and may yet explain the alleviation of anxiety in others.

5.5 The victim

Individuals with Asperger's Syndrome are often subject to bullying. This is one of the main reasons for breakdowns in mainstream schools. It is important that all aspects of bullying are addressed and not just accepted – a culture of reporting and addressing bullying should be adopted within any school. You need to clearly define what constitutes bullying as 'what offends the individual or victim'. You can waste a lot of time trying to explain that what had happened was or wasn't bullying, but to the individual with Asperger's Syndrome this can make their life intolerable, so it doesn't help to be told 'That is not bullying, just ignore it.' The individual with Asperger's Syndrome is often going to be a target due them being 'uncool', taking things literally, saying things that are perceived as rude, or having 'strange' interests. The other students should be educated in how to tolerate and explain the social rules within any setting. It is important in a school or college setting that there is a culture of acceptance and an understanding of people's differences. This at times is difficult as the school may have a clear academic focus which has high expectations and not be aware of the issues that affect youngsters with Asperger's Syndrome.

There are strategies that the individual with Asperger's Syndrome can develop to assist. It helps not to argue, contradict or correct every student and teacher on every point, and if you feel it is essential to do so, doing it discreetly helps. It helps also if you are clear of the expectations within each setting and these are written down. It also helps to know the rules and to stick by them, not only the school rules but the unwritten ones, of not sitting in someone's desk or taking their place at lunchtime and being aware of others.

It is difficult for someone with a socially isolating communication difficulty to understand and learn all the rules of engagement. It is vitally important that the establishment understand what cultural difference they can make to assist the student. It is important within the school and within the individual classroom setting that strategies to assist students with Asperger's Syndrome are adopted. Strategies such as: predictable timetables; explaining any changes and giving reasons; visual timetables; considering a 'multi-sensory' teaching approach; pairing up students with Asperger's Syndrome with a sympathetic student (buddy system); getting the students with Asperger's Syndrome to sit near the front; being aware of the minefield of the corridors, changing rooms, and lessons, and general organisation. They will need as much support out of the classroom environment as in it and the unstructured situations are difficult for them to cope with. All these strategies will help to lower their anxieties and cope with mainstream school settings, and without them the changes of success are slim.

It does help if the student speaks to the class about their Asperger's Syndrome traits, habits, obsessions and strategies and explains how the rest of the class could help. I have witnessed a whole change in attitude to students when this has happened. This strategy has changed individuals' lives and they have become accepted for what they are after months of being an outcast and teased behind their backs.

CHAPTER 6

INDEPENDENCE AND FRIENDSHIP

Most of what I really need to know about how to live, and what to do, and how to be, I learnt at nursery school. Wisdom is not at the top of the University Mountain, but there in the sand tray in the nursery.

These are the things I have learned:

Share everything.

Don't hit people.

Put things back where you found them.

Clean up your own mess.

Say you're sorry when you hurt somebody.

Wash your hands before you go out.

Flush the toilet.

Freshly baked biscuits and cold milk are good for you.

Live a balanced life.

Learn things and think about things, and draw and paint and sing and dance and play and work every day.

Have a sleep every afternoon. When you go out into the world, watch out for traffic, hold hands and stick together.

Beware of wonders. Remember the little seed in the plastic cup? The roots go down and the shoots go up, and nobody really knows how or why, but we are all like that.

And remember the book about Janet and John, and the first word you learned. The biggest word of all 'LOOK'. Everything you need to know is in there somewhere.

Think what a better world it would be if we all – the whole world – had biscuits and milk about 3 o'clock every afternoon and then lay down for a nap. Or if we had a basic policy in our nations always to put things back where we found them, and we cleaned up our messes.

And it is still true, no matter how old you are, and when you go out into the world, it is better to hold hands and stick together.

– Anon

As a school we often asked the question what is more important, developing social skills or academic attainment. I certainly feel that they are both as important as each other. The individual with Asperger's Syndrome will often be very intelligent and knowledgeable, but in a specific narrow field. This knowledge and analytical skills give the young person some 'street cred' among his family and peer group, while external qualifications will give them choices in career opportunities or higher education. However, one without the other will make it confusing and restrictive for the individual with Asperger's Syndrome: having the academic qualifications without the social skills may make them unemployable; and the social skills but no academic qualifications will make the choice of employment very restricted.

I still hear of adults with Asperger's Syndrome who have gone through university and obtained an excellent degree but are unable to get work or to use the qualifications they have gained. Thus you end up with the individual still living at home dependent upon their parent for support and protection.

It is important that we understand that independent skills just do not develop overnight. My youngest son when going to university would only think of washing his clothes when he had no more clean clothes to put on. Then he asked how to use a washing machine and iron and after a couple of weeks had mastered both skills (although is still happy to bring his black bags of washing home at the end of the term). The young person with Asperger's Syndrome will continue to wear the same clothes each day and not think that there is an alternative and may never develop the skill of using the washing machine.

We then need to think how we can break each of these social skills into very small steps that can be practised and 'over-learnt' over a period of time. Also the skills need to be practised in different situations, as individuals with Asperger's Syndrome find the transfer of learnt skills very difficult.

There are many characteristics that we may feel are genetic and difficult to learn and which make up our personality. Yet it is also true that these can be developed or learnt. I am referring to those qualities of patience, empathy, understanding how to make, develop and keep relationships, and understanding the needs of others.

6.1 Development milestones

When we compare the development milestones of children with Asperger's Syndrome with those of other 'neuro-typical' children we see that there is some disparity between the two. They initially seem to meet the normal physical milestones but there is often a delay in speech or the speech comes in full sentences. The social interaction and interest levels may seem normal for a toddler but they seem to get 'stuck' on specific interests. For example, space and travel, which becomes the centre of a two- and three-year-old's world, remain such with the youngster with Asperger's Syndrome for many more years. The emotional differences seem to grow as the child reaches puberty and beyond, with the interests remaining immature, and there becomes an inability to understand the social rules of the playground, classroom or the world at large. The cute eccentric little 'Lord Fauntleroy' appearance and behaviour at three years old becomes annoying in an eight- or nine-year-old and is seen as very odd in an 18-year-old. There is a desire for sameness and predictability. There is often a mismatch between the physical maturation and the emotional maturation which causes problems when trying to make friends or develop relationships with members of the opposite sex. This often causes difficulties as there is desperation to be liked and to be part of the group but a misunderstanding of the concept of 'cool'.

Children with Asperger's Syndrome are often seen as 'cute' and 'little grown-ups' when they are toddlers but become annoying teenagers with strange individual interests. The differences grow when the individual realises that he is not wanted in the group and becomes lonely and is not sure what he is doing wrong or how he can change the situation. The onset of adulthood is often when depression, anxiety and suicidal thoughts start to become part of the symptoms of having Asperger's Syndrome. This is usually when the young person realises that people are avoiding them and they are no longer cute or desirable to be with, if they ever were. Loneliness and isolation become the norm and there is an awareness that this may be for life.

The individual develops a 'learned helplessness' where they will be content to play the victim as this is easier than trying to change the situation.

6.2 Towards independence

It is important initially to provide a 'wrap-around' environment for the individual with Asperger's Syndrome which will allow them to feel secure and hence help lower their anxiety levels. They need to be in a secure environment which becomes their comfort zone and then allows you to slowly and sensitively consider how they will develop strategies and independent skills. It is also important once the student has started to make progress that you peel away those layers of support to expose the individual to the stresses of life. The pace of this will depend upon the individual student and be different for each one. It is also crucial that once the student makes some progress then the support is not totally removed:

> One would not expect a physically disabled student who has been provided with extra support and starts to make an improvement with their mobility to suddenly have this support removed. So why do we propose it with other difficulties?

The student may have been subjected to bullying and been a victim; they will still have this naïvety and gullibility that needs to be protected. It is vitally important that parents are involved in this process. They will have looked after and protected their child for many years and will be very anxious about them experiencing new things, even if these are simple everyday occurrences for children of the same age. It is essential that parents and the school become a real partnership, understanding each other's points of view and needs and agreeing a detailed programme that can be continued and reinforced by both sides. When there is a disagreement between the parties the main person that suffers is, of course, the young person. You will have to 'risk assess' formally every activity to look at the safety factors and the risks involved. Each activity will need to be broken down into small achievable steps and completed over a number of weeks or months.

For example, for one student who was going home on a regular basis we decided that it would be excellent if by the time they left school they were able to travel independently on their own. The process was:

- First to travel on public transport from one bus stop to the next with a member of staff for a reason, either to go to the leisure centre or the local shops. The member of staff bought the ticket, found the times of the bus and escorted the student. There was also a risk assessment form completed for this journey and every subsequent journey.

- Secondly, the journey with the member of staff became a regular trip out for a number of weeks.

- Then one piece was changed at a time. First the student found the times of the bus, then they bought the ticket on the bus, and then the journey was changed – all still with the member of staff escorting the student.

- When the member of staff and the student was confident in taking this short journey the student would make the journey with the member of staff sitting elsewhere on the bus, or already on the bus observing.

- Then the student would travel on the bus on their own having purchased the ticket, with a member of staff at the end of the journey to make sure they got off at the right place.

- This process would be continued over a matter of months; the student would also carry a mobile phone and have the numbers of the members of staff in case there was any change.

- Then the journeys were extended, still with someone being at the beginning and end of the journey. All these journeys would be 'risk assessed' and the parents kept fully informed. In many cases the parents were involved in the 'shadowing' of their child on the bus.

- If everyone was confident then the mode of transport would be changed, to train or even plane, and the whole process would start again.

Some students may never get to the stage where they are able to travel independently on their own, whilst others are capable of flying home to Northern Ireland or Switzerland at the end of the term. The process was followed for many other experiences: going to concerts, football matches, cinemas, youth clubs, shopping, and all the events that one would associate with the life of an adolescent.

It was not without its hiccups and pitfalls. When taking a group of students to London we failed to remember that mobile phones wouldn't work on the underground trains. One student who travelled regularly to Birmingham was asked to leave a bus because his ticket was not valid; he calmly refused and asked if he could ring the school for advice. It was a matter of taking risks that were calculated but allowing the students to make mistakes within a controlled environment.

As with all of us, developing independence skills takes a great deal of practice, some trial and error and a lot of common sense – which isn't always the main strength of young people. It is important that young people with Asperger's Syndrome are also given the opportunity to try new things, and they will often amaze you by their resilience:

One of the very first students at Farleigh College, who was very nervous about trying anything new on his own, amazed all of us by announcing that he was going to fly to Australia to see a friend of the family on his own one summer. This he did, although we did have visions of him not making the connection in Singapore and getting the phone call asking, 'What should I do?'

Many parents and students mention the independence training in their responses, found later in the book (Chapters 10 and 11), as something that was traumatic for parents but gave students a step towards full independence.

It is important to develop a whole-school step-by-step approach to independence, then students will see it as part of their education and it becomes something they aspire to rather than dread. The social skills and independence programme extended to budgeting, shopping, cooking their own meals and entertaining others, developing those social skills within a controlled secure environment. These life skills must be embedded in the curriculum and need to be explicitly taught as the individuals with Asperger's Syndrome will not learn them by observation or osmosis. It is also something that can be continued at home with their parents and siblings.

I remember sitting in a review with a student, just before the half-term break. The mother made a comment about having to come home from work every day for the next week, at lunchtime, to butter the bread, cut the cheese and make up his sandwich. The room fell silent. It turned out that the mother had so little trust in her son's capabilities, and was too afraid to allow him to take risks in such areas, that she left work each day in order to make his lunch, before returning to work once he had eaten, forfeiting her own lunchtime to do so. However, at the college he was cooking evening meals for himself, peers and staff, and he enjoyed doing so and was very proud of his achievements. It was agreed as part of the review action points that over the break he would be allowed to cook an evening meal for his family, to show that he was safe doing so, and hopefully build his mother's trust.

It was a success.

The opportunities for re-integration into mainstream life were viewed as a chance to be able to practise newly learnt social skills. It was then important to retain excellent working relationships with the local mainstream secondary schools, which enabled the students to have some level of integration. The difficulty was not the academic ability of the students, as usually they were more than able to cope with the level of the work; it was the organisation of the school and the teaching methods that were the most challenging. It meant that re-integration into the mainstream school was done at the same pace as much of the other independence training. It did allow some students to broaden their curriculum opportunities to take four or five A-level courses or to be involved in specific curriculum areas, whether they were languages, physics or mathematics, at a much higher level.

One of the students who joined a mainstream maths group wanted the lesson to progress at his rate and not the rate of the rest of the class. The teacher was trying to teach the use of spreadsheets in presenting different information. The information gave a monthly management account of a small business. The students were asked to put the information in the different cells and then see what happened to the rest of the spreadsheet when they changed one cell. Our student was ahead of the rest of the group, doing spreadsheets in different currencies and annualising the figures and explaining how they could be improved. This became very threatening for the teacher who admonished the student for not keeping within the parameters of the task. Our student thought he was working on what he had been given.

As part of the curriculum the students would be involved in work experience, which became an art of matching sympathetic employers with suitable businesses with the skills and interests of the students. Again this didn't always go to plan:

One student who worked in a book shop would enthusiastically engage customers in conversations about the book they were looking at and had to be reminded by the owner of the shop that the purpose was to sell books and not to tell the customers their endings. Another student working as a library assistant also decided to classify the books in his own manner, which meant that nothing could be found without his knowledge of the system he had designed.

We do have to remember when working with young people with Asperger's Syndrome that they are also adolescents and bring their own level of angst, stroppiness and deviance. The art is to work out which behaviours are due to the difficulties with Asperger's Syndrome and which are because they are going through adolescence.

6.3 Transitions

One of the most difficult things for an individual with Asperger's Syndrome to cope with is change and the transitions that happen throughout life, whether these are physiological changes such as puberty or psychological changes such as adulthood where expectations change and sympathy lessens. The educational and social care systems also have clear changes and expectations. These are often abrupt and fraught with difficulties. The education structures of primary, secondary, tertiary and higher education become more and more difficult for the individual with Asperger's Syndrome. I explain the culture of these different education stages in some detail in Chapter 8.

The other transitions that take place are when puberty arrives and individuals try to make sense of different hormones which create feelings that they don't understand. Although they may have a different cognitive style there is no impairment in physical development. This can cause problems where the individual is desperate for attention and someone to care for and love them, thus becoming the vulnerable 'victim'. They simply do not understand the 'rules of engagement' for developing friendships or long-term loving relationships. This is not to say that girlfriends/boyfriends are out of the question but they will need help in understanding the steps to achieving a loving/giving relationship.

The transition into adulthood is often punctuated with periods of loneliness or depression as the individual realises they are different from their peers and are often viewed as strange and weird. This is also the time when the onset of other difficulties appears: anxiety, depression, obsessional behaviour, bipolarity. It is not unusual for episodes of mental health issues to develop. It is also the time when the level of statutory help diminishes.

6.4 Adult services

Adult services should be a continuation of children's services. In other words, if an individual requires a certain level of support pre-18 then this support should continue to assist with the development of independent skills into adulthood. Unfortunately this is not the case, unless the student is in a service that has a link with adult services, which in my experience is the exception rather than the rule. The whole cycle of assessing need and finding the appropriate support or provision has to start again from the beginning. Some individuals may have the academic ability to study at university but not the social skills to look after or organise themselves. It always seems that those with visual disabilities are able to obtain the support, albeit with some difficulty, while the student with Asperger's Syndrome who looks capable and is articulate does not receive the same sympathy or understanding. The question of support goes back to what the family can do, for it is important to realise that some students will need a level of support for life.

It is important that when an assessment is made of what is required then all the aspects of life are considered and linked together in a clear action plan. So accommodation, health issues, social care, vocational opportunities and emotional support are all considered not as individual aspects of the individual's life but as integral parts of the path towards independence. Far too often one aspect such as accommodation is resolved and there is an expectation that that will be the total solution, and professionals are surprised when the individual cannot cope. The expectations should still be high and the desired outcomes clearly stated, as individuals with Asperger's Syndrome can lead full lives becoming integral, contributing members of society.

6.5 Friendships

It's like a curse as the Asperger's amplifies my unstable personality. So interacting with others is very difficult as I don't have any friends to socialise with so I feel isolated. (Student at Farleigh)

Friendships and social interaction is one of the most fraught areas for individuals with Asperger's Syndrome as they are desperate to be part of the social world and have friends, but often get it so wrong they can end up alone. Thus it is very important that we do not assume that these skills will just develop or arrive at some stage in their development – they need to be taught and practised in a secure environment and then attempted in real situations with support and guidance. It is important that we realise that individuals with Asperger's Syndrome will want friends and partners, and in time loving and physical relationships. We need to talk to them about the 'rules of engagement' and not leave them to experiment through trial and error.

The importance of play in the sand-pit and at the nursery cannot be over-emphasised – it is where all these rules are learnt. The rules of sharing, turn-taking, saying sorry, being patient, clearing up your mess and making friends are all important in any social interaction or developing friendship. It is as if the child with Asperger's Syndrome misses out on the 'play' part of their development and doesn't learn these lessons at all. It is only later that it becomes evident that this part is missing. It is not that the child with Asperger's Syndrome is totally selfish – it just seems they are totally self-centred. They are the child at their own birthday party who is playing on their own in the corner or under the table unaware that they should involve others, or the child in the playground playing on their own. It is not that they will not participate in activities or play, it is that they will often dominate or set the agenda according to their rules. They are often not interested in deviating from their script and involving others. They will often interact with younger children or older adults where they feel more comfortable.

> I just can't make friends... I'd like to be on my own and look at my coin collection... I've got a hamster at home. That's enough company for me... I can play by myself, I don't need other people. (Wolff 1995, p.7)

Parents of children with Asperger's Syndrome initially are not too concerned about the child's behaviour as they are usually bright. It is when the child starts to socialise with other children that the inappropriate skills become apparent.

Individuals with Asperger's Syndrome find the concept of friendship extremely difficult, and will have very little empathy towards other children. It is what Simon Baron-Cohen (2011) describes as 'Zero Empathy Positive'. He feels that although individuals with Asperger's Syndrome may have little or no empathy they do not wish ill on other people, as opposed to individuals with no empathy who commit serious crimes and intentionally hurt people, who he describes as 'Zero Empathy Negative'.

This lack of empathy will obviously impact upon the turn-taking and sharing of the 'sand-pit' environment. They will not understand how others feel through their own behaviour and see 'friends' as those who can give them something material and not consider it as a reciprocal arrangement where they need to consider what the other person is getting out of the relationship. It is no good saying 'How do you think they felt?' when something happens as they are not able to consider other people's feelings and everything is focused on their own needs.

6.6 Friendships and rules

The difficulty with taking things literally and assuming there is only 'black and white' means that individuals with Asperger's Syndrome will regard the guidelines as 'laws set in stone'. For example, many of the students learnt a range of greeting skills, varying from saying 'Hello, I'm...' to shaking hands and introducing themselves. Unfortunately the greeting skill used was not always appropriate: from a student introducing himself to others at a youth club by shaking everybody's hands to a student being introduced to a school governor saying 'yo bro'.

It is extremely difficult to give a script that will match any scenario, as most social interactions are similar to a table-tennis match: you say something, if the response is friendly and open you try with something else, if it is short and sharp you will change your response appropriately. So to every conversation there will be many different outcomes depending upon many different factors, none of which are predictable.

It is important that we understand how individuals may think and act so we can guide them through the minefield of gaining acceptance and long-lasting friends:

- They will often only have one friend at a time and that friend is their 'best friend'.

- It is important that the concept and the social 'rules' of friendship are explained and taught. Taking things literally and saying what you think, which is often a symptom of Asperger's Syndrome, is not always a positive way of getting and retaining friends.

- It is often what is not said that is as important as what is being said, but individuals with Asperger's Syndrome will often misunderstand the implications. For example, 'Shall we' or 'Do you think we should' has to be interpreted in the setting within which it is said, what has gone before and who is saying it to whom. It is easily misunderstood.

- The phrase 'telling the truth with sensitivity' was often used to students when trying to explain how things that were true actually hurt people.

- The obvious, 'Does my bum look big in this?' doesn't want the reply, 'Yes, and it looks big in most things.' Or telling someone they have a spot on their face or they have put on weight or their new hair style looks awful are not comments that will assist in getting friends.

- The individual with Asperger's Syndrome is also more likely to misunderstand and misread other people's intentions.

- They are very vulnerable in relationships. Their desire to be liked, wanted, and have friends of either sex will make them an easy target.

- They are often used in adolescence as the 'fall guys' and the focus of amusement as they will do things to gain acceptance and be encouraged by peers without seeing how they are being used.

- The understanding and strategies of gaining friends or acquaintances need to be explained often with a script and practised in a safe environment. Individuals with Asperger's Syndrome will also not understand that there are differing levels of friendship.

- You may have 'friends' at work whose company you enjoy and will have a laugh with, but they are only acquaintances – although they may become real friends. Then there are relatives and friends of the family, and then your peer group at school or college.

- Shaking hands with someone at a youth club may not be the correct greeting, or kissing a relative or colleague on the lips may be too intrusive. This is something they often get wrong. For example:

At the end of the term at one of the schools, the school secretary was saying goodbye to the parents and students who were leaving the school at the end of that year. She was affectionately giving the parents a hug and kissing the students on the cheek saying good luck and farewell. One student who was not leaving but observing this behaviour was curious, and when beckoned over by the secretary to say 'goodbye' then took this as an open invitation and went into a full cuddle and kiss on the lips. Both the student and the secretary landed on the floor. Obviously the student had read the wrong signals and wasn't aware of the boundaries that people expect you to know.

So, greeting skills, personal space, appropriate touching, all need to be explained and practised in a risk-free setting. It is also important to explain when these rules become suspended. A case in point was when we worked with one student to explain what the safe distance was for each level of friend or acquaintance, and that getting any closer gave different messages. Invasion of personal space is something that many of our students had difficulty with.

This student would stand as close to your face as he possibly could when talking, and would make no attempt to move away if he needed to cough, sneeze, burp, etc. So we taught him, by using our arms, that when speaking to someone (we began with 'anyone') he must stand one arm's length away. To practise we would hold out our arms and encourage him to move into the correct place. We then progressed to him guessing the arm's length and checking once in position, until he no longer needed the arm as he was aware of the distance himself. However, he then travelled on a packed underground train during the rush hour. He was not aware that the rules no longer applied and became very anxious being so close to other people, feeling he was invading their space and they were invading his and that he would get in trouble for not following 'the rules'.

It is similar when travelling in a crowded lift. These situations have to be explained and practised and a clear explanation needs to be given as to when and why the rules are not applied with the same intensity.

6.7 Peer relations

The next relationship that needs to be explained and learnt is the student's relationship with other students and people their own age: the peer relations. It is essential that the students understand the concept of peer relationships, that they don't have just one exclusive friend but may have differing acquaintances depending upon their interest, whether it is computers or cars or a sport, and they may have many different friendship groups. Obviously with students with Asperger's Syndrome this becomes more difficult as they focus on their 'special interest' and have a great desire to have a 'best friend'. It is also vital that they understand that the peer group is not just a group of individuals who will meet their needs solely. This must be a two-way process, again where the needs of others are considered and met. This needs to be explained in detail and played out in role-play.

One of the students at the school explained that he had many friends. When asked what made them his friends he stated that they would let him play with their different toys if he gave them money. When asked if he felt they were 'real friends' he said that he thought they were as they shared things.

Another student was allowed to borrow some computer games in exchange for using his football. He assumed that the computer games had been given to him to keep as the other student wanted to be his friend. The ensuing misunderstanding took some time to resolve.

Students have to be taught that friends are not need-based and cannot be bought or sold as commodities. It is essential that some ground rules are explained, such as:

- Friendship needs to be a sharing relationship where the 'rules of the sand-pit' are explained and practised, where students learn how to turn-take and share through the formal social skills sessions.

- These sessions need to be structured. It is also important that they learn the meaning of words like 'give' and 'lend' and don't confuse them and don't try to buy friends through giving them material presents.

- This should then lead onto the meaning of friendship and how acquaintances can sometimes over time become friends and that this process cannot be rushed.

- The staff should moderate any disagreements between students immediately and intervene where necessary, deconstructing the disagreements to ensure they are resolved quickly and amicably. It is vital that the students learn that friendships are not just possession-based or based around their own needs but there is a reciprocal arrangement.

The social network site Facebook is an interesting phenomenon. It was set up by an individual who may be described as having many of the characteristics of Asperger's Syndrome. The Internet site is the perfect tool for individuals with Asperger's Syndrome to use to communicate and list their friends. The concept where individuals can have their own page and invite people to be their 'friend' is perfect for someone with Asperger's Syndrome. They are able to communicate and 'chat' online, giving their opinions on any subject they feel free or able to without having to interact with people face to face.

Facebook does have its positive side. It puts people into contact with each other. It allows a sharing of information and photographs and has been instrumental in organising events in many parts of the world. I used it to locate previous students and their parents to get their views on this project.

The negative side is how many people that agree to be friends on a social network site are really friends – how many of them care about each other? There have been some tragic examples where individuals have asked for help from friends to find that they are totally alone.

It seems that we all need our self-esteem and egos massaged from time to time to ensure we have an extensive network of friends and colleagues who think well of us. This is a natural expectation but one that is highlighted in individuals with Asperger's Syndrome.

The following is taken from the Friends Reunited website with the student's permission. He was one of the first students at Farleigh College in 1996:

> To anyone who remembers me – especially from Farleigh College, I miss all you guys – and can find time to correspond, I REALLY WANT TO HEAR FROM YOU! I might even come to a reunion, if anybody is organising one!

> Thank you for taking the time to read this, and do feel reassured about who I am today.

6.8 Best friend

This is one area where those with Asperger's Syndrome appear to have significant difficulties, as there is a real desire to have a 'best friend'. This does seem to be stronger in females with Asperger's Syndrome but that may be a reflection of the general population.

Many will be desperate to have a 'best friend' and ask people to be their 'best friend' and can only have one 'best friend', because 'best' means 'better than' anyone else, so how can you have more than one 'best friend'? They also find it difficult if the 'best friend' has other friends of any kind – in fact they can even struggle when their 'best friend' so much as talks to another person the same age.

They will not want their 'best friend' to play with anyone but them. The best friend concept will be based on their needs or on some material gain rather than a reciprocal arrangement.

I have observed many frantic days within the school when two 'best friends' have fallen out. Of course this is perhaps overly emphasised due to both friends having Asperger's Syndrome, so the rules become intertwined with the difficulties they both have already. It is made even worse when the students are new. A new student can change the dynamics of the school within seconds of arriving. Unlike most schools these 'best friend rules' are not governed by popularity. They are simply dependent on who gets there first. As soon as a new 'best friend' friendship is established, the old 'best friend' friendship no longer remains, making this very difficult and unfair for the third person. As I stated before, these rules are more predominant in females with Asperger's Syndrome. Males tend to prefer their own company, or are happy to join in with any group dynamic, especially if there are females in the room, simply to be part of what is happening and perhaps talk to the opposite sex.

6.9 Girlfriend/boyfriend/life partner

The most difficult relationship for the individual with Asperger's Syndrome to understand and come to terms with is the emotional relationships where they have romantic feelings towards someone which may or may not be reciprocated. This is a minefield for most adolescents and even more so for the individual with Asperger's Syndrome. They need to understand what is appropriate touching, when and how, that sexual relationships grow out of a consensual, caring, loving relationship and there are life-changing consequences for getting these 'rules' wrong.

It is worth mentioning that over the years I have become aware that many of the students fit into three distinct groups. First, those who just want to have sex, with anyone, at any time (even if the person went out with their friend before them, etc.). The second group is seeking a 'normal' happy, stable sexual relationship; and the third group simply does not ever want to have sex. Very often the connection of having feelings for another person and having sex with them are very tenuous. They will often see sex as a physical act that is part of finding out whether they like the other person or not. Thus it is important that clear guidelines and rules of engagement are established for all students whether they appear emotionally mature or not.

Appropriate touching is important to explain and teach. Many parents will state that their children with Asperger's Syndrome will not naturally come for a cuddle and this has to be taught. But also it is important to know who to cuddle, when and how. Children with Asperger's Syndrome will often not differentiate between parents, siblings, school friends, partners or pets with cuddles unless this is explained and taught.

It is important as relationships progress, and students are taught about appropriate sexual relationships, that they do not just assume that what they are doing is acceptable. They will know that inappropriately touching the family dog is wrong because they will have been told and taught.

Sexual relationships are a major issue with *all* adolescents, and individuals with Asperger's Syndrome are no different. They will be curious, interested, excited by relationships and these must be discussed. Far too often parents and professionals think if it is not discussed then it will not become an issue. They somehow think that those with Asperger's Syndrome will not develop the curiosity of other teenagers and will be immune to making any mistakes.

A member of staff was asked by one of our girls, 'When could you legally have sex?' and replied, 'I think it's sixteen.' So on her sixteenth birthday she found some unsuspecting boy and led him to the toilets to have sex with her. Afterwards she then told everyone including the staff what had happened. It was necessary to involve the child protection team and interview the two students. Her parents were distressed whilst his parents were quite pleased as they thought he would never have had a relationship, however brief. She declared that it wasn't that good and she didn't want to try it ever again.

I am making light of quite a serious incident but it makes the point that unless sexual relationships are discussed then they will still occur without any boundaries or understanding of the rules.

That incident in school did ensure that we had the 'no sex' chat with all the students and were able to talk about what was appropriate and what wasn't. A clear policy and procedure followed that all students agreed to which was explained to students when they were first interviewed.

On another occasion a student had taken to masturbating at different times of the day. He was told that if he found the need or desire to masturbate then it was only something he should go into the toilet to do. The following day at college, when a support worker was looking for the student they went into the toilets and there he was sat on the toilet with the door wide open, trousers around his ankles, masturbating. No one had thought to tell him that it should be done in private with the toilet door closed, just that he should do it in the toilet.

Again it is important to have a set of rules or guidelines that can be worked through to develop the concept of what the social rules are. For example:

- It needs to be explained how physical relationships should happen, within a loving, caring, and consensual relationship, no matter what the individual member of staff's own view on these matters is.

- It is essential that there should be an agreed school policy on sex education so the messages are clear and unambiguous.

I remember a health visitor giving a series of health and sex education discussions with a group of 15- and 16-year-olds, explaining carefully different forms of contraception and demonstrating to the class how to put a condom on. She used the example of how to put a condom on using a banana. It was clear that this confused most of the group until one boy eventually said, 'How will putting a condom onto a banana stop a baby!'

I remember another time when a female student came bursting into the office. She shouted that she was pregnant and appeared very upset by this. She was calmed down and spoken to. It transpired that she had held hands with her boyfriend. This was obviously not a problem, except that her mother had told her that holding hands with a boy would get you pregnant.

This proved to us that honesty was the only policy we should have at the school, and how dangerous mixed messages, or the wrong thing being taught, could be.

It is vital that the student has a clear view of what is acceptable, when and who with. This is often an area which adults are embarrassed to discuss openly, but without clear guidelines students will get it wrong.

6.10 Relationships with authority figures

The relationship with authority figures – teachers, the police, priests, doctors, and anyone else who seems to be in a position of authority over them – is often fraught with difficulties for many adolescents. Students with Asperger's Syndrome often have difficulty understanding that this relationship should differ from that with their peer group or family. Most people understand that if someone is in a position of authority they expect to be treated with a certain amount of respect.

It is important that children with Asperger's Syndrome learn that treating people in authority with respect will make their interaction with them so much easier. This is a difficult concept for such students, who feel that they are equal to all others and that adults should earn respect rather than just expect it. We can see their point, but not responding suitably to the police often escalates the difficulty rather than resolving it. For example, they will often only answer direct questions: any statements beginning with 'Well' or 'So' will get little or no response as they don't regard them as questions therefore not requiring an answer. These situations need to be taught and practised just as we would practise a job interview in advance.

Interaction with the police can be very difficult as they will often assume guilt and expect the individual to prove their innocence. Questions like 'What are you doing?' will be answered factually and directly. But if they are asked 'Is it possible that you could have committed this crime?' they will answer 'Yes', as it is possible even if they didn't do it.

This is explained perfectly in the first chapter of Mark Haddon's book *The Curious Incident of the Dog in the Night-Time* in the interaction between Christopher, the boy with Asperger's Syndrome, and the policeman, and highlights how misunderstandings occur:

'Did you kill the dog?' he asked.

I said, 'I did not kill the dog.'

'Is this your fork? he asked.

I said, 'No.'

'You seem very upset about this,' he said.

He was asking too many questions and he was asking them too quickly. They were stacking up in my head like loaves in the factory where Uncle Terry works. The factory is a bakery and he operates the slicing machine. And sometimes the slicer is not working fast enough but the bread keeps coming and there is a blockage. I sometimes think of my mind as a machine, but not always as a bread slicing machine. It makes it easier to explain to other people what is going on inside it.

The policeman said, 'I am going to ask you once again.'

I rolled back onto the lawn and pressed my forehead to the ground and made the noise that Father calls groaning. I make this noise when there is too much information coming into my head from the outside world. It is like when you are upset and you hold the radio up to your ear and tune it halfway between two stations so that all you get is white noise and then you turn the volume right up so that this is all you can hear and then you know you are safe because you cannot hear anything else.

The policeman took hold of my arm and lifted me onto my feet.

I didn't like him touching me like this.

And this is when I hit him.

6.11 So how do we teach how to develop friendship?

The first place we need to start is with our own behaviour as members of staff. We need to ensure that we are the role models, that there is a consistency to our behaviour and a moral code, so the student will learn that every relationship has a moral agreement and honesty to it. If a student feels that a member of staff is dishonest or has told him things that are not true this can damage the relationship.

This often creates problems for parents, who, as all parents do, like to maintain the mystique of childhood for as long as possible with stories about the tooth fairy and Father Christmas. The child with Asperger's Syndrome often feels they should have told the truth about these fictional childhood characters from the beginning, as they are not real. I am not advocating that all children with Asperger's Syndrome should not be told about Father Christmas but it is clear that once they start to question the logic of the story then it is time to explain fully and why we tell such stories. This is why many individuals with Asperger's Syndrome find religious stories baffling as they want to understand them literally. Believing without seeing is a difficult concept for them.

Once the guidelines are given and discussed and the students start to understand how relationships work, they need to be practised in social situations, initially in the school and then in social situations in the community during everyday activities, such as going to the cinema, at the local youth club, out shopping or in the café.

There are different strategies that can be used in schools to assist individuals in learning how to develop and nurture friendships. Carol Gray's social stories are excellent for teaching social skills within different settings. I recently heard of a parent who became a registered childminder so there was always a group of children in the house who her child with Asperger's Syndrome could play with and regard as friends. The utilisation of a buddy system, where students with Asperger's Syndrome are twinned with supportive and understanding peers who can advise and assist in different circumstances during the time at school, is a helpful strategy in mainstream schools.

'Circle of Friends' is another strategy that can be used, as can formal communication groups and support networks, role-play and the use of video to explain and practise different scenarios which will increase the likelihood of gaining more acceptance and friends within the peer group.

Outside of the school environment the strategies should include inviting home a friend of the same age, gender and with similar interests, joining a club or youth club, and encouraging positive relations.

It should be pointed out that many friendships grow over time and the young people should not expect a relationship to just happen. Sometimes you have to work hard to develop it.

Often individuals with Asperger's Syndrome will be drawn to others with similar interests or difficulties. The difficulty grows as the relationship becomes more intense, and romantic interests are sometimes too difficult to manage. It should be explained what friends actually do together – that they may just enjoy time together and being in each other's company, share the same interests, share material things, be kind to each other.

If you can, define what a friend is for them, and help them to understand that it will be different for each person. A generic explanation will help. For example: someone who is kind to you, talks to you and shows an interest in you, doesn't bully you, listens to you, who you are able to trust and gives you emotional support which is not just material based.

You should also have a similar list of what they should do for a friend, which is actually the same list, and highlight that they need to listen to the individual and not just talk about themselves, but ask about the other person.

It is also interesting to ask the individual with Asperger's Syndrome what their view of 'a friend' is, and what they want out of a 'friendship'.

It is often difficult for us to tell the difference between a true friend and an insincere friend, but for individuals with Asperger's Syndrome this can be many times harder.

We are all social animals and we live in a social world. Some of us may thoroughly enjoy making social connections and others may view it as a chore or an intrusion into our world.

Individuals with Asperger's Syndrome are usually desperate to have friends, although there are others who need to be drawn out to be social or do not seem to care. It is important to help them to develop the social skills required to maintain basic relationships, whether it is with a friend, teacher, grandparent or neighbour.

As I have said before, these skills have to be taught and practised. This instruction needs to be very specific and presented with lots of repetition. It is important that when an individual acquires a playmate you, the teacher or parent should discuss the importance of taking an interest in what the other person does. You should get the child to be appropriately inquisitive about their friend and teach him or her that to ask questions in a kind, courteous and sincere manner will help any relationship blossom.

It is also important that the individual with Asperger's Syndrome knows how to start a conversation and keep it going. This again should be taught in communication groups and practised within the safety of these groups. A conversation should be broken down into three separate components: the person saying the words, the non-verbal response from the recipient and then the response or an indication that the other person has understood the words. Far too often we as parents or teachers do the first part and wonder why the child hasn't responded. It is also important to remember that individuals with Asperger's Syndrome are often visual learners and as such will not pick up the verbal instructions and know they should even respond.

Teaching respect, empathy and turn-taking is often a challenge for children with Asperger's Syndrome who do not have Theory of Mind, but this is vital to the process. This should be undertaken through social skills sessions.

Another strategy that for us was successful in assisting social skills training was the video recording of social settings. Watching the video after the sessions enabled the teacher and student to observe how they engaged with their friend. It allowed the teacher to ask the student if they could have done something differently. Videos of different films also enable asking the 'What happens next?' and 'What would you do or say?' questions. This helps in trying to interpret different situations.

You cannot practise social situations too much. It helps in habit creation and will help the student to generalise their skills from one situation to the next. The student should also have as much contact as possible with all other children, not just those who like themselves have Asperger's Syndrome. They should be exposed to social situations that offer varied opportunities to interact.

EDUCATION

Chapter 7

Working with Social Frameworks

One young person was unaware that his sister was seriously ill. His parents decided that he needed to know. They were very anxious about his reaction, and so they carefully rehearsed their speech and chose the moment with care to tell him sensitively to avoid raising his anxiety. After hearing the grave news he instantly responded with a nonchalant, 'OK... Is the toy shop open today?'

7.1 The concept of a social framework

We all, across broad aspects of life, share a common ground and we adjust our behaviours to comply with the expectations of the situations in which we are engaged. My own behaviour will be different when in the family house, the work situation, and watching football at Old Trafford. In general we all share this *common social framework*, and understand that there are different ways to behave in different situations and generally comply with the way in which social interchanges operate. We are usually intuitive and are aware of the subtle interactions, behaviours and signals that occur between us. We understand the social rules of a great number of contexts and are able to respond in a general way which is not only understood, but accepted, by others. We might be with the same group of people in the same room but in a different situation and so with different rules of behaviour. The office party is a classic situation where the rules have changed yet you could be with the same group of people in the same environment. We generally conform and have common ground, although maybe the office party is an example of how often many people get it wrong and suffer the consequences. It is as if the individual with Asperger's Syndrome initially gets it wrong more often than they get it right by not understanding the rules of the particular social framework.

We are bound by a range of conventions, sometimes formal as in manners or etiquette, and often informal, even unconscious. There are many situations where unless we experience them we will never learn their social rules. Situations such as board meetings, High Court, Parliament, Council meetings, operating theatre or a Royal garden party all have their own unwritten rules and procedures which we may never experience but understand there will be different social norms, procedures and language associated with them. Our behaviour in different social settings, whether it is the restaurant, the classroom or the football stadium, will conform to the social norms and rules within that situation.

Although these responses seem unconscious and unconsidered, they are born out of years of developmental experiences and social and cultural conventions where we learn to react and respond appropriately to the expectations of others. These conventions and common ground are the social glue that binds us together as a communicating society. In reality, this is Theory of Mind in practice – awareness that others have not only self-awareness but a perception of what others may be thinking. I remember at school being reminded that some behaviour was 'not the Grammar School way', which meant that you were expected to abide by an unwritten code of behaviour that everyone was apparently aware of.

The social framework is not fixed, but is dynamic; it may change in time and different places in the world. As we approach new situations we learn from the experiences and we adapt. This is essentially a cognitive constructivism approach embedded in the approaches of Piaget, Vygotsky and others. Arguably, children with Asperger's Syndrome are in a similar position; it just appears that their social framework is skewed and more rigid.

7.2 Social rules and manners

It is worth considering the social rules in a little more detail. Often we pay little attention to the root and effect of the manners we exhibit, learn and teach to our children. On deeper examination I would consider that they have one thing in common, which is making other people feel better. When we queue, we join a common order – in reality we would like to go to the front, but we understand that this would be offensive and unacceptable for those who have waited longer than we have. We open doors and beckon others through before us as a sign of respect. We eat with our mouths closed, not just to stop food from spilling out, but because it is unattractive to sit opposite someone churning their dinner in their mouths in front of us. The very young learn these skills and the very old often have to relearn them.

All of these instances require us to have a Theory of Mind, a concept that people have a perception and expectation of others in a range of situations. If we fail to comply, to meet these expectations, we are considered ill-mannered, rude or insensitive. No wonder then that a young person with Asperger's Syndrome would be liable to fail socially given the need to comply with rules that are so puzzling. Why do we try and put peas on the back of a fork to eat them when it is much easier to use the fork as a spoon to scoop up peas and other vegetables? Why do we eat soup by pushing it away from us? It does remind me of a poem I learnt in primary school:

I eat my peas with honey
I've done it all my life
It makes the peas taste funny
But it keeps them on the knife.
— Anon

But what about conventional eating, using a knife and fork, or just a fork – the 'American way' as my father would call it?

I recall working with a young person with Asperger's Syndrome who always chose to eat food with his hands, irrespective of what the meal was. It was very clear from conversations with him that he was unable to understand why this was unacceptable, as he felt it was much more efficient, and quicker.

The problems occurred when we tried to explain the 'rules', the guidelines regarding eating. It is very difficult to explain why we use cutlery when some of the reasons are based on how others see us. It is only then that we realised how complicated and intuitive our lives are. We recognised the ease with which we decide to eat pizza slices with our fingers but whole pizzas with a knife and fork, how we eat buffet food with our fingers, as indeed we often do with take-away fish and chips, and how it is also acceptable to eat ethnic food with our hands. We realised that our rules are also culture-dependent, that manners too do not transcend the geographic borders of the world. Thus eating habits, manners and gestures practised in one culture could be viewed as odd or unacceptable in another.

When we first encounter new social settings, say a formal dinner or a garden party with buffet or a barbeque at an important function, and are totally unaware of the correct etiquette, we watch what others were doing and slowly follow rather than jump in and assume we know the social rules. The rules are rarely explained and never written down in a form that would make sense. When trying to explain these rules to individuals with Asperger's Syndrome they often respond with 'Why?' and challenge them. This is not a problem as such, providing they have understood the social norms for that occasion. However, individuals with Asperger's Syndrome will be unaware that the social norms may change in different environments and cultures.

When having food prepared as a buffet it was always interesting to watch some of the children take all of one type of food and not leave any for those that follow. When challenged they would say, 'But I just like the prawns.' Once again, very little awareness of the social rules of that situation.

It is important that social rules and norms are taught and explained so the individual may make sense of situations that initially seem totally bewildering.

7.3 Social frameworks and different contexts

All my life I have been an observer, and I have always felt like someone who watches from the outside. I could not participate in the social interactions... I just did not fit in. I never fit in with the crowd, but I had a few friends who were interested in the same things, such as skiing and riding horses. Friendships always revolved around what I did rather than who I was. (Grandin 1996, p.132)

When we think about our social framework with regard to contexts the picture is equally confusing. Consider how we know how to respond to this situation for instance, even though it is hypothetical example:

If you were to be invited to attend an interview for a job, you would have expectations of the interviewers and the process and you would in turn understand that they would have expectations of you: perhaps how you dressed, behaved, and certainly the responses you made to their questions. You would know value judgements were being made based on your demeanour, perhaps whether you smiled, how you engaged the listener or managed the conversational exchange. There may be judgements made of the way you might manage your anxiety, your confidence and hand gestures or the body posture you adopt. In essence, beyond your individual skills and knowledge, interviews are underpinned by a code of interactional skills which the interviewers seek to discover. You would know that eye contact and a firm handshake are essential.

In this situation a young person with Asperger's Syndrome without a clear understanding of how they impacted upon the social framework of the interviewers and the context is likely to struggle, almost irrespective of the skills they have to undertake as part of the role. Therefore it is vital that they are helped to gain the insight of others. The most effective way to work with individuals with Asperger's Syndrome is to acknowledge and understand the different social frameworks in which young people tend to function and seek to bridge the gaps in understanding.

There was one occasion when a very bright student was going for an interview for a university placement. I did fear for this student, who often would say nothing or give just one-word answers. However, explaining this to the university and ensuring that the assessment was not just on the spoken interview helped. The student having been briefed was able to say enough to highlight his obvious talent and the university accepted him. However, not all employers or universities are so understanding. As Temple Grandin states:

Figuring out how to interact socially was much more difficult than solving an engineering problem. (Grandin 1996, p.138)

In contrast, a completely different set of skills is required in the context of interaction when shopping. There are queues to be stood in, particularly in the supermarket, and payment to be made in full. Yet as always in our society there are exceptions: if an elderly person in the supermarket is standing behind our full trolley carrying only a few items, manners would dictate they be invited to check out ahead of us. Even with regard to fixed price there are hidden conventions: in the market or at a car boot sale there would be an expectation to haggle over price and negotiate an agreed sum. Consider the conventions regarding buying and selling a motor car: there is an expectation that the price is negotiable; how would a young adult with Asperger's Syndrome cope with this?

Many of our students think that rules are rules, with no areas of grey, black and white, and are written down. In a local supermarket many of our students will note if there are people in the 'eight items or less' queue with nine or ten items in their basket. Not only do they think it is incorrect but they will say so to the offending person.

We cannot forget these subtle differences in the contexts in which we live and learn. We gain experiences from a range of environments and situations and use these to direct our actions in new situations we encounter. We also are acutely aware of how we might be perceived by others and seek to avoid embarrassment by complying with the general expectations of the situation. Once again, embarrassment is a result of Theory of Mind. We are aware of the social norms and care about how we will feel if we get something wrong, if we say or do something that we know could cause us to be singled out and create embarrassment. This feeling is completely dependent on self-awareness, perception of others and actually caring about other people's judgements. This is rarely the process with regard to Asperger's Syndrome.

We often had groups of students visiting the theatre and it was important to explain to them the expected rules for each production. Although often the cast and venue was similar, the audience participation and interaction was completely different for each production. Shouting out 'He's behind you' may be appropriate at the pantomime but not at a play or the ballet. It is not even funny, and anyone who participates in that behaviour may find themselves ejected from the theatre.

It is only by empathy and addressing the gap between the common social framework and that of a child with Asperger's Syndrome that we are in a position to help them to move forward. It does mean that often we challenge our own social framework to ask 'Why'. Temple Grandin's view is that individuals with Asperger's Syndrome constantly challenge traditional thinking.

7.4 The use of social frameworks to understand others

Trying to understand the world from the student's point of view is one of several key principles that underpin my model for working with children with Asperger's Syndrome. Remember, our world works because we all understand the rules and as such conform to them. If we aren't clear of the rules we will observe those around us and follow what we regard as the norm for that situation.

If we flip the concept of social frameworks, it is likely that a child with Asperger's Syndrome lives their life to a set of rules, but *we just don't understand what they are*. From our social viewpoint we often miss crucial points because unless we think as the child we simply will not be able to understand what the problem is. It is similar to trying to understand the responses of infants and young children; they will learn that by making a noise, initially crying, then their parents are able to ascertain that something is just not quite right and they require something, which may be comfort, food, clothing or just attention. Often the art of parenting is to work out what the child requires and make the response to that or not as the case may be.

With youngsters with Asperger's Syndrome it is useful to try and work out what set of rules they are adhering to or what anxieties they are trying to avoid. As mentioned in the previous chapter a great deal of behaviour with young people with Asperger's Syndrome stems from their anxiety and trying to control the situation they find themselves in. We will often hear from parents that a child with Asperger's Syndrome will wear a favourite shirt all the time and the only time they can get this shirt away from them is when they are asleep. They are then able to wash and return it for the next day's use.

Obviously, trying to understand how someone else thinks is not a new concept with regard to social interaction; we do it all the time, with friends, work colleagues and in personal relationships. We achieve greater closeness with others through empathy and understanding; we know how other people will feel and behave accordingly to forge relationships. However, by failing to consider others, or by choosing to ignore the rules, we can also create rifts and disruption.

In order to work effectively with young people with Asperger's Syndrome, not only do we have to look at the world from their individual perspective to understand their slant on the world, but also we have to seek to address the differences with the shared common social framework. We have to deal with the 'primary behaviour' and not the 'secondary behaviour' that accompanies it. This secondary behaviour often creates anxiety and leads to major points of conflict. This is where a great number of schools and teachers make their first mistake in dealing with students with Asperger's Syndrome: they deal with the secondary behaviour rather than trying to find out how the student is thinking and what are their own rules. It is a difficult skill to master, as adolescents are exactly that – adolescents – and will always challenge and not conform at various times, and some behaviours cannot be ignored. But if the teacher always deals with the secondary behaviour and ignores the reason for the behaviour the relationship will not develop, and the individual with Asperger's Syndrome will dismiss all the teacher's efforts.

7.5 Creating bridges to plug the gaps in social frameworks

The inability of young people with Asperger's Syndrome to cope with change has meant that it is often the member of staff who has to adjust their way of thinking to be able to draw the children closer towards the shared understanding of a common framework. When I started teaching, the advice I was given was to be assertive and exercise control. I was assured that by establishing a clear hierarchy of power I would retain control over the behaviour of the pupils in my class. This relationship teacher/pupil or adult/child was always thought to be based upon respect but it leaned more towards one of power and control.

With experience, I rapidly learnt that control has very little to do with effective teaching and learning, and factors such as differentiated lessons, delivered through a stimulating pace, style and passion for your subject within a well-organised environment were far more effective. It is also more important that you develop a relationship with your students, that you know their learning style and adapt your teaching style to it. Teaching is not about a pedagogic model of imparting knowledge, but rather of creating an environment conducive to learning. However, the more we as teachers struggle to maintain the behaviours of young people in our care the more we resort to assertive control. We use set phrases which are aimed at asserting dominance:

'Now just listen to me...'

'I am not asking you, I am telling you...'

'Would you like to take over and teach this lesson?'

These have little to do with effective teaching or behaviour management, and are even less effective with students with Asperger's Syndrome. An effective teacher evaluates what the learning objectives are and seeks to overcome the barriers that exist or develop. This can be personally very challenging and requires a well-grounded worker confident in their own practice. We know that a young person's social framework may be very different to our own but we need to bridge the gap and work out what is really important. It is important that sarcasm and rhetorical questions are not used, as the student is likely to reply to the rhetorical question or take the sarcasm literally. You really have to get to know your students, what motivates them, what raises and lowers their anxiety and what makes them tick. If you are aware of these 'trigger points' then it is much easier to avoid them or develop coping strategies knowing they will arise. The teacher needs to know the 'trigger points' for every individual and how these are acted out and what would help if they do happen.

The teacher/pupil or adult/child relationship is traditionally one that is based upon power, where one will give the instruction and the other will follow. This model is one of the most difficult to overcome for the adult who has worked with children in this way in the past. It requires flexibility from both the staff and the school as well as flexibility in thinking. It is very easy to be judgemental and to fall into the trap of value judgements according to our own social framework and code with regard to the behaviours of students with Asperger's Syndrome. Again I recall several key examples where it is difficult to resist this judgement:

We had one student who would collect signatures from famous people. He did this by writing to them explaining that he had Asperger's Syndrome and would welcome any contact or support from them. Normally he would have a signed, kind letter in return that stated that unfortunately they had defined charities they supported but wished him well. He would then sell the signatures to collectors.

On the occasion of Princess Diana's unfortunate death he seemed visibly upset. On further investigation it turned out that he was annoyed that he had written to Diana but she had failed to reply. His response was that if she had replied her signature would be worth double because she had died young.

At a time when the world was shocked and upset, it would be easy to view this response as callous. However, it is unsurprising that there was a lack of sensitivity since, in reality, there was no awareness of the emotions regarding death and suffering. He was also indignant at why the staff were so annoyed by the behaviour, as he saw it as disproportionate.

7.6 The process of deconstructing each incident

This leads us onto the next most important aspect of bridging the void between social frameworks, which is by the use of *deconstructing the incident*. It is also a reality that young people often fail to see the consequences of their actions, which is probably true of all of us at some point in time. However, when the consequences of the insensitivities are pointed out, we are usually able to recognise the mistakes we have made and thus adjust our social framework to avoid the same issues in the future. This common-sense approach appears rational and yet the model is severely compromised when applied to young people with Asperger's Syndrome.

The problems focus on assumptions: firstly, a common understanding that everyone has emotions. Once again, this is not the social framework of the children we are working with. Secondly, there is an assumption that they will learn in one context and carry it to another, and again, we are very aware that this is a major issue. Finally, and perhaps most importantly, there is an assumption that everyone must care. This is rarely the case with regard to those with Asperger's Syndrome: the young people often fail to exhibit the very emotions that forge society together. Amongst these fundamental emotions are remorse, empathy and sympathy. I was often rebuked as a child and it would be accompanied by comments like:

'How do you think they felt?'

'Would you like it if it happened to you?'

'Now apologise and say sorry.'

'…and mean it!'

These comments would obviously not work with young people with Asperger's Syndrome, as you can easily see that this approach is in a language of understanding, completely removed from that of the student. The boy in the example did not have the capability to understand the impact of his behaviour. It was simply not within his repertoire of emotional understanding. As a result he did not understand that he had to care. With regard to apology, which is an accepted way for someone to acknowledge they are wrong and take responsibility for their actions, clearly this is an unrealistic option.

You understand emotions because you feel them; you have a mutual exchange and can personally relate to situations if you find yourself in the same position. Without these skills you would be unable to understand society and gel with others. This is the world of a young person with Asperger's Syndrome.

When working to bridge the gap between social frameworks you have to use any and every way to help the student to try to understand the situation in greater depth. Fortunately you do have a range of opportunities: you can use verbal language, stories, social stories, role-play, etc. But irrespective of the approach, you are seeking to probe down into a child's understanding, to get to the root of a situation so that you can try to build alternative ways for the student to learn to manage and integrate.

7.7 How to resolve conflict

Following incidents or altercations our students were encouraged to seek out their personal tutors to discuss any outstanding issues, or a member of staff would follow through with the student. To leave an issue unresolved from the student's perspective is to allow something to fester and re-emerge later. It is important for the member of staff to talk through the build-up to the altercation. If the member of staff's account was factually incorrect they should invite the student to intervene and correct them. This was designed to avoid re-creating the argument, as opposed to causing it to be re-enacted. Over a period of time, in the calm atmosphere of the room, guided by the staff, the scenario would unfold. Often when the member of staff probed further and deeper into the situation it would transpire that the entire problem hinged on something quite small.

This process was to try to establish gaps in understanding by focusing on the root cause and seeking to address it, resolve the problem and adapt the way in which the student's social framework was operating. Another example of how a conflict could only be resolved by deconstructing the conflict was when a pupil wanted to make a formal complaint about a member of staff who he felt had assaulted him:

The conflict arose when the pupil failed to get out of bed at the allotted time and missed his time to have his shower; times had been allotted to ensure that all pupils had access to the shower without interruption. He was allocated another time which meant he had to wait an extra 15 minutes. He was not happy about this and tried to leave the room, barging past the member of staff to gain access to the shower. The member of staff blocked his way and wouldn't allow him out of the room. This resulted in a physical stand-off with the pupil claiming he had been assaulted. With the use of a third person as an intermediary the incident was discussed as the pupil would not move on or go into school until it had been resolved. It was obvious that the pupil felt he should have not been stopped or his way been barred by the member of staff but also accepted that he was in the wrong. The only way for this to be resolved was to ask the member of staff to apologise to the pupil for the altercation and the pupil agree he was also in the wrong and if a similar situation reoccurred there would be clear guidelines. The pupil suggested this resolution. The member of staff found it very difficult to accept that they should apologise as they were not in the wrong. However, it was resolved by the member of staff apologising and the pupil going straight into school as agreed.

This was quite a turning point for the member of staff, who accepted that traditional views of who was right and what was their own perception of the incident would not have resolved this conflict.

It was important to remember what the desired outcome always is and work towards that outcome using different strategies.

The previous example could be classed as a misunderstanding, but often these situations can appear as much more bizarre:

We had a situation where the entire school drainage system was brought to a halt and required the professional intervention of a plumber. The blocked drain had caused a toilet to overflow and had created massive disruption for the residential school. The plumber resolved the issue after an hour or so, and the blockage was found to be due to a young person flushing an entire bath towel down a toilet! Further investigations narrowed the problem down to only one or two students, and with a final investigation it was clearly ascertained it could only be one child. Even with the knowledge of who had created the problem the child was initially unwilling to accept responsibility. Eventually, they admitted they had created the problem. The staff, who were strained by the entire episode, then asked the young person to help clean up some of the mess that had ensued.

'Why?' he replied. 'That's why you employ cleaners.'

Questions and judgements automatically flow into our minds as this story unfolds. 'Why?' is the first reaction. Then, after considering the disruption and expense the episode created, amazement at the child's lack of responsibility and subsequent remorse.

This situation demonstrates several key themes previously addressed: the 'naughtiness' which required addressing as it would with any student; the failure to take responsibility; and finally the lack of remorse. This final point is crucial. One of the key ways in which you seek resolution is to apply your social framework to the values of students by asking them to say sorry and apologise for their misdemeanour. This is such a high order thought process and could not be further from the understanding of most individuals with Asperger's Syndrome. How can we expect a student to apologise, and to mean it? This would require that they understood what they had done was wrong; accepted responsibility for it; understood that it had an impact on others; that it could be upsetting for others; understood what upsetting meant, etc.

These are high expectations for any individual, but impossible if the individual has an inability to recognise emotions in themselves or others as a result of impaired Theory of Mind. The entire concept of an apology is that it is embedded in sincerity. This is dependent on mutual respect and understanding – so much of our lives is governed by unconscious awareness of others and our compliance to the expectations of each other.

7.8 The use of language and humour

When we initially started to work with a group of young people with Asperger's Syndrome, as a staff group we spent a great deal of time debating our use of language. How we should use simplified language, reduce the use of idioms, similes and metaphors and use clarity in our direct communication with students. Over a period of time, however, we began to realise that all of these elements of language occurred routinely within the real world and we were duty-bound to equip students with Asperger's Syndrome to comprehend them. Language is a huge part of our social world, and humour is a vital part of social integration. As time passed, we increasingly used humour in everyday conversation with the students and as part of de-escalation. Many of the young people I have met have a very astute sense of humour, and they are often fascinated by word play. Some really enjoy hearing the sounds of certain words.

For example, the students would come up with many words that sound like their meaning, onomatopoeic words such as 'splash', 'thud', 'crash', 'skim', 'fly'. There were also words they just liked the sound of, words like 'serendipity', 'epiglottis', 'bobbly' and 'gobbledygook'.

Humour can also be used to help students with Asperger's Syndrome understand more about the way people think. One student was beside himself because he understood that when he was going to attend a wedding someone was going to 'toast the bride'. Out of this literal thinking came a great opportunity to explain the mechanism of how elements of humour worked and so his anxiety could be dissipated into something he could understand as being humorous.

Many of the students enjoyed the slapstick type of humour. In one art lesson a boy (called Peter) painted his hand red, and when asked by another boy why he had done that he replied, 'It's because I want to get caught red-handed,' at which the second boy wiped a brush of blue paint across his face. 'Why did you do that?' the first boy demanded. 'Well, now you can also be Blue Peter.'

In our first few years we would be constantly pulled up by the students for what they misunderstood and only regarded as the literal meaning of a phrase, such as 'skeleton timetable' or 'wanting to pick their brains'.

We also realised that labels were often confusing, or at least not meant to be taken literally, so we started collecting our own unusual labels. Here are some examples:

- In a London department store: *Bargain basement upstairs*

- On a night-club door: *The most exclusive disco in town, everyone welcome*

- Warning of quicksand: *Any person passing this point will be drowned. By order of the district council*

- Sign on a toilet in Heathrow Airport: *Toilet out of order, please use floor below*

- Leaflet explaining literacy classes: *If you cannot read, this leaflet will tell you how to get lessons*

- Notice at a safari park: *Monkeys please stay in your car.*

Our interactions are bound by generally acknowledged generic codes, which we call a social framework. This framework is often hidden and is constantly developing and adjusting. By having broadly common social frameworks we are able to share understanding across a broad range of contexts. The lack of social understanding is founded in an inability to understand emotions, feelings and the needs of others, probably in part due to a deficient Theory of Mind. In working with students with Asperger's Syndrome you are seeking to understand their individual social frameworks and bridge the gap through deconstructing issues to develop a new way of thinking more closely aligned to a general set of expectations. It is important when working with such students that you have a consistent agreed approach, that you share common ground and have a shared language.

When I first started working with children with Asperger's Syndrome I asked the staff to agree that we would pronounce it 'Ass' 'perger' – with a hard 'g' – and spell it with an apostrophe. It didn't matter if this was right, if there is a right and wrong, as long as there was a consistent approach. It is important that we all understand contexts and have a common understanding.

Over time we have become intuitive and have learnt by our experience. I developed an approach as I learnt what worked and what didn't. Although every individual with Asperger's Syndrome is different and will present in a different way, there is a common theme running through and the approach needs to reflect that. We know how to react to situations and not over-react and we don't often get it wrong. It is important that we explore the way our understanding of different social frameworks underpins the way in which we work.

You must also remember that not all problems stem from the association with Asperger's Syndrome – many will be due to adolescence or normal child development and testing and exploring the boundaries. You need to understand that one context is not the same as another and to expect a different reaction. You will know how and when subtle differences in context apply.

It is important that you evaluate issues and experiences with the student when the opportunity arises so they and you can learn from those experiences, and it is important to deconstruct the incidents to get a greater understanding. The use of humour and everyday language using explanations and jokes will often help with new learning contexts.

CHAPTER 8

THE CULTURE OF THE SCHOOL

8.1 The pedagogy

Before we consider classroom management we need to understand the present pedagogy within schools, their culture, the reasons why students with Asperger's Syndrome so often struggle in those environments and what would help to improve their chances of success.

> It is ineffective and unfair for the school to treat all children the same... In order to treat children equally one has to treat them differently. (Jordan 1999, p.33)

When considering the management of pupils with Asperger's Syndrome you cannot consider one aspect and try and make that fit the pupil – you must look at the culture of the school, unit or classroom. Our education system is academically driven, with league tables and inspections considering how well the school performs against defined criteria which are often alien to the teaching of special needs. This is not a case of round pegs into square holes – the pegs are multi-shaped and by definition 'non-inclusive'.

The culture of mainstream schools has changed considerably over the last 20 or so years. When I was at school the method of teaching was very formal: we sat in rows, worked on our own, and were given information verbally and then asked to regurgitate that information at the correct time, and the examination system reinforced that culture. It became the external accreditation of regurgitation, not to think too much about what you had been told or how credible the source had been but to recount the information verbatim. The teaching method was very much a verbal and written transfer of information and, hopefully, knowledge.

The culture of mainstream schools today is very different. It is one of working together, in twos or in groups, working collaboratively, discussing and hypothesising and then collectively coming up with conclusions. Students rarely sit alone and would be regarded as rather strange if they wanted to do so. This for a student with Asperger's Syndrome is a minefield, an area they dread. Add to that the chaos of the playground, the corridors and the dining room, and the need to relate to 20 or so staff members a day, and it is little wonder that some of our students with Asperger's Syndrome fail to thrive in mainstream schools.

You have to consider how to adapt this culture but also give the student with Asperger's Syndrome the strategies to cope with differing ones.

The different phases of education hold differing degrees of difficulty for the student with Asperger's Syndrome. The primary schools in the UK have a culture that for the majority of the time is more suited to catering for the student with Asperger's Syndrome. The teacher is one who will be aware of the pastoral needs of their students. They will adopt a 'mother hen' approach, looking after their brood, ensuring that individuals are not lost or left behind, coaxing, cajoling and prompting them through all aspects of education. The schools are traditionally smaller, serving a smaller area of the community or a sector of the community. The students are more forgiving at this age, are less aware of the differences in other students, and will often make allowances for those that are different. However, even at the primary stage the student with Asperger's Syndrome will find that they are the last to be selected for a game in the playground, will be the butt of many students' jokes and will not be invited to birthday parties or to stay over at other students' houses and not have any real friends. Nevertheless, their perception is that they are liked, and that they have many friends.

They survive the primary phase to be told that they now are going to the 'big' school. This is due to them reaching a certain age. One day in July you stop going to a small, warm school and then in September you are sent or taken to a large secondary school where there are students from many primary schools. If you are fortunate your parents are articulate enough to ask for or demand a choice of schools, and the school meets your needs (or says it does). If you are very fortunate then you will have spent a day in this large school and therefore know what to expect. The expectations in this school are that no longer do you have someone who is interested enough to make sure all your pastoral and education needs are being met; this is now done by a number of people, including your Year Head, your class teacher (who just takes you for the registration session) and your subject teachers. You have a different teacher for each subject and a different room for each lesson. This means you have to be organised and be able to relate to a number of adults and get on with them and be aware of differing expectations. Most students can adapt and take this in their stride. The size of the school increases tenfold, thus the break times and dinner times are a nightmare; these times are unstructured and supervised by another group of adults. The corridors are places of total chaos which at change-of-lesson times have what seems like hundreds of students going in the opposite direction to you.

The learning style is no longer geared to the individual but becomes one of a collaborative approach; discussion and group work becomes the norm. The inspection process is one of judging the teacher in control and how effective their teaching methods are. Paraphrasing the Ofsted Handbook for School Inspections in the 1990s, inspectors were asked to evaluate the teaching:

> Remember to consider the following issues carefully when evaluating the teaching in lessons:
>
> - How effective is the teacher's voice control?
> - How effective is the teacher's pupil management?
> - Are the pupils attentive and focused on the teacher?
> - When given a task, do all pupils engage in their work appropriately?
> - What is the general level of behaviour?
> - Do the pupils appear to respect the teacher?
> - Do pupils work well whether individually, in pairs, in groups or as a whole class?
> - Do pupils cooperate with each other?

- Do they collaborate successfully on tasks?
- Do pupils display high levels of concentration and perseverance?
- If given the opportunity do pupils use their initiative and take responsibility for their learning?

Everything is based around pupils collaboratively working together.

This is also the time when puberty kicks in, your body gives you messages that you don't understand, feelings you cannot work out. Your body starts to change and you may look awkward. This at a time when the peer group becomes the most important thing in your life. This need to be part of the group and one of the gang has never been stronger. The peer group takes over from the family as the most important social group to the teenager. Yet for the student with Asperger's Syndrome, who seemed to be able to understand things in a logical way at primary school, they are thrown into confusion and chaos. Is it any wonder that many students with Asperger's Syndrome reject mainstream school?

Teachers who are aware of the teacher–pupil power relationship start off the term in a 'no compromising' way. The way that is advised, so later you are able to ease off. They are in to control, control of the class and control of the individual. They will not back down or change their teaching style for anyone:

'It's worked for 20 years so why should I change?'

'I can't change everything for one student.'

'They are not going to win.'

These are comments that have been made many times by teachers when working with students, including students with Asperger's Syndrome.

Many secondary schools are aware of special needs and do assist many students with Asperger's Syndrome to fit into the school. But it is the student with Asperger's Syndrome that has to fit in and not the school which has a change of culture.

Unfortunately, as we progress through the educational phases it gets even more difficult for the student with Asperger's Syndrome to make sense of the organisation. At tertiary, further education, stage, no longer is anyone concerned if you attend the lectures. That is your own responsibility and if you choose not to attend then that is your problem, not an issue for the lecturer. If you want help you must go and ask for it, and this is usually situated in the Special Needs department if you are able to locate that. If you fail to hand in some work or just don't attend, no one will chase you. You are expected to be an adult and behave as such – there is no pastoral care.

The size of the establishment has risen to massive proportions, usually on more then one campus. Again you are expected to organise yourself, find the room and the lecturer, do the work and find the references from the library. The Special Needs department is for pupils who are cognitively or physically impaired; if you don't look different or have an above average IQ then you will not fit into this department either. The corridors are even more of a nightmare and the dining room has now become a canteen. The most important part of your life continues to be your group of friends, and you are judged by the clothes you wear and how grown-up you are. The word 'cool' becomes the most important part of your vocabulary. Once again this becomes a major area of conflict for the student with Asperger's Syndrome who does not understand the concept of 'cool' and becomes more and more ostracised.

Going to university doesn't get any better for the individual with Asperger's Syndrome. The establishment is even bigger, usually on a number of sites. You will usually have to be residential with a few hundred other students, far away from the home comforts you understand. If you fail to get up in the morning then no one will wake you or even notice, as many students oversleep. If you fail to turn up for lectures this may not be noticed until after a few weeks. If you fail to hand in essays or work then eventually someone will ask you why. The canteen will not notice if you never eat and the main area of social interaction is the student bar which will welcome you if you are loud, outgoing and popular, not the place to be on your own. The main purpose at university is to join in as many clubs you can, either sporting or otherwise, to meet new exciting friends, and, oh yes, get a qualification at the end of it if you are fortunate.

The whole education system seems to be unwelcoming at best and a complete nightmare and totally inappropriate at worst for anyone with a difficulty in social communication. Whereas the system can make allowances and cater for the majority of students with special needs, for students with Asperger's Syndrome it is the culture that needs to change or for the student to develop strategies to cope with the alien culture.

Individuals with Asperger's Syndrome are the perfect victims in our education system; they look reasonably normal, although they do not understand the subtle differences in behaviour and clothes. The subtle and minute differences between being 'cool' and totally 'uncool' are not things that the individual with Asperger's Syndrome is aware of. In school you get the perfect victim and the perfect victimiser in the same establishment, and therefore difficulty. People with Asperger's Syndrome do not know why they are being picked on. They have no idea that they are irritating to other people. Many students with Asperger's Syndrome become paranoid, since as they do not understand why they are being picked on they assume that everyone is going to do so.

The adult support networks also mirror this 'slipping between the cracks', in that they have a Learning Difficulties budget for adults of low cognitive ability and a Mental Health budget for adults with mental health issues, but the adult with Asperger's Syndrome does not fit into either of these groups. Thus they often end up with no support as they enter adulthood.

8.2 The whole-school ethos

There are no difficulties too big to be overcome. I believe you can achieve anything. (Student at Farleigh)

Education is of particular importance because it may help to develop special interests and general competence sufficiently to allow independence in adult life. The teacher has to find a compromise between, on one hand, letting the child follow his own bent completely, and, on the other, insisting that he conform. She also has to ensure that he is not teased and bullied by the rest of the class. ... Education progress depends upon the severity of the child's impairments, but also on the understanding and skill of the teacher. (Wing 1981, p.115)

Lorna Wing goes on to say:

There is no type of school that is particularly suitable for those with Asperger's Syndrome.

With Lorna Wing's words echoing, it is important to think briefly about the key elements of the overall model I adopted for working with children with Asperger's Syndrome. It is important that the strategies and techniques run seamlessly throughout the whole day and underpin the work undertaken. It is also important to try to ensure an overall consistency of approach from all members of the team and to formulate plans and policies as a whole school.

I do not believe there is a single, magical methodology that works effectively with all children with Asperger's Syndrome. The model that I developed is based on an eclectic gathering of ideas, programmes and strategies. I felt that it is a mistake just to take another model used with children with autism and try and adopt it with students with Asperger's Syndrome. Rather, it was better to take the best from each, and add to that my own experience. I did feel that the most important part was the relationship with the student and trying to understand the condition. My approach is guided by some theory, and a lot of experience. It is dynamic, reviewed frequently, and refined in the light of new experiences. I and the team had many 'eureka' moments when we suddenly realised why something worked or why a student did something.

It is important that many of the changes are small and subtle ones, ones that can be adopted by any teacher in any school. These may be changes in the environment of the classroom or the school or the approach that the teacher or Learning Support can make themselves, changes that will impact upon the student's ability to grow, develop and achieve. Making these changes is not as difficult as you may imagine.

There are, however, some crucial, key elements that run throughout the approach, both within the classroom and during the extended curriculum:

1. Team approach

2. Highly structured day

3. A predictable timetable

4. Individual education and social care plans

5. Monitoring progress

6. Students should be kept closely informed

7. Activities for weekdays and weekends organised in advance

8. Valuing students' opinions

9. Close supervision

10. Structured free time

11. Communal mealtimes

12. Regular exercise

13. Direct working with students

14. Resolution of issues

15. Staff awareness and training

16. Access to a wider team of professionals.

8.2.1 Team approach

It is important, when considering a team approach, who is on the team and what the approach is. Simply put, every member of the staff team is on the team – it is the Brian Clough [a former football club manager] school of thought, that everybody on the field is interfering with play, or all the actors on the stage impact on the production. They all impact on the delivery, whether they are the Headteacher or the cleaner; they are all important and can all be as effective as each other. So, it is necessary that they all understand what the school is trying to achieve, all have the same level of training and all have a consistent approach. The direction or vision may come from one person, and the rest of the team may not agree with everything that person does or says, but it is important that they are facing the same way and are receptive, open to discussing and learning from each other.

This is what I did, try to provide the leadership and pace and bring the team with me. Many describe the management system as a flattened one but it still requires clear direction, and the structure encourages teamwork and promotes support, thereby valuing each staff member. The plans for activities and strategies were made together, thus endeavouring to maintain similar working patterns for the students. It is important to maintain a whole-school approach and consistency in working with this particular group, especially with boundaries, school discipline and sanctions. Communication is very important, if not critical, and has to be managed through handover meetings, log books, staff emails and visually using white boards.

It is also important that the students and staff team have access to different therapists. Obviously nothing works perfectly with so many different personalities on any team but a cohesive, holistic, consistent approach is what is required and it helps if people are able to discuss and challenge what is done by everyone for the sake of getting it right for the students. This is obviously underpinned by regular training sessions through the school year. But it seems as if we were all learning about what worked and what didn't work with students with Asperger's Syndrome. From the beginning, there needs to be a passion to 'get it right'. Most schools will describe their approach as holistic but forget to include the auxiliary staff, that is, the admin, catering, cleaning and caretaking staff, in training and an understanding of the ethos. These groups are important as they will come into contact with the students in many unstructured situations.

8.2.2 Highly structured day

It is important to realise that the programme needs to mirror mainstream schooling in many ways. It is important that the student with Asperger's Syndrome is not taught in a 'bubble' but a protected environment that will allow them to have a full broad and balanced curriculum. It is also important that these students do have some access to mainstream schools, however brief and staged. This will allow them to understand and cope with the different demands in different situations. A highly structured day is also something that can be adopted by teachers in every classroom. In other words, 'even the free time is structured' so the student with Asperger's Syndrome knows what they are doing and where they should be at all times. The timetable needs to be visual, available at all times and clearly understood.

The aim is to ensure that the day is structured, but there is flexibility for the individual child within the allocated times. There is clear demarcation between the sessions, which are easily punctuated if there is a change of venue, but even within the classroom with the same teacher the lesson has a distinct start, middle and end to it. If it is in the same room and the teacher then changes then there is a clear 'stop and start' to it. It is also helpful if the lesson has a clear structure, with objectives clearly defined, learning objectives written down, a recap of what has gone before and a plenary session of what has been taught. These are the demands of the National Curriculum and should therefore be in all lessons in all schools. Even though each student may be working individually and with individual support on work that is differentiated, it is important to commence and end with the whole group understanding what had been achieved.

8.2.3 A predictable timetable

Once again, predictability is something that can be adopted by teachers in all settings. Things do change and events will occur that make it difficult for each day to be exactly the same as the last, and that would be very boring anyway, but it is important that each school and teacher tries to ensure that the timetable is predictable and if things do change they are planned and the minimum of disruption occurs. It is also important that if change occurs, for example, if a teacher is ill and replaced by another teacher, then the only thing that changes is that, the teacher. The room, the subject, the support, the material used, the delivery, should all stay the same so the change is kept to a minimum.

In the schools I started, every student and adult within the school had a copy of the daily timetable, for the whole school day, for the lessons within that day, for the evening's activities and for the activities planned for each term. In this way anxiety for the student was kept to a minimum through predictability and avoidance of change. This will always require a great deal of work and coordination from the staff, but it was effective. Another important aspect is to ensure that predictable problems are catered for, bad weather on school trips for instance, and that the students are fully aware of alternative plans.

8.2.4 Individual education and social care plans

The use of IEPs (Individual Education Plans) and ICPs (Individual Care Plans) are now commonplace amongst teachers and schools, and have spawned Individual Behaviour Plans, Individual Communication Plans and Individual Learning Plans, all of which are important if not essential. However, in 1996 they were not so commonplace. It is important that the plans stem initially from the student's Statement of

Special Educational Needs and the written assessments that usually accompany the student to any new provision. It is essential that you check that these reports are recent and reflect the student before you. Often when a parent is trying to make a case for resources the reports may be written highlighting all the negative aspects of the young person's behaviour and mask their cognitive ability or ability to cope, or conversely the Local Authority or previous school may want to portray the student in a positive light and ignore some crucial behavioural difficulties.

Thus at our schools during the first few weeks of arriving the student is assessed by the teaching, care and therapy teams to create a baseline assessment which enables us to establish a programme to meet the student's actual needs. These needs are then formulated into a programme for the child that is often highly individual. The individual education plan prioritises the specific academic needs for the child into small manageable targets in class, which will then be monitored by the teaching team. Additionally the social and communication difficulties highlighted by the speech and language therapist, parents and psychologists' reports are formulated into targets monitored by the school team. The students are then formed into communication groups on the basis of their needs, for intensive work with the speech and language team.

Students with Asperger's Syndrome often exhibit difficulties with attention; sometimes this is additionally associated with hyperactivity. The occupational therapist will make recommendations with regard to exercises that may well help with energy levels and attention span, and these are built into individual pupil timetables.

One particular student was unable to stand still, he was so full of energy, and medication options had been previously exhausted as a means to control energy, attention and hyperactivity. The occupational therapist worked closely with the teaching and support staff to include a target of ten-minute exercises every half-hour throughout the day. The activities were built into an interactive timetable; this was then put on the wall next to the child's place in class. This then simply became an integral part of the student's programme as a target monitored by the occupational therapist.

8.2.5 Monitoring progress

Strategies and programmes are ineffective without detailed monitoring. In turn, monitoring is ineffective if it is awkward and time-consuming. There are many recording and reporting systems available that are electronically based and should also influence planning and target setting. It is important that several key aspects of the student's progress are monitored by specific therapists working with the child, whilst academic progress and social skills need to be monitored by the whole school. The individual education plan, individual care plan, and outline goals for the student during their time at school are broken down into achievable targets that are monitored by teaching and residential care staff. In the case of socialisation, behaviour and communication skills, these targets are monitored twice daily using a progress log. This enables a quantitative measurement of the pupil's progress that can easily be graphically represented for those concerned with the care of the student. The important aspect when setting and monitoring these targets is that they are set in small achievable steps with an attention to detail yet are able to show progress and motivate the student.

8.2.6 Students should be kept closely informed

I believe that the student will perform better and have confidence in the programme set if they are totally involved in every aspect of it. They need to know what is occurring in their school and they should be kept closely informed of the daily events, usually through announcements at early morning assembly. In this way they are more able to cope with guests and visitors, who can often unwittingly disrupt the timetable. We are honest with the students, and they are often refreshingly honest with visitors:

We were to be inspected by a Social Services Inspector, and the children had been encouraged to tidy their rooms in anticipation, especially their drawers. Later that day the inspector entered the classroom and one of the children asked if he was the man who was going to inspect his sock drawer.

8.2.7 Activities for weekdays and weekends organised in advance

The care team carefully plans the weekday and weekend activities and these are subsequently published and posted on each student's personal notice board. In this way the student knows exactly what is going to happen and anxiety is once more reduced.

8.2.8 Valuing students' opinions

I remember walking into your office when I came to look round during the summer holidays (so there were no pupils running around, etc.) and on being introduced to you, thinking, 'Aren't you a bit young to be a Headteacher?' Seriously, that is what I thought. You were nothing like the common 1950s image of a Headteacher who wears glasses and a tweed jacket with leather patches! (Student at Farleigh)

I would always actively encourage students to contribute to the school and to air their opinions, although in the socially accepted way and in the correct context. The students contribute to school rules, and have a large input into the menus and activities; they also work with the teacher to produce a range of acceptable rules for the classroom. The students also worked on a reward system that was implemented. The students can make suggestions informally, through any member of staff, or through formal systems – the school council, for example. At the end of each week I introduced a 'positive assembly' which was intended to ensure that we could end the week on a positive note and the students could focus on the positives rather than the negative events of that week. Before this assembly the students would meet with their personal tutor to discuss what had been positive. When I started the assemblies I would ask either the tutor or the student to give me one positive event in their week that we could celebrate. This was a positive activity and the students soon got into the full swing of participation. The 'rules' for this assembly were that:

- Only one person could speak at a time and everyone else would listen.

- The subject discussed had to be positive.

The first week one of our more negative students was keen to voice his opinion, and eventually he was given the floor to speak:

'I want to say that Fred (not his actual name) is a complete arsehole.'

When reminded of the rules, he said:

'It was a positive comment. If it had been a negative comment I would have to use "wasn't" something, but he "was" an arsehole.'

Sometimes you are just speechless!

8.2.9 Close supervision

It is important to realise that although students with Asperger's Syndrome can appear confident and outgoing, they are also are highly vulnerable. Often they are frequently bullied, and are easy victims. They will frequently show little fear, often seeming to not understand the very nature of fear. They are often headstrong and determined, and at times outside the classroom need very close supervision to ensure their safety. It is important that you are aware of where the students with Asperger's Syndrome are and don't assume they are coping, especially in areas such as the corridors, dining rooms and the playground. It is important when students complain of bullying that they are aware of the meaning of words they use. There were times when students said that certain things had happened and used emotive words such as 'raped' or 'assaulted', so that it was necessary to be sure that they were aware of exactly what had occurred and they were describing it correctly. It is true that students with Asperger's Syndrome actually will be bullied but they also have the perception that the whole world dislikes them and everyone is bullying them. Perception is reality to the individual with Asperger's Syndrome so this needs sensitive handling and should not just be dismissed.

8.2.10 Structured free time

The students frequently struggle with break, playtime and relaxation periods, and will often seek to fill them with their obsession or enthusiasm. Whilst these needs must be met, these students may often require careful and enthusiastic support to use free time in more creative ways. It is not sufficient to let students with Asperger's Syndrome out to play at break times, as at best they will fail to socialise and at worst may be teased or bullied. The students need to be supervised and provided with ideas to stimulate them; this could be a range of outdoor games, or swings. It is important that the adults are active at these times to stimulate social interaction.

I would try and get the students to play football at lunchtimes, though this would only happen if there were staff members involved in the game, and even then it was a spectacle to behold:

Picking sides was a skill in itself to try and ensure that there was a balance of numbers, skills and coordination. Then the rules had to be explained. Very few would understand that it was a team game with the aim of putting the ball in the opponents' goal. So we had students tackling each other, often from the same sides, one student always wanting to pick the ball up, one wanting to be referee, another running up and down parallel to the pitch, another commentating on the match. When trying to explain the 'unwritten rules' it became even more bizarre and impossible; rules such as not trying too hard, making the 'top students' look good, not fouling the major players, passing to a recognised 'star', telling people how good they were, always praising and looking 'cool'.

All these aspects of the game had to be taught or introduced one at a time. Thus, free time in school is always difficult, but a balance between a variety of activities, personal freedom, space and time to indulge in their interest is essential.

8.2.11 Communal mealtimes

It is crucial to realise how important mealtimes are. They are a learning experience, a social occasion and one of the highlights of the day, both for the satisfaction and enjoyment food brings for the students and for the wealth of opportunities for social interaction. It was therefore essential to get as many adults in the dining room to interact with the students, thus all of the staff and any visitors ate with the students. Students initially sat at set places, marked with their own distinctive placemats. They were expected to adhere to the conventions of mealtimes, using a knife and fork, cutting food properly, using table manners and eating within an appropriate time span. Some students found using a knife and fork tedious, perhaps because it is an inefficient way to eat and like many table manners conventions it serves merely to make eating more visually acceptable for other people sharing the meal. Students also learnt the meaning of sharing food, that despite wanting all of a particular food that is available, they need to leave some for their peers. Most students have food preferences based upon their likes and experience. Students with Asperger's Syndrome often have obsessions, rituals and fads surrounding food and diet; these are countless. I have encountered children that will only eat certain colours of food, some that had a very restricted diet of one or two things and others that would not eat hot food. Many children with Asperger's Syndrome used food as a something they exercise control over. Additionally, food choices are difficult. We developed a system of ordering the evening meal in the morning: children can choose from three items on the menu. This appeared to ensure their choice is their own, and they will eat. It also helps with not having to make choices later in the day at dinner time. They did have a problem with choice and remembering what they ordered, but that is not so unusual – I have a whole family who have that particular difficulty!

8.2.12 Regular exercise

It is essential that the students exercise daily. We introduced a system where the students exercised early in the morning after getting up and having a biscuit and a drink, and once the routine had been established they enjoyed it.

Regular daily exercise is important for the students for several key reasons. From the perspective of health, generally children with Asperger's Syndrome are susceptible to inactivity and daily exercise goes some way to ensuring they will gain a reasonable level of fitness. It also helps develop team cooperation and socialisation for a new purpose in a different context and enables them to practise hand–eye coordination in fun and stimulating ways.

The additional effect of early morning exercise is to make breakfast a little later. This allows all staff to join the children for this first meal of the day.

8.2.13 Direct working with students

All of the students have a personal tutor who deals with issues beyond the classroom. They act as confidante, guide, support, conscience and parental liaison; they also act as intermediary in disputes or difficulties the student may have. The personal tutor is usually a member of the residential care team and is responsible for coordinating annual review reports and setting social targets in conjunction with the whole-school staff team. A close bond forms between student and tutor; this enables direct work with the student on a range of issues, dependent upon the individual needs of the student.

We did have one student who would constantly ask questions and would only respond if he was asked a direct question. In order to monitor this I decided that it would be important to limit the number of questions he could ask and the number of questions he could be asked. He agreed that five was a reasonable number per half-day and would try and stick to that.

The following day I needed to contact this student's mother and was passing him in the corridor so I casually said to him, 'Edward, can I ask you just one question?'

To which he replied, 'Is that the question?'

'Is what the question?' I said.

'That,' he replied.

Once again I was speechless.

8.2.14 Resolution of issues

The importance of resolving issues and conflicts for children with Asperger's Syndrome cannot be over-emphasised. What may appear to us as tiny, trivial or insignificant 'hiccups' are likely to be considered in completely different proportions for the student with Asperger's Syndrome. If a conflict or difficulty is not resolved it will not disappear, and will return to cloud future difficulties or will radically affect the child's forthcoming day. I have known students to carry a grudge for years. One student who was exceptionally bright would refuse to do a subject if that teacher had not resolved an issue to his satisfaction or had mis-handled a situation. It is crucial that adults help students to resolve difficulties and then sign off on them. Techniques that are used are discussion, role-play, and careful reframing of conversations, deconstructing events step by step for the student, in order that they can begin to understand the issue, hopefully from the perspective of another. I introduced written contracts, signed by those involved, to ensure that a student stayed within agreed targets. The use of written and signed resolution certificates to underline the finish of a difficulty for the student is certainly beneficial as it gives closure to an incident or event that the student is then able to move on from. The student would be expected to sign this and a copy is pinned to their personal notice board.

Sometimes this doesn't always go to plan:

Following a conflict, one student signed off on his resolution certificate, which was prepared by the pastoral tutor. However, the following day the issue emerged once more. The student was reminded that the issue had been resolved and they had signed off on it. The student replied that he hadn't used his Gothic handwriting, and so the contract wasn't binding. The situation was once more resolved, a new certificate signed in the correct script, and the staff were informed by the tutor that they needed to ensure any binding signatures from the student needed to be in Gothic script.

8.2.15 Staff awareness and training

It is important that all of the staff receive training before they start working with students with Asperger's Syndrome and understand the basics of the difficulties the students will have. It is also important, if not crucial, that there is a consistent approach and the staff follow the agreed procedures. There is always a forum to discuss strategies that are used with the students and changes in philosophy, but once there is an agreed strategy and way of working then it must be followed. This did help new members of staff who may have arrived with different preconceived notions of what Asperger's Syndrome was and how it should be dealt with, or made different value judgements. Consistency is one of the crucial building blocks for working with students with Asperger's Syndrome. Staff would be involved in regular training, either internally through the school or through conferences and externally verified courses. The awareness of the characteristics of Asperger's Syndrome is essential for working effectively with these students.

Your staff and the quality of training and understanding of Asperger's Syndrome was your greatest asset. (Parent of one of the students at Farleigh College)

The staff group needs to be diverse and come from a variety of different backgrounds; the experiences they will bring to the team are invaluable and ensure the students have role models from all aspects of life. It is important to have not only a skills balance but a balance of gender, age and outlook on life which mirrors society at large. Students with Asperger's Syndrome do not need to be constantly wrapped in cotton wool but slowly exposed to as many different experiences as is possible, firstly in a secure safe environment then eventually in a riskier situation. A diverse staff team assists this process. There does seem to be a predominance of female teachers and support workers in schools for autism, and I do think that any establishment needs to be aware of this imbalance.

As previously stated (Chapter 2), I worked alongside the University in Bath to produce a training programme on Asperger's Syndrome. A report on the programme was first prepared by the team led by Tim Bilham at the Department for Health, University of Bath, in 2003, and is reproduced at the end of this chapter. It outlines the reason for the training, the process and the way the pilot scheme was introduced to the staff at the school.

8.2.16 Access to a wider team of professionals

Students with Asperger's Syndrome may also have difficulty with expressive language, and certainly social communication, and may be described as clumsy. It is therefore important that a therapy team is part of the provision in schools. Where this goes wrong is when the therapy team is not an integral part of the staff team and working hand-in-hand with the rest of the staff team. The first example that occurred was when we appointed a nurse to assist with medical overview: she wanted to wear her nurse's uniform at all times and be called 'sister', and wanted to be the only person to deal with medical issues. This obviously was not going to work and didn't last very long. All too often this input seems to be a 'bolt-on' one where the therapist will work independently, away from the teacher, seeing the student on their own and staying within their own professional bubble. So when setting up the schools I ensured that the therapists were able to work as a team and involve the teaching and care staff teams. The team of professionals involved with the school includes a speech and language therapist, occupational therapist, educational psychologist, paediatrician, psychiatrist, general practitioner and counsellor. I looked for therapists who wanted to work as part of a multi-disciplinary team and work alongside other teachers and care staff with the students rather than write a report and see the students out of the context of their classroom or living situation. Students with Asperger's Syndrome present with a wide variety of needs, and while all students will not see every professional, referrals are made to meet the individual needs of the child. The professional involved with the school acts primarily in a consultancy role, thereby supporting the staff working directly with the child.

It is important when working with young people with Asperger's Syndrome that one considers the culture of the school and how that will assist those youngsters. Far too often it is expected that the young people will adapt to the culture and expectations of the school, but with youngsters with Asperger's Syndrome it is the other way round. The school needs to be able to wrap around the individual student and lower their level of anxiety.

It is important in the mainstream setting to consider what individuals with Asperger's Syndrome find difficult and how the school can adapt its own culture. The education system creates abrupt transition stages which students with Asperger's Syndrome find very difficult. The change from primary to secondary stage takes the student from a warm, secure environment where they relate to one key adult to a secondary system where they have to organise themselves and relate to many different adults in different rooms and where the expectation is that the student will organise themselves. This is too big a step to take in one move and the school should be aware of this. The change from secondary to tertiary is equally large, where the expectation of the establishment is that the student will be mature and organised enough to cope with a completely new educational culture.

Individual teachers can make it much easier for students with Asperger's Syndrome to cope if they align their teaching style with the student's learning style. Good teaching is good teaching for all students and there is no mystery about teaching young people with Asperger's Syndrome, but it is important that the Syndrome is understood, training is clear and support of the students is evident in meeting their needs. A 'tag team' approach and access to a multi-disciplinary team make life much easier, but the most important is to get the culture accepting of the differences.

Report on the pilot scheme[1]

We know today that Asperger's Syndrome (AS) and Autistic Spectrum Disorders (ASD) result from abnormalities in brain function and structure, not emotional trauma or bad parenting (Gillberg and Billstedt 2000).

Most individuals with AS have limited access to psychiatrists, psychologists, and other medical professionals experienced with the disorder. Appropriate educational services, training and certain beneficial therapies are also hard to come by. Although AS is considered rare, current estimates place the prevalence at 1 in 300. Given the alarming rise in diagnoses of all forms of autism – the California Department of Health, for example, found an increase of more than 210 per cent between 1987 and 1998 – it is likely that the AS rate will rise in coming years.

Given this situation, even if public awareness of AS is low, people with the disorder are commonly recognisable via 'lay diagnosis'. They are often seen as individuals who, as children, might have been perceived as uncooperative, spoilt, or the product of poor parenting. Adults with AS might avoid eye contact, fail to comprehend instructions, dress oddly, lack good personal hygiene, or talk about seemingly irrelevant subjects (Szatmari *et al.* 2003). While researchers continue to debate the diagnostic criteria, individuals with AS can also exhibit an inflexible adherence to non-functional routines and rituals, stereotyped or repetitive motor mannerisms, and preoccupation with parts of objects. (These behaviours must be sufficient to interfere significantly with social or other areas of functioning.) At the same time, there is no significant associated delay in cognitive function, self-help skills, interest in the environment, or language development (Prior *et al.* 1998).

---

1   Report prepared (2003), by the AS project team following the pilot scheme led by Tim Bilham, Department for Health, University of Bath

The need for training

Useful as these diagnostic criteria may be, they fail to show what it's like to be or live with an individual with AS. For example, parents and carers soon recognise the presence of a different view of the world, as expressed in communications, and understandings of self and others. Some social behaviour, like using appropriate tone of voice or facial expression, is often viewed as beyond young adults with AS, while others with AS tend to see the world in black and white and may have difficulty carrying over what they learn in one situation to another. Indeed, they may seem to lack 'common sense' (Howlin 2000).

Other common features associated with AS include emotional labiality and inappropriate responses to stress – for example, laughing at the sound of another child crying. Young adults with AS may exhibit motor clumsiness, have difficulty following directions related to physical movements, and have sensory integration problems that prompt strong, unusual responses to touch, smell, sound, taste and visual stimulation (Ghaziuddin and Butler 1998). People with AS may also have trouble describing the degree and type of pain they experience.

Because most young children with AS do not present with what we often regard as an autistic profile – they can be quite talkative, bright and emotionally connected to family – many are not diagnosed until the early school years and far too many not until their teens or beyond. While there is no cure for ASD, correct and timely diagnosis and an appropriate, intensive, multifaceted intervention programme can vastly improve the young adult's quality of life and future prospects. It goes without saying that healthcare professionals and educators should take seriously every parent's concerns about unusual behaviours, developmental delays in motor skill development, and problems with socialisation among peers. In these cases, a full neuropsychological workup, not a wait-and-see approach, is indicated (Ziatas et al. 1998).

Factors affecting training

As people involved in the provision of care for young adults with AS in the UK, we are cognisant of a number of factors in developing training courses for care and support workers in this area:

1. While there are many training courses for ASD, very few are purely for AS. Moreover, ASD courses may not be suitable or easily adopted, owing to their provision (or not) for the distinctive nature of young adults with AS (e.g. high functioning, and wanting to be part of the group).

2. Relatedly, there are very few training programmes in the world dealing with AS, and hence few, if any, training models that have been researched or published.

3. Care staff often come to work with young adults with an awareness of AS but without the necessary skills, yet are very keen to develop their 'skills set'.

4. AS manifests very individualistically and therefore a single, overall approach to care does not work; support requires awareness and understanding before training and implementation.

5. In the UK, there is no obvious graduate route to qualification in this area.

In short, with these factors and those of life roles, occupational status and geography often limiting opportunities for discussion and training amongst stakeholders in AS, we chose to pursue an online solution, combining face-to-face meetings with online activities and resources in a virtual learning environment, which we describe below. The authors developed the training programme within a wider course development team of stakeholders (parents, carers, professionals, academics, etc.) who tested, piloted and validated the philosophy, framework and approach of the training. The theoretical framework was strongly influenced by insights from theories of adult learning, situated learning and communities of practice, which can be found in work in online learning communities (Salmon 2002). In the following section, we discuss key features of the training programme that will be elaborated further in the full paper.

The development of learning communities using 'blended learning' approaches

There are many restrictions in both time and location that prevent care and support workers meeting for face-to-face [f2f] training. The f2f component of the course was restricted to 2.5 days over a 12 week period. In order to make best use of this time, we adapted the blended learning approach advocated by Lewis and Orton (2000) where the blend is determined with reference to the attributes of the content. Thus f2f meetings were chosen for learning highly interactive skills and online delivery for subject-related information, as shown in the themes and structure of the course plan:

Week	1	2	3	4	5	6	7	8	9	10	11	12
AS Awareness												
AS in Context												
AS Support												

■ Face to face: f2f1, ... f2f4   ▒ Online: Sessions 1–3

The division into face-to-face and online components was made transparent to stakeholders and participants. The course as a whole was designed to 'flow' such that it:

- seamlessly built a learning community that models participation in a community of practice

- provided meaningful routes through content

- supported a variety of learning styles.

A constructivist and situated learning approach was appropriate in this context as it mirrors how learning naturally occurs in the 'communities of practice' found in the care teams (Kimble et al. 2001; Wenger 1998). The course commenced with a short f2f session (f2f1) where the learning approach was explained and the rationale and potential benefits of sharing knowledge and experience online was discussed and practised.

A pre-requisite to this mode of learning is that participants should develop a mutual respect and trust. The first online session (Session 1) was devoted to a series of online activities, or E-tivities, which followed Gilly Salmon's five-stage model (Salmon 2002). This provided a framework for establishing the necessary relationships for knowledge construction around AS. Further opportunities for informal exchanges between participants and tutors were created both online (e.g. Cybercafe) and face to face (pre- and post-meeting). Participants themselves recognized the need for mutual respect as messages were posted to the discussion board voicing the issue. Some participants found the large public arena of the general discussion board inhibited some of the connections they wished to make with others in the training group, so additional private spaces were set up to support exchanges with a trusted few.

At f2f2, participants were able to continue the socialization process by picking up on the discussions they had had online. The session comprised expert and group presentations and an AS case study analysis workshop. The workshop was then mirrored by an online case study analysis that ran in the following online session (Session 2). It also supported follow-up discussions arising from the presentations and workshop.

The quality of the online case analysis exceeded that in f2f2. Evaluation suggests this was because the learning community was maturing and had moved on towards level 4 of the 5 stage model (Salmon 2002). In particular, we note that the case analysis task itself was probably better supported in an asynchronous conferencing online environment where there was time to reflect on and revisit ideas.

The online AS case study analysis was reviewed at f2f3. At this session the quality of the discussions was notably higher and the group interaction had changed markedly. All participants, including the course tutors, seemed to be making equal contributions and trainees were willing to contribute personal experience in a way that hadn't happened previously. Increasingly, the f2f interaction showed marked similarities in terms of the quality of interactions that had been occurring online via the E-tivities.

The role of E-tivities in fostering learning and the exchange of information

Gilly Salmon (2002) describes E-tivities as motivating, engaging and purposeful online activities. In order for an online group to learn together individuals must participate over an extended period of time.

Motivating them to make repeated visits to the virtual environment requires that the learning experience is both pleasurable and that the benefits are clearly stated, for example, they carry a built-in reward for participants as they always encompass a response element.

Forums were set up on the discussion board in the VLE for individuals to participate in E-tivities. There were additional discussion threads that had more open-ended discussions, for example, Ask a Question and Cybercafe. Participation in the E-tivity lead forums was markedly greater than in the open-ended forums. The E-tivities provided both a framework and a purpose for interaction.

For many participants the online environment is an alien one and early apprehension has to be overcome. E-tivities give clear consistent instructions and in so doing provided an effective handrail to gaining confidence. For example, none of the participants on the first training course had used a VLE before and only one had used asynchronous discussion, yet all succeeded in effectively participating in the E-tivities using the discussion board. The focus of the learning was the E-tivity, not the discussion board, so there was a reason for becoming proficient in its use. [Worked examples on AS will be included in the full paper.]

Conclusions

The blended approach has successfully supported different learning styles within the training group and contributed to building a cohesive AS learning community. Those participants who were most active in f2f sessions were not those who were most active online. By meeting both 'on' and 'off' line the group were able to value the contributions made by those with different learning styles.

Our approach lends support to what Cohen and Payiatakis (2002) have observed in connection with e-learning, 'what makes the difference between quality e-learning from "tabloid training" is process, not content. It is the L, not the E, that makes the real difference.' E-tivities give everyone an opportunity to participate when the task is broad enough to allow each to attach their own slant. In contrast, unstructured discussions, face to face or electronic, are often vulnerable to domination by a few who say everything. Or, if the task element becomes too narrow then this closes down participation as everyone posts a similar message. When time boundaries are used with E-tivities they help to pace the learning process by keeping momentum and providing direction. These online time boundaries approximate to the physical boundaries of f2f learning in giving the participants a sense of place. Such outcomes would not have been available to us if a f2f approach had been adopted throughout in the AS training programme, hence the importance of considering the use of blended learning and E-tivities in making AS training available online.

CHAPTER 9

MANAGING STUDENT BEHAVIOUR

9.1 The student

As stated previously, there are many things a teacher or learning support assistant can do when working with a student with Asperger's Syndrome that will make a tremendous difference. There is no mystery about teaching these students; rather, you need an understanding and a willingness to challenge your own practice. This takes me back to when students were described as not being able to read when the actual truth was that we, as teachers, had not found a strategy to teach them to read. It is the same with students with Asperger's Syndrome – we need to challenge our practice and discover ways of teaching them in differing settings. In order to work effectively with students with Asperger's Syndrome we must reflect radically on our practice, training and ethos. The differences the student with Asperger's Syndrome presents require changes in practice for the adults working in the classroom, at personal and professional levels.

It is not important to dwell upon the philosophy of education, but it is crucial to consider the purpose of school when considering educational approaches for students with Asperger's Syndrome. The school should not merely be seeking to ensure that all of the students have a range of formal accreditations in a broad range of subjects, but to enable students to function in the social setting of a classroom and to begin to unravel and understand the wider social world in which they function. The majority of our learning in everyday school is social.

One of our students was particularly able in mathematics and computing and so we arranged for him to join a small group of students at a local college with the additional support of a member of staff. The student was very able and quickly completed the tasks, but was then unable to wait for the remainder of his group to catch up or complete their tasks before he could move on. He would become increasingly frustrated and kept making demands on the teacher that went beyond her remit within a group situation, to the degree that she would need to be a one-to-one tutor for him if he were to be kept busy. He was not prepared to wait for others, to learn in a group situation. Neither did he consider that he should have to wait for anyone, but he should be able to move through the syllabus as he wanted. Eventually his demands on the teacher became too great: his lack of social skills meant he appeared blunt, rude and selfish, and despite his skills in computing, the college was unable to cope with the student in the class scenario, even with additional support.

This illustrates the dichotomy with which we are frequently faced: often students with Asperger's Syndrome could academically succeed in a subject but would be unable to cope with the social structure and rigidity of traditional education establishments. If the teacher is aware of the pace the student is able to proceed at and be prepared to differentiate the work at that level, the student would not be a threat to the adult within the classroom. The philosophy therefore was to maintain the student's self-worth and confidence through academic achievement while seeking to educate them to thrive socially in the future in a range of contexts.

Traditional teaching methods need to be modified. For example when teaching a new mathematical concept, say long division, the process may be to explain the concept and workings to the students using one example. The next stage would then be to ask the student if they are able to complete a similar problem using the same format and process. If they are able to follow the process and achieve the correct answer we would give them a series of different problems on the same theme to ensure they have understood the concept and could apply it to a number of differing problems. The student with Asperger's Syndrome, however, once understanding the concept and getting it correct the first time will not see any point in practising it over and over again. They either get it or they don't. Nor do they see the point of showing all their working-out – the answer is either correct or not. Saying that the teacher would be able to see where they went wrong, or examination boards will award marks for seeing the working-out, they see as pointless. Understanding this way of working allows you to adapt your teaching style to their learning style.

9.1.1 Traditional classroom control

Traditionally, the authority of the teacher in the classroom is intrinsically linked to control. Student teachers throughout their training are encouraged to consider classroom management and organisation effectively from the perspective of control. You need to reconsider whether this power base is essential to create an environment conducive to learning: do you need to deliver a lesson from the front of the room or are there other ways that the students will learn and find learning fun? As a teacher I was taught to be in control of the environment and the learning and the teaching opportunities this affords. I would organise the class into groups or pairs, and encourage collaborative learning situations. I was encouraged by my colleagues, mentors and inspectors to consider a range of different organisational strategies designed to promote and encourage learning. Teachers in mainstream settings control the classroom and school and what occurs within it, and anticipate that students will conform to classroom conventions and rules.

You need to consider your own teaching style. It is possible to have clear rules for the classroom which the student with Asperger's Syndrome will accept and abide by, if they are explained to them and they seem relevant, yet have flexibility within those rules. The students who do not comply with this model may well be the very students we need to learn to understand: the student who becomes anxious when confronted with the assembly hall in the morning or at lunchtime, because they can't cope with crowds; the student who needs to go though a ritual before starting a lesson; the student who needs to take a certain route to a class. I have taught many students who have a total aversion to crowded rooms, who as a result needed to skip assembly or to have arrangements made to eat lunch alone. These are typical behaviours of students with Asperger's Syndrome; it is important that the teacher learns who needs what and adapts their approach appropriately. You need to be looking to reduce anxiety for the student; only then can you expect learning to follow.

It is unrealistic to expect students with Asperger's Syndrome to just conform to the daily school routines – sooner or later there will be a problem. You simply cannot expect that by imposing a system the Asperger's Syndrome will simply go away; indeed, the opposite is more likely. Anxiety for the student will increase and obsessive, bizarre or non-compliant behaviours are also likely to increase.

You need therefore to recognise that it is important to make small but significant changes in the system for the student rather than require the student to change to fit into the school system.

As teachers the methods of control in the mainstream system hinge on rules, order and structure. These rules, order and structure can continue, and they certainly were there in Farleigh and North Hill House, yet the model is modified from that of mainstream education.

Those unwritten rules where the students sat in the same place, shared books and the computer, changed for PE, and used certain-coloured exercise books for specific subjects was clearly a teacher-imposed structure essential to the smooth running of a busy class. When the student with Asperger's Syndrome is introduced to such a system the rules need to be clear and explicit, black and white and written down. There needs to be an understanding that they are highly anxious students, often with obsessive and ritualised behaviour. They have major difficulties with social understanding in a range of different contexts, they find socialising at best confusing and at worst threatening, are frequently self-centred and have a literal, often pedantic, understanding of language. The model needs to have clear rules and expectations but also flexibility and understanding. As I have said, the changes should be subtle and flexible but will make a great difference to the student with Asperger's Syndrome. I would always have the aim with a segregated provision such as Farleigh and North Hill House that some students would integrate back into mainstream education either on a part-time or a full-time basis. However, the most socially aware children I have worked with have sometimes behaved in ways we might consider bizarre or unthoughtful, highlighting the necessity of support from workers with an understanding of Asperger's Syndrome.

One student from the school was studying for his GCSEs at a local mainstream school, attending several sessions a week as an opportunity to broaden his opportunities, both educationally and socially. One particular morning, his teacher was ill and the student, faced with a cover lesson, went to the school office to get his usual teacher's phone number so he could call him at home. In this way he thought he could get details of the lesson the teacher would have taught them that day. The school told him this was unacceptable, and that his normal teacher was ill. The student was very confused, and stated that his teacher would have prepared the lesson, so what was the problem phoning him in order that he could fax the lesson plan and work in?

This illustrates the tendency of students with Asperger's Syndrome to put logic before socially acceptable behaviour and also serves well to illustrate the massive task ahead for teaching how to deal with the complexities of social situations and normal conventions. In order to work effectively with students we must learn to understand them. Through understanding their point of view we can begin to explain 'acceptable' and 'unacceptable' behaviour, thus helping the individual to unravel the complexities of our social world.

9.1.2 The student as an individual

I have said before, but it is worth repeating, that as a teacher it is important to try to see the world from the perspective of the child with Asperger's Syndrome. The world we live in only works well when we all understand the rules and conform to them. Similarly, an individual with Asperger's Syndrome is likely to live their life to a set of rules, but we just don't understand what they are. We often miss crucial points because unless we think as an individual with Asperger's Syndrome we simply will not be able to understand what the problem is.

One student at the school, despite being bright and intelligent, at the age of 13 appeared unable to work with maths; it appeared he simply could not master 'carrying' numbers. Working one-to-one with him, the teacher asked him what he didn't like about these sums. 'Tens', he replied, 'I don't like the number ten.' This student had a total aversion to the number ten, he hated it, and therefore refused to include it in his work. If the student hated the number it was not surprising there was a reluctance to use it. The teacher worked extensively with the student using tens as a range of numbers in games, empathising with the student when tens were part of the game but encouraging their use. The teacher openly accepted the student's dislike of the number. It took a long time, but eventually the student accepted that ten would simply have to be used. With patience and understanding the problem was resolved.

Another student only ever used the same pencil for every single piece of writing. He would never use a pen. If the pencil wasn't with him or was lost, he would not produce written work. The teacher accepted that the student had a special and exclusive pencil, and also that as each lesson went by it was getting shorter! The teacher shopped in a local stationery shop and purchased an unusual and individual pencil, which he gave to the student to look after, hoping he would adopt it as his new pencil. This became the case. The success of this approach led to the anxiety of the student (and the teacher!) being reduced, and ensured the student had a writing implement. The provision of the new pencil also strengthened their relationship and with encouragement (and the right colour pen!) the student felt comfortable to start using new writing media. He now uses pens willingly.

The expectation within mainstream provision is that the student enters the accepted system of educational management. However, within North Hill House and Farleigh I looked to 'wrap the school around the student'. This is possible through resources, and the size of the class and school, but is mostly facilitated by interpersonal skills and awareness of Asperger's Syndrome. I would suggest that, even without additional funding, but with careful evaluation of the structure of everyday schools, many of the methods I have found successful with students with Asperger's Syndrome could be translated into the mainstream environment.

It is also important to remember that you do not always get it right. Students with Asperger's Syndrome can be masters of deception and may willingly lead you to tackle all kinds of problems they convince you exist. This is a very difficult area, sorting out the behaviours and difficulties associated with Asperger's Syndrome from those that are designed to push boundaries, assert control or are just the normal stubbornness of young people's development as they progress through puberty and adolescence.

The staff produced a map of the school and grounds to illustrate the out-of-bounds areas and coloured all of these with a luminescent lime-green pen. The out-of-bounds posters were announced in assembly and placed around the school. The following morning five students stood in a corridor they never needed to access, and which we had designated out of bounds. When challenged, the students highlighted the one poster in which a tiny piece of corridor was uncoloured. This was duly rectified; the students never stepped into the corridor again without permission.

Later I was able to identify the 'out-of-bounds areas' just by red stickers on the door and subsequently green stickers for places they were allowed to go. These became the accepted 'rules' and once explained to the students there was no challenge to following them.

When we were designing the gardens and lawn playing area, the boundary with the next door mews houses was on one of the boundaries. I approached the residents to ask what type of fencing would be suitable to mark the edge of their boundaries. They didn't want a large six foot high fence as it would cast most of their garden into shadow. So we decided to leave the boundary open with a line of plant pots to show where the division was. This was explained to the students and the reasons for it. Not once was this boundary crossed: even when the football went over the lawn, they asked permission before retrieving it.

Within the classes at North Hill House and Farleigh the rules and structure are applied, but more importantly they are also applied at an individual level. The students will have some specific needs and behaviours catered for but this instantly highlights possible major conflicts: if rules and order are imposed at an individual level, must this essentially mean that students are in control?

That is why 'negotiable and non-negotiable' became such an important phrase in our development of boundaries and rules.

9.1.3 Negotiable and non-negotiable

It was much easier when starting with a group of individuals with Asperger's Syndrome to have various rules written in stone, 'unchangeable, unchallengeable and non-negotiable'.

> For people with autism, rules are very important, because we concentrate on how things are done. (Grandin 1996, p.103)

It was important that the staff team did not enter into discussion with a student on these aspects; they are outlined clearly in the school handbook, at interview with parents, during any assessment periods, and daily during the day-to-day running of the school. These rules are the obvious ones: safety, not hurting others, respect for yourself and others, attending school. There are few of these rules – the fewer the better. For example, students would all be told the following and asked if they feel it is fair and that they can abide by it:

Some things are negotiable and some are not. Those things that are not negotiable are called the 'rules' and we must abide by them, for example, not hurting others and going to school. What is negotiable is what you do in school, your programme, what is achieved in school, and how it is achieved.

I have always found that arguing with a child with Asperger's Syndrome is pointless. Their language skills are excellent and they enjoy the arguing process. This also puts you, the adult, in direct confrontation with the student and a satisfactory resolution is highly unlikely. By using 'negotiable or non-negotiable' in this way we avoid these long, protracted, fruitless arguments. Using clearly defined expectations the student is left in no doubt as to what is expected of them. The argument is also the secondary behaviour and it is an intentional avoidance strategy, which the adult should not get drawn into.

So what happens when the child refuses to comply with the non-negotiable rules?

Firstly, it will happen! This is where a clear, well-defined, whole-school approach to discipline is essential. There must be a policy established by the whole-school team for working through difficulties, tied in with rewards and sanctions where appropriate. Every member of the team must speak as one in dealing with situations and difficulties, otherwise the student will see that the structure of control and discipline in the school can easily be undermined and manipulated. This is far from easy but we have found some techniques useful.

I have utilised some of the experiences of those working in the past with students with emotional and behavioural difficulties in the formulation of a method of working with students. In particular, I have drawn on the excellent work of Bill Rogers, the Australian behaviourist. Several techniques have been useful; none are new or magical, they just need to be applied consistently:

1. Assume that what you want the student to do is going to be done by using 'please' and 'thank you'. 'John, can you go into class now please, thanks.'

   Give the child space and time for take up.

   Make sure first of all that you are tackling the real problem, not just the 'smoke screen' the student has put up to mask the real underlying concern. Make sure you have thought about why the student is behaving in this way at a level deeper than the behaviour that is manifest. Is anything underlying it? An anxiety, a change, a previously unresolved situation? This needs to be considered carefully before moving on.

2. Always deal with the primary behaviour you want to change, not the secondary behaviour that often comes with it. For example, if you request a student to put their chewing gum in the waste bin, and they do this but mumble all the time, just thank them; don't start complaining about the secondary behaviour.

3. Remind the student of the rule. Ask politely for compliance. Always assume that the student will comply – don't stand over the student waiting for it to happen.

   Give the child space and time for take up.

4. Remind the student of the rule once more and the sanction for refusal to comply. This is a big step: think of the confrontation you may be faced with, what is likely to happen and whether you will be able to see the 'if you don't do it' sanction through.

   Give the child space and time for take up.

5. If there is no compliance, apply the sanction.

6. After the sanction is completed, ensure that at some point you spend some relaxed time with the student one-to-one to make your peace and resolve the situation. If you fail to resolve the situation it will not simply go away and will affect the child's day.

To reiterate the issue of control: establishing control in the school is through imposing some *non-negotiable* boundaries and then working with each child to make targets for learning and socially adapting to everyday school.

Another excellent strategy is working as a 'tag team':

As a Headteacher or later as a Principal of all three schools, I would often work somewhere that was very visible to the staff team and the students. If a student or member of staff were having a particularly difficult day I would be able to observe the interaction and at the right time intervene just to give the member of staff a break. This would be done by me approaching the member of staff and student and asking if I could 'look after' little Jonny whilst the member of staff went and got a 'cup of coffee' and could return in 20 minutes or so when the student may be more receptive to discussing the issue. Usually when the member of staff had left the student would then try and use me as a focus for their discontent. I always retorted by saying, 'Excuse me, don't start having a go at me, I'm not any part of this argument,' or 'Don't be rude to me, I've not been rude to you.' The student would then feel aggrieved but have nowhere to vent their frustration. When the member of staff returned I would ask the student, 'Are you now ready to return and resolve this?' If they said 'No', I would ask the member of staff to return in another 30 minutes. I would then ask the student to return with the member of staff.

Another example of 'tag team' is when you adopt a completely different strategy to your colleagues. If a student has been out of class for some time and not responding to staff requests to return to the classroom and get on with his work, I would walk by the student and member of staff and just say abruptly, 'What are you doing out of class? Now get straight back in.' This would usually have the desired effect as the student was so shocked with the response they complied immediately.

It is important when dealing with students in highly charged situations that you remember that this is not a personal attack on you or your ability or relationship with the student. You need to take the emotion out of it and look at the situation objectively. Once again this is not a natural thing for adults to do, but with experience and practice it becomes far more effective. It is also a positive strategy to involve a third party. This does not mean you have failed, but that you are using the resources at your disposal.

Another example was of a very intelligent male student who would become very anxious at times and revert to hiding in his bedroom, taking all of his clothes off and pulling his drawers out and hiding in the space left. A female member of staff who had an excellent relationship with the student felt it was totally inappropriate to go into the student's bedroom when he was undressed. Thus there was an impasse, the student using a technique that allowed him to keep control and not do what was being asked. I suggested to the member of staff that she talked to the student, ignoring his state of undress, and tried to divert his attention by talking about his favourite subjects of black holes and space. She would have a colleague in the corridor who would be able to observe everything and give her confidence. This she tried, and after two or three incidents the student stopped taking his clothes off as a strategy to gain control over the situation.

As teachers we strive to understand the child by analysing situations from their perspective, and make some *negotiated* adaptations to the aspects of the school with the primary purpose of reducing anxiety for the student. Once anxiety is reduced, learning readiness is more likely and individual learning targets can be jointly formulated with the student and parents. The targets are formalised as the Individual Educational Plan (IEP).

Students with Asperger's Syndrome are just as likely as other children to push boundaries within school and the home. Often, when something has been negotiated, the child will return to question a decision when it suits them, perhaps the next time they are asked to comply by an adult. In these instances it is helpful to chart areas that have been mutually accepted, in fine detail. This means that areas where boundaries and acceptable behaviours, rituals and routines which have been successfully sorted out with the student do not need to be revisited. The student and the adults can then sign off on this list and add to it. Again, it then becomes a useful tool to record progress, and to identify areas of conflict for future resolution.

One student insisted on wearing a baseball cap everywhere. Whilst there were times this was acceptable, it was decided that in class was a non-negotiable place to not wear the hat. With work from the staff an agreement was reached about where the hat could be worn. Generally, there was no problem with this rule, but if the pupil was particularly stressed, irritated or having a difficult day, this rule would be disputed. Rather than continually having battles over previously negotiated areas, a list was drawn up with the student about individual agreements. This in turn helped when the issue was raised in future conflicts, thus acting as a reminder for the student and as assistance in resolution of the difficulties.

9.1.4 Child-centred control

Students with Asperger's Syndrome certainly need their world to be predictable: they require sameness of the environment if the structure of their life is to be maintained; they find change difficult and need some rituals preserved to maintain a reduced anxiety state. Equally, the individual with Asperger's Syndrome is a child first and thus also passes through normal child development patterns, though often delayed or less distinct. Through normal childhood the infant will be demanding and egocentric as they grow, yet met by the challenges and external controls of the parents, the young child learns to understand they are not in control of the world around them. It is important to remember that children with Asperger's Syndrome are just as likely to be naughty and even more demanding than 'normal' children. They will need to be reprimanded and told 'No' when their behaviour is poor. All children are egocentric and seek to control the adults around them and their environment to ensure their needs are met. This is an area where Asperger's Syndrome can cause real anxiety for parents and carers; faced with poor behaviours and a controlling child the adult feels self-doubt about challenging the child as it could be caused by Asperger's Syndrome. Understandably, faced with a challenging situation, the adult questions whether it is appropriate to challenge the child:

Is this a normal pattern of development requiring boundaries to be set, or a manifestation of Asperger's Syndrome and therefore inappropriate to challenge the child as they cannot be responsible for their behaviour?

However, left unchallenged, the success the child experiences in controlling the adults and immediate environment is reinforced and behaviour worsens. One of the major difficulties with managing children with Asperger's Syndrome was that adults allowed the child to be the centre of everything they did. The result was often an increase in obsessive behaviour. Often, faced with a late or indistinct diagnosis, parents feel remorse and guilt about not spotting the difficulties earlier in childhood, though this is extremely difficult to do. This guilt can be worsened if the child needs to be reprimanded. If the child remains unchecked, the poor behaviour is reinforced and leads to a downward spiral in which control over adults is increased. Of course this is an over-generalisation, and is valuable only as reflection for parents and adults working with children with Asperger's Syndrome. No single situation is the same, but in my experience, the issue of the child's control within the family is very significant, and a difficult task for parents raising the child can be made into a wearing, impossible one if the child remains unchecked. A strong, physically mature adolescent teenager in a full-blown tantrum over relatively minor issues centring on control is every parent's worst scenario.

Individuals with Asperger's Syndrome are largely unaware of the needs of those around them; they are very need-orientated, so this person-centred control worsens. This is likely to lead to increased tantrums, perhaps even violence, as the child seeks to gain what they want at that particular moment. Frequently we see the manifestation of these factors, a student of perhaps 13 or 14 with total control of the parents and carers, yet when challenged by teachers in the normal course of a school day, a tantrum equating to the behaviour of a young toddler may result. As the young person becomes older, physical strength becomes another factor. This is a most frightening scenario, and extremely difficult to deal with, and a potentially huge problem in society as a whole; the young person uses strategies that have worked with parents and carers to establish and control the environment as they move into society as a whole.

Thus a distinct pattern is created from failure to challenge the control of the young person over the adult. Whilst difficult and often heartbreaking for the parent, failure to reprimand the young person can lead to massive, serious problems in the future.

I have had numerous phone calls at holiday times from distraught parents who have had incidents that they are at a loss to resolve, or some bizarre behaviour has occurred. Each time the parent has asked me what to do or whether I can speak to the young person. Once having ascertained what has happened, I always ask, 'Did you tell him "No" or did you say "Don't do that"?' Many parents had not and the young person would have done something that they did not think was inappropriate.

It is important that students with Asperger's Syndrome are told what is and what is not socially acceptable, otherwise how will they know and understand that they may just be behaving like any other adolescent in seeking to find out how far they can push the boundaries?

One of the most bizarre examples was of a student who came from a family with many social connections and would entertain often in the form of a dinner party. The parent asked me to have a word with the student because he was always rude and inappropriate in his language.

I asked the mother to tell me exactly what would happen on these occasions so I could address the situation informally with the student. She said that the dinner party would always be a large gathering and someone would ask this student what he was doing or what was his favourite pastime or passion nowadays. He would then say the same phrase that would silence the room and she would feel very embarrassed and ask him to leave. It followed the same pattern. I asked her what exactly did he say. 'Oh I couldn't possibly tell you, it's so bad.' I explained that I would need to know or couldn't really help. 'Well', she said, 'whenever a female member of our dinner asked him what he liked doing he would state in a loud voice "eating pussy".' This always had the same reaction – guests would spit out wine, not sure whether to laugh or cry and the mother would explode and the student would leave the scene with a large smirk on his face.

On this occasion he was aware of what he was doing and the reaction was what he intended it to be. There are other occasions when the same individual wasn't aware that he was being rude or his comments were inappropriate. It is your role to differentiate between the two cases but explain that neither is acceptable.

9.2 The physical environment

The classroom environment does not need to be expensively modified. Good organisational and methodological practices are more important than physical adaptation of the teaching area. It is important that the classroom environment is well organised and everything has a place and is clearly labelled. Pastel colours work best, with some detailing in primary colours. A well organised 'primary school classroom environment' is what is required. The furniture should be simple, and flexible enough to allow group, paired or individual work. Each child should have a designated place at a table; this should ideally be marked with a small piece of card which outlines the child's individual education targets in conventional and visual symbol writing. This order and 'sameness' plays to the youngsters strengths and lowers the anxiety levels.

> I am indebted to the good teachers at that school, who ran an old-fashioned, highly structured classroom, with lots of opportunity for interesting hands-on activities. (Grandin 1996, p.97)

It is also helpful if the student is able to work in a variety of ways within the classroom: on their own using 'TEACCH' style booths or individual tables so that they are not distracted; in pairs; and in a large group.

Most of the students I have encountered with Asperger's Syndrome seem to be very computer literate. They enjoy using computers, often primarily games, perhaps because the computer is an easier tool to work with than people, showing no emotion and responding to clear instructions. Thus it would assist if the students have access to IT as a learning tool. It does seem that many students with Asperger's

Syndrome prefer the relationship with technology rather than people and some go on to develop IT-based vocations. At one time I felt that all students with Asperger's Syndrome had this compulsion, but it seems to wane as they get older. The students find sharing anything difficult, and it is easier if each student has access to their own personal computer on a network. The network needs to have stringent internal security, firewalls and Internet filtering software loaded as the curiosity of the student is high and they would be very tempted to try and explore restricted areas or unsuitable Internet sites.

There was one occasion when a student visited the local further education college and hacked into the computer network, putting on a 'restart loop' so each time the computers were started they switched off then restarted constantly. When the college rang and asked if any of the students were capable of doing such a thing, the answer was obviously 'mmm, yes'. It is an area where the student with Asperger's Syndrome can excel – they have the attention to detail and the patience to work at a problem until they solve it, and the computer seems to be the ideal companion for these students.

In addition it is important that there are daily visual timetables on display. The timetables are essential and inform the students of the details of the lessons of the day and provide an overview of the week. The students should have some degree of input into these timetables, and in some instances the order of work should be adjusted in negotiation with the teacher.

It is better if the classes are kept small and well structured with extra adult support. The amount of attention and guidance required cannot be underestimated. They may appear to be coping, but this is not always the case. It is important to consider the level of extra support, though, as too many adults are counter-productive and many students will get into a 'learned helplessness' situation if there is always an adult to do everything for them.

It is important for students who have sensory difficulties with noise or light that the classroom environment is an area of low arousal. The levels of arousal are not the same for each student so the teacher will have to be aware of their different sensory needs.

Fluorescent lighting causes severe problems for many autistic people, because they can see a sixty-cycle flicker... Fluorescent lighting in the classroom was a big problem... Reflections bounce off everything, and the room looked like an animated cartoon. (Grandin 1996, p.74)

9.3 The curriculum

Special schools do not have a good record of developing the curriculum to meet the needs of children with SEN.

Ofsted in 2010 reinforced this view in the *Special Education Needs and Disability Review*, stating:

SEN was good or outstanding in less than half the providers visited. The review found that no one model – such as special schools, full inclusion in mainstream settings, or specialised units co-located with mainstream settings – worked better than any other.

The keys to good outcomes were good teaching and learning, close tracking, rigorous monitoring of progress with intervention quickly put into place, and a thorough evaluation of the impact of additional provision.

The best learning occurred in all types of provision when teachers or other lead adults had a thorough and detailed knowledge of the children and young people; a thorough knowledge and understanding of teaching and learning strategies and techniques, as well as the subject or areas of learning being taught; and a sound understanding of child development, and how different learning difficulties and disabilities influence this. (Crown copyright 2012)

It is important that the teacher and learning support assistants not only have a thorough working knowledge of their subject but also of the students and their cognitive styles. Students should always have access to a full broad, balanced and differentiated curriculum; in the United Kingdom that is the National Curriculum. An important area where the student may need some extra input is in their ability to communicate and understand what is expected of them and the expectations of the curriculum. An easy way to achieve this is to build in additional sessions during the week on social communication skills and thinking skills. These sessions really require the input of a speech and language therapist, but teachers can quite successfully run these sessions using Carol Gray's social stories. It is important that these programmes are an integral part of the timetable and not an extra 'bolt-on' component. Social skills work continues throughout the day as a cross-curricular theme, and it is imperative for us to use every opportunity to introduce, explain and teach the children new social skills in a range of contexts. Every part of the day becomes a 'social skills' lesson where the unwritten rules are explained, the reason for those rules and what the expectations are in different contexts. So lunchtimes are another social skills lesson where adults will eat with the students and explain what the rules and expectations are.

If possible, a primary model of education is more appropriate, but with the appropriate key stage work – that is, the students have a class teacher who will take them for the 'core' subjects, while the specialist subjects of Physical Education, Science, Music and Technology are taught in specialist rooms. Students with Asperger's Syndrome find moving from class to class and from teacher to teacher very taxing. The class teacher model enables the teacher to maintain consistency of expectations, social structure and discipline within the class; I believe this ensures more rapid progress for the students. It is imperative to move students towards internalising their work and self-motivation, which is particularly difficult for students with Asperger's Syndrome as they have little concept of the future and what that may mean for them. In addition to standard classes it is important to have a 'transition' group for students who have begun to progress in terms of internal motivation. This class focuses particularly on independent learning – the rewards are not concrete, but are the honour or pleasure of working in a mature setting, and the feel-good factor this instils.

Lessons which involve sharing of any kind are almost impossible:

One student I taught for four years never shared any science experiment equipment with anyone, and point-blank refused to share. In another instance a teacher decided to read a book with the children – one student refused to do this because he wanted to read at his pace, duly completed the book and told everyone the ending!

9.3.1 Curriculum subjects – general observations

This is by no means a definitive review of the subjects with regard to how they affect pupils with Asperger's Syndrome; rather it is a set of observations and anecdotal evidence based on my awareness of students in the classroom.

Mathematics

It is very common to have students who excel at mathematics. They enjoy working with numbers and can do a lot of the mental arithmetic at remarkable speed. They are capable of achieving excellent examination grades and taking these exams early. This was exciting and positive for the schools I ran but also posed a problem for timetabling. Differentiation in the classroom is stretched to unacceptable levels in these instances, and the maths students need to be taught in separate groups or individually. It is important to try and guard against the competitive element between students, as whilst this might be seen as a good motivating force, in reality it becomes a source of argument and friction.

English

The teaching of English poses a very different set of problems from maths. Generally the students are excellent readers, though occasionally some will struggle and there will often be other factors that impair their work. Many children with Asperger's Syndrome are reading addicts, and will read avidly from textbooks and works of fiction. They are usually quite rigid about the type of reading material they prefer and it is a major task to persuade them to access a broad range of material. Their reading and use of language is often far ahead of their comprehension and they can learn set passages without understanding the meaning at all. At times it is difficult to get them to stop reading and change task, as they become so absorbed by their books.

Writing is a totally different picture. Generally students with Asperger's Syndrome do not enjoy handwriting. In my experience as a teacher, this is not unusual with many normal children, but what is different is the massive resistance and reluctance of the students to writing, and it can become a battleground in teaching. You need to use a variety of ploys to persuade students to produce acceptable pieces of written work. Whilst computers are a useful way of generating work, and the students' resistance to using computers for work is minimal, the ability to master handwriting is an important skill.

Story writing remains a particular difficulty for the students, especially when they are called upon to write creatively about areas in which they have little interest or awareness. If they are asked to describe what their day was like or the usual 'what did you do in the school holidays?' essay, they will struggle to write anything. But ask them what their friend did and they will happily describe it in great detail. This is very frustrating for parents or teachers who are trying to get any information out of them. Often free-written stories are adapted from those they have read or seen, or are limited to their area of interest. Nevertheless, in my experience of teaching literature the students have been able to demonstrate good quality work in analysing and comparing pieces of written work. Many have excellent memories; this is particularly useful in remembering lengthy Shakespearian quotations.

Science

Science is a popular subject with students with Asperger's Syndrome. They are fascinated by the way things work and often learn about areas to frightening depths. In these instances, students may develop a huge knowledge base in a specific area, space for example, but often to the detriment of other areas. In these instances the task of the teacher of science is to ensure breadth to the subject, and this is often where resistance is met, as students are frequently highly resistant to study in areas beyond their specific interest.

Information Communication Technology

As I have previously stated, many students with Asperger's Syndrome have an affinity with technology and seem to be able to relate to an object that shows no emotion and will give the appropriate response providing the correct data is put in. At one time I did think that all individuals with Asperger's Syndrome are obsessed with computers but it does seem in my experience that this dependency does lessen with age. That said, it is an excellent teaching tool and a good source of information. However, it does need to be time restricted and the Internet needs to have restrictions against inappropriate sites.

9.3.2 Examinations, accreditation and anxiety

As the student settles into school and progresses through the key stages, they will be ever confronted by tests and examinations. Against the backdrop of performance tables and high parental expectations, these are times of heightened anxiety for all concerned. The student enters the examination phase with high expectations. Examinations and tests prove difficult for all students but pose particular difficulties for children with Asperger's Syndrome: firstly a massive change in routine and structure to the day; often a change in venue, an unfamiliar 'exam-cleansed' room; an environment in which the familiar adults are now distant and seem unsupportive; a task or paper presented in an unfamiliar way. These effects alone will cause massive anxiety for the student but pre-examination nerves may further compound them.

It is essential to prepare all students for the inevitable tests and examinations by reducing anxiety, but this is particularly important for students with Asperger's Syndrome. You need to decide well in advance if the student is going to be able to cope with other students in the examination room or if special provision is necessary for taking tests individually. They need to know well in advance where they will be, who will be there, how long the tests will take, when they can leave the room, if they can go to the toilet, etc. These facts need to be written down and the student taken through them, point by point. They need to visit the examination room and see where it is and what it is like. They need to know where they will sit and see their allocated desk. The student will need to be told how to attract adult attention in the right way and what they are able to ask. The invigilator will need to be empathetic to the needs of the student and recognise the need for clarity and explanation of their responses should the student with Asperger's Syndrome require help in the room.

When confronted by the examination paper many of us have experienced the cold feeling in the stomach and the temporary panic of a blank mind, such is the nature of examination anxiety, but steadily as we become accustomed to the environment and begin to calm down we gain greater clarity of thought. Perhaps by reading and re-reading the paper, jotting down some key words or phrases, we steadily plot our responses to the questions posed. This is not always the case with students with Asperger's Syndrome — the initial panic serves only to reconfirm and boost their underlying anxiety to a pitch where we have frequently witnessed students simply storming out of the room, unable to cope. Forewarned is partly forearmed, and teachers and carers need to take students through these possibilities, explaining the nature of anxiety, how it is likely to feel, emotionally and physically. The students need to be taken through the scenarios and prepared, their anxiety needs to be put into the frame of normality in this situation, and perhaps most importantly the feelings they will experience need to be labelled for them so they are aware of what they are.

Physical props can be supportive too; anyone who has invigilated will bear witness to various mascots and props in exams, from small soft toys to special 'lucky' pens and pencils, special pencil-top rubbers or furry pencil cases. These are all soothers, and are carried to help us cope; they give some modicum of comfort and familiarity in an isolating and alien situation. These soothers can be even more important for the student with Asperger's Syndrome; they may well have the need for these calming influences to merely cope with a normal day, so it is essential to ensure they are with the student prior to entering the examination room. A phone call to parents or a check with care staff in the residential setting can ensure the student has the items they need to help allay anxiety. Ritual practices, perhaps dropped by the student, may return in these instances of heightened anxiety. Again, providing they are not damaging, the student needs to undertake these to get though into the examination setting.

As previously mentioned, examination questions cause anxiety for us all. As we seek to relate our knowledge to the framing of the question, we align the knowledge we have studied with the crucial elements of the question. We are able to tease out the information the question seeks from irrelevant elements of the question that perhaps merely seek to set the context. Not so the student with Asperger's Syndrome. Consider the effect of focusing on detail to the detriment of seeing the whole, the underlying principle of the theory of central coherence. The student may never get to the point of the question. This is perhaps best illustrated by some examples:

One student was undertaking an examination and was asked to consider at what point the business went into the red. He was unable to get past the concept of colour, taking it literally as opposed to seeking the negative financial balance the question was addressing.

Another student faced with a question on health and safety in an ITC examination, 'What advice would you give a medical secretary using a computer?' focused not on the user of a computer who might want to consider proper seating, lighting, wrist rests, etc., but on the word 'medical'. 'Wash their hands before using the computer' he wrote.

Yet another student confronted by a geography GCSE question that asked students to consider the final destination of the Australian cricket team who landed at a certain airport and made a series of journeys of specified distance and compass direction wrote, 'I have no idea. I don't even like cricket.'

In the last two examples the students were confounded by the two words 'medical' and 'cricket'. They merely served to set a context of the question and arguably had no function, yet the students were unable to answer the question because of them. I am aware of the enormous difficulties that confront the examiners but it is easy when setting a question to lose sight of the context as they seek to frame a question to address a particular area. I was invigilating in a mental arithmetic test in which the questions were presented via a pre-recorded tape. Generally the questions were clear and succinct, but one question, clearly aimed at getting students to calculate in thousands, stated, 'I have a hundred pounds in 5p pieces, how many 5p pieces do I have?' At this some of the students laughed, some grinned, and many of them, as I did, tried to visualise what 2000 5p pieces looked like and wondered why someone had such a collection. It has long been considered that people with Asperger's Syndrome think in pictures. This being the case it is easy to see how a student would never get past the word that to them is the key to the question, but was intended by the question setter as merely to frame the context. It is easy to criticise, and this is not the purpose of these illustrations, but hopefully they may serve to aid clarity of thought and context in setting questions.

There are also the questions that the student with Asperger's Syndrome will answer literally, when asked.

If asked 'Do you know why...?' They will often answer 'Yes.' One student when asked 'Do you know why Hitler invaded Poland?' answered 'Yes.'

Or when asked 'What is ...?' will give their own literal answer. The question on a philosophy paper 'What is courage?' would expect a clear description of what the word courage meant to them. My daughter answered 'This is' to that question in a practice examination.

On another occasion when the SATs first came out the instructions for the teacher administering the Key Stage 1 Science SAT were to ask the student to perform the same experiment and record exactly the words the student said when they discovered the answer.

The test was to see if three different substances floated. The student was asked before to say whether they floated and afterwards whether they had been correct and to record what they said.

The first object was a piece of wood – 'This will float,' the student said.

He placed the wood into the tank full of water – 'Told you,' he said.

The second object was an orange – 'This will half float,' he said.

He placed the orange in the tank – 'Well, that did as well.'

The third object was a piece of metal – 'This will float – because ships are made of metal and they float.'

He placed the metal in the tank of water. 'Bugger me, the bastard's sunk,' he stated – which the teacher wrote down on the recording form.

9.3.3 Reward systems in the classroom

Our students respond very differently to the concept of exams, but often nervousness as such is unknown to them. Many students simply have no 'exam nerves', yet may become extremely anxious in areas we find difficult to comprehend from our social viewpoint. The nervousness we describe as 'stage fright' is also sometimes missing, and the young people will willingly perform plays and celebrate their work in assemblies, providing of course that the difficulties of interaction are overcome beforehand. I have always encouraged the students to celebrate their work; often their self-esteem is very low, and they need every opportunity to increase self-worth and receive praise for their academic and social achievements, linked to a tangible reward.

As you would expect, the motivation of each student to work varies from individual to individual and subject to subject, but generally it is greater in the area of their enthusiasm, often maths, reading or computing. Equally, they are very difficult to stimulate in areas in which they have little interest. They are frequently masters of avoidance tactics and you need to safeguard against time-wasting. In these instances, each student has a target with a realistic expectation of when the work is to be completed, and the student is praised if the target is reached. However, if the time taken falls below the target, the student is kept in to finish it. This may seem simple and obvious, but often we can react differently to students with social and learning differences, and we must temper these ideas with a need to make progress in class.

At times students can become completely non-compliant, and this behaviour is usually underpinned by an incident, concern or unresolved issue. In these instances it is pointless to continue until the issue is resolved, and the pastoral tutor or a 'free' member of staff is brought in to take the student and work through the issue. If these instances are not recognised in time, the student may react in a range of ways: silence; non-compliance; obsessive behaviour; repetitive behaviour; aggression; total meltdown – all are possible. To avoid these instances we negotiate 'time out' procedures with the student in times of calm.

9.3.4 De-escalating anger

In order to have strategies for de-escalating incidents and anger, it is important that these have been negotiated with the student in times of calm. The pastoral tutor will talk with the child and they discuss 'triggers', and frustrations which increase anxiety. They will discuss how it feels to become frustrated and what happens when the anger rises, the purpose of which is to identify for the student the feeling of escalation, and for the adult to be aware of the signals and for the student and tutor to be able to defuse a situation before it gets out of hand. The tutor discusses in what way this feeling is alleviated for the student, which in our experience could be, for example: 'twiddling' with cotton; playing with Lego; spending time with a favourite toy; listening to music or a taped voice; walking around; or sitting in the garden. Most frequently, however, it is the opportunity for the student to withdraw to their own space. These quiet areas are identified and a 'time out' contract negotiated, typed up, signed and circulated to all staff. Within the contract the student describes how they would indicate they need time out. This is usually a very simple sign as the student may get too angry to use language to express what they are doing, and this is why whole-staff communication is crucial. The time out can be invoked by the student in class, and allows for de-escalation of anger. During time out, the student is left alone, but monitored from a distance, for a period of usually five minutes, after which they are expected to talk to an adult, who assesses if they are ready to return to class, or alternatively attempts to resolve the issue that caused the raised anxiety for the student.

One student who arrived at the school asked if he could have a very small area into which he could retreat to at times of heightened anxiety. We created a cupboard in the corner of his bedroom which was just large enough for him to crawl into under the staircase and he was allowed to stay there for ten minutes before he had to inform staff that he was to return. This was very successful for him and we knew where he was. Within the first three months this was used on a daily basis but reduced over time and after nine months was still available but no longer used.

9.3.5 Academic expectations

One of the criticisms commonly aimed at special schools and students with special needs is a low expectation in academic areas. However, students with Asperger's Syndrome can be exceptionally able in some areas and I have always felt that expectations of success should be high. Education is a therapy in itself and educational achievement will increase self-esteem and self-confidence and give the individual a certain amount of 'street cred' amongst his peers and the staff group. The majority of students are capable of getting to university and the expectation should be that this is a realistic option. Not all students are able in class, however, and there appears to be no common profile for all of the students with Asperger's Syndrome: frequently a student may be above average in one area and below in another. I would often describe this as a 'Toblerone' profile, and even within a single subject there is this discrepancy. This makes planning in the classroom exceptionally exacting for the teacher, who must carefully differentiate all the areas taught to ensure an appropriate challenge for each student. This can lead to fragmentation of the class in subject teaching, with all of the students working individually though within a classroom environment. Whilst this may sometimes be appropriate, teachers endeavour to teach to themes and then differentiate work – in this way the students are able to share the learning experience of the subjects, but remain stimulated by the work set.

9.3.6 School phobia and separation anxiety

All of the students placed at North Hill House and Farleigh had Statements of Special Educational Needs, but not all students with Asperger's Syndrome have a Statement. Although the diagnosis is now far more common, it is still difficult for a student to get extra resources through a Statement of Special Educational Needs. The students had often been in many previous schools and as a result of difficulties experienced had an extremely negative view of the educational system. Many of the students would have been out of school for months, on several occasions in excess of a year, with the student remaining at home in the interim receiving home tuition, lessons from parents, or very little education at all. During these times the bonds between child and parent increase, and yet are strained because of the difficulties of everyday management the young person presents for the parents. This was always a difficult time for the family, usually further complicated as parents tried to find a suitable school for the young person. Finally, when placed, the student had to comply to an entirely contrasting environment to that at home. At the same time, parents' anxiety was raised as they would worry about the student settling in.

I often talked to parents about the three things that I felt should/ would occur once the young person was successfully placed:

- The Crusade should now be over – that is, now the young person is placed at the school. The 'fight' that the parents have had to get the young person's needs agreed and assessed and placed in the appropriate school, and which has taken over most of their lives for the last few years, is finished. It is time now to end the crusade and work with the school.

- They should stop feeling guilty and that they have failed because their 'baby' goes to a residential school. They have not failed – the young person now has an opportunity to 'grow' in a caring environment.

- The umbilical cord now needs to be severed, to be superseded by a period of self-reliance and independence for the young person. Most parents want their children to grow into independent adults who are resourceful and can find their own way in the world, but sometimes it is very difficult to let the child go.

The student will frequently suffer from separation anxiety. They will find it difficult to settle; they will suffer from homesickness, but be unaware of what this is. The student will find that they are faced with a classroom, and experience again the feeling of failure that they had previously experienced in that environment. This is a very stressful time for the student and one in which adults need to have empathy, yet firmness to ease the student back into school. Initially, in the first few days, stress is kept to a minimum, but the student would have to attend school, perhaps supported by the tutor. The quantity of work at this time is unimportant – the key issue is to get the student into class, and happy. Only then would the work levels increase. We use all kinds of ways to reduce these periods of anxiety, yet a creative, simple and flexible approach could be very productive:

One particular child started with us after a long period of time at home. His anxiety was high, as was the control he exerted over his environment. He was very homesick, but gained great solace from his collection of large soft toys, from which he was inseparable, and which helped him reduce his anxiety. On the first day in school, he wanted to carry a large toy to school. This would clearly have made him a target of derision, a poor start for a new class, yet we recognised the need for him to carry some toy. Searching around, we found in his collection a very small teddy bear, about 15cm tall, which fitted in his pocket under his sweatshirt. He was happy to carry this toy and seemed relieved at having 'a familiar friend' with him. This helped reduce his anxiety and helped him settle in class.

These early days at school are critical, and it is imperative that the student is helped to settle whilst learning that there are firm boundaries.

It is essential that the student is having fun, but at the same time we need to be realistic and recognise that the student is likely to react to some aspect of the rules and boundaries. The student will always try to see how far the rules can be pushed and how many of the non-negotiable rules can be tested. This is where fairness, firmness and a whole-school approach comes in, the staff choosing carefully where they need to be assertive, gain control, and enforce the boundaries.

9.3.7 Teaching strategies

It is important to realise that when teaching young people with Asperger's Syndrome it is essential that you are explicit. Everything needs to be in black and white and written down. It is not an exaggeration to say that you cannot be too explicit. You also need to ensure that your teaching style meets the students' learning style. Remember that most individuals with Asperger's Syndrome have a visual learning style, so 'talking at' the student will not be effective if it is not followed up with explanations either in writing or diagrammatic form. Students with Asperger's Syndrome will learn a concept or skill in one subject, say graphs in mathematics, but then find it difficult to transfer that same skill into, say, geography. They will struggle in history with checking different sources for facts, preferring to regard 'facts' as 'facts', whereas teachers will ask students to check their sources, interpretations and background. It is important that lessons are well planned, use a lot of different sources and have a multi-sensory approach. This is only what a good teacher will deliver every day in a mainstream school, so providing they are flexible and understand the difficulties the student with Asperger's Syndrome has there is no reason why they cannot work with these youngsters in a mainstream setting.

The behavioural management of students in any educational setting is vitally important. However, with students with Asperger's Syndrome it needs to be viewed with a completely new outlook.

It is important that the teacher considers the traditional 'locum of control' and asks, 'Can I create an environment conducive to learning without this traditional level of control?' There needs to be a negotiated learning environment where everything becomes predictable, any unforeseen change is explained in advance, the rules are clear and written down, and everything is clearly either negotiable or non-negotiable.

The teacher needs a thorough knowledge and understanding not just of teaching and learning strategies and techniques and a sound subject knowledge. Also they are required to have a sound knowledge of the students and how their difficulties will impact on their learning. Without this knowledge then difficulties will arise:

It is often only when people know about the fundamentals of Asperger Syndrome and have in depth knowledge about the individual with the diagnosis that they can provide a good environment that does not cause concern, anxiety or extreme stress. (Gillberg 2002, p.103)

Students' and Parents' Views – Perception of Reality

CHAPTER 10

STUDENTS' VIEWS

ATTENTION, ANYONE WHO REMEMBERS ME!

For those of you who remember yours truly as the vulnerable, hyper-active, over-reacting kid, I can explain it all: I have Asperger's Syndrome, a form of mild autism. This disability makes it difficult for people to socialise, fit into crowds, and handle jokes; strengths often appear in the form of sensitivity, frustration, and sometimes taking it out on other people.

Although Asperger's can also be seen as something of a gift (i.e. where there is a lack of communication skills, there is a presence of immense knowledge in some people with AS).

I do still wish that, more for your sake and that of my family, than for my own sake, I did not have a disability. But I do, and I have to live with it, especially at a time when society is increasingly showing awareness of it, and more and more help is being given to people with AS, as each year passes.

For more information, visit a biography of Nick Hornby, or read *The Curious Incident of the Dog in the Night-Time* by Mark Haddon. Have any of you seen the film *Rain Man* with Dustin Hoffman? That's a good source of info, too.

To all those I was at school with whom I hurt verbally or physically, or gave a hard time, often out of frustration: I AM SORRY I HURT YOU, AND CAN ASSURE YOU I AM NOW ENTIRELY CONFIDENT AND EASY-GOING, AND NOT VULNERABLE OR IRRITABLE.

I am about to finish a degree course at university called BA (Hons) Media With Cultural Studies. After I finish, I hope to work in the media – but who knows where?

To anyone who remembers me – especially from Farleigh College, I miss all you guys – and can find time to correspond,

I REALLY WANT TO HEAR FROM YOU! I might even come to a reunion, if anybody is organising one!

Thank you for taking the time to read this, and do feel reassured about who I am today.

This is taken from the Friends Reunited website with the student's permission. He was one of the first students at Farleigh College in 1996, still keeps in touch, and never forgets my or any of my family's birthdays. I thought it was a useful insight into Asperger's Syndrome and how some students progress.

It was important when considering a 'model' of education and social care for individuals with Asperger's Syndrome that the views of those involved was considered carefully. This chapter is their explanation of their experiences and what worked for them and what didn't. I initially sent out about 20 emails to ex-students asking if they would like to contribute to an account of how the schools developed and the model I used. I gave them three open-ended questions:

1. What were life and education experiences like before coming to North Hill/Farleigh College?

2. What was life like at North Hill/Farleigh College for you?

3. What has life been for you after North Hill/Farleigh College in terms of how prepared it made you?

A few students responded to these questions but many found it difficult to structure their thoughts around them. I then sent out a fuller questionnaire, which many replied to. The questions in that questionnaire are included below with their replies. We all have different perceptions of events and people. It is often described as reality and perception of reality. For individuals with Asperger's Syndrome, perception *is* reality: they cannot see any difference. This at times makes their rigidity of thought impossible to change and it is pointless trying to argue or change their views. These accounts from former students are their perceptions of their educational and social experiences through their adolescence, and may differ from others' perceptions or what actually occurred.

I was hoping to discover what, if anything, the students thought had worked at the schools, what didn't work, were they interested at all or was it just part of their education that they expected? I also wanted to know if they thought the same as me in the bits I would change if I were doing it again. Hopefully I am still refining the model with each school I become involved in. I certainly am still learning about this fascinating syndrome and trying to make a difference. This surely can only be judged by those who experienced it – far too often we as educators feel we know best and meet the demands of the examination boards or the inspectorate, which is understandable, but we also need to take account of the views of students as well.

I have kept the descriptive explanation of each student intentionally brief to preserve their privacy. Many of the students came to the schools with poor social skills and behavioural and family complications; it would be unfair to describe these in this format. I think it is fair to say that independent residential schooling is an expensive option for Local Authorities and is not chosen lightly or as a first option to assisting students with Asperger's Syndrome, so most of the students at North Hill House and Farleigh had not received a positive educational experience.

I have copied the responses as they came in, just removing any personal comments about people or their names to try and disguise their and others' identities.

I am sure you will find these insights fascinating and enlightening.

10.1 Responses to the questionnaire
Student A

This was one of the first students I accepted at Farleigh College with a diagnosis of Asperger's Syndrome, though I already had a number of undiagnosed students. The school still had students with dyslexia attending and the mix at times was very volatile. Initially he was unable to cope with any form of teasing (bullying) and found it difficult to develop relationships, yet now is able to see what progress he made through the school.

When this student first looked around the school he was engaged in conversation by one of the established boys trying to involve him in their conversation. The conversation went something like this:

Boy: Do you like rabbits?

New Student: Yes I do. Why?

Boy: Because we have a number of rabbits in cages round the back of the science room you could look at.

New Student: I think you'll find that rabbits live in 'hutches' not cages – it's rabbit hutches.

Boy: Well **** off then.

When I contacted him initially we had an email exchange before he completed the questionnaire. In that exchange he asked me what I remembered of him, and I replied. Here is his response to my reply:

Hello again,
I appear to have underestimated how you would respond to my big question. While it is very detailed, multi-layered, and quite different to what I expected...I am surprised at the complete absence of that time when, during a farewell speech in assembly, I took you by surprise with a massive insult, whilst everyone else erupted with laughter! Surely that is lodged in your mind, somewhere?

But in answer to your question, I remember walking into your office when I came to look round during the summer holidays (so there were no pupils running around, etc.) and on being introduced to you, thinking, 'Aren't you a bit young to be a Headteacher?' Seriously, that is what I thought. You were nothing like the common 1950s image of a Headteacher who wears glasses and a tweed jacket with leather patches!

Anything else? Well: there is the time I corrected you in assembly about a piece of trivia related to the '60s, and you politely accepted that without looking at all annoyed; there is your tendency to mock yourself, one way or another (on one occasion, you were holding a bowl of trifle, and you commented 'Look at it wobbling – a mirror image of me, that is'); there is your less-than-serious approach to teaching geography (making it fun, with the odd joke here and there); there is the way in which, when dealing with a trouble-maker, you could be more intimidating than any one else (I am not joking); and above all, the way in which, through speech and mannerisms, you were more all-over-the-place and jolly as well as a serious, no-nonsense straight-talker.

I had no idea that I had an ability to teach anyone about Asperger's – to be honest, I am still learning about it myself, and feel the need to ask certain questions about it, once in a while. You are (amazingly) correct in assuming that it was Meat Loaf who I was going to see in concert – when it did go ahead, I went, and enjoyed it without any anxieties.

Finally, I remember that my only visit as a former pupil (in July 2000, to hand out a prize with my name on it) was the last time I came into contact with your family (if I remember correctly), and meeting both your parents in your office. Your father said, 'How are you?' and your mother was sitting on the sofa, with my 'award speech' in her hand; I thought for one moment I was going to be walloped with her handbag for mocking you!

Once again, I promise to have that questionnaire filled in and sent to you by next week.

Enjoy the rest of this week.

Bye for now.

Here is his response to the questionnaire.

Since 2007 I have worked mostly as a Library Assistant, and have also been a Records Assistant and Clerical Officer.

Whilst at Farleigh, I was encouraged to take part in certain sports – some I liked (such as swimming or trampolining at the leisure centre in Bath) and some I was less keen on (such as baseball or football on the site of Farleigh itself, mostly due to peer pressure). Sports aside, I was encouraged to take part in certain other activities, even if they were not exactly stimulating – I liked horse-riding in the countryside, and even more (though this may seem lazy) I loved using computers.

I did not get involved in musical theatre at Farleigh, as the means to do so was not on offer. As for travel, I could not possibly do this by myself until I was 18, possibly out of fears that I may get lost or end up in some sort of danger – this may still have been the case, even if I did not have a disability of any sort.

'Mild' is one way of putting how my Asperger's manifests itself. Even as a child and teenager – and despite having enormous difficulty in reading other people's body language, knowing what to say and what not to say, and getting anxious about trivial matters – I was told that my weaknesses were few, compared to others with worse cases of AS for whom interaction and living can be more of a struggle.

Overall, being Asperger's means not quite being able to analyse or interpret people or situations as quickly or as accurately as ordinary people would.

I used to have enormous difficulty in knowing whether or not other people were interested when I spoke to them at great length, and difficulty in knowing when to stop talking or not go into too much detail – but now I can mostly tell when people do or do not want to listen, and not talk too much.

I overcame my difficulties first by becoming more aware and able to think very carefully as I got older – although what really helped was learning how to interpret people's emotions through facial expressions, with the help of training sessions at school, whether these were one-to-one (with an expert in behavioural therapy or anything similar) or in a group with other pupils.

One thing I still really struggle with would be knowing the right way to solve a certain difficulty in a way that 'ordinary' people would find no difficulties with – but a more likely answer is being a bit slow in performing certain tasks, compared to normal people, and needing other people to be more patient regarding progress.

The only way to deal with this is to pause, think carefully, and take deep breaths – anything to avoid yelling at others, or conveying signs of being visibly aggravated and frustrated.

As years go by, this hindrance – whether or not it can be overcome – has produced less stress, and so one day it may become totally unnoticeable.

My AS continues to show itself in a variety of ways, actually – anxieties, being too focused on one person or object at a time, thinking unrealistically about future goals in life, and never being on the same wave-length as ordinary people, in terms of how to achieve a form of success or tackle a complicated situation.

The one way in which these defects can be dealt with, is simply to think long and hard about what really matters (especially choosing something current or urgent to focus on, as opposed to anything current but not at all urgent, or even something in the past that cannot be changed).

A more sophisticated or detailed means of defining 'ordinary' would be the word which experts on disabilities use to describe those without any form of disability whatsoever – simply, 'neuro-typical', or 'NT'.

Very few strategies have helped, but they have made much difference – to start with, there is thinking more positively about life in general, and the various difficulties it can throw at anyone, anywhere. Then, with regard to past events, there is accepting that the only solution to confronting them is to learn, and be sure not to make such mistakes again – and accepting that everyone moves on.

The strategies I have used, either I learned from my parents, or I learned them through helpful adult figures at school (such as care staff) and after that, counsellors.

Being at Farleigh helped, because the size of the school (no more than 75 pupils) and a greater understanding of Asperger's than can be found at any previous school proved instrumental in the preparation for life in bigger environments, such as college and more importantly university. Frequent discussions with teachers also helped.

To give an example of how life at Farleigh proved more helpful than life at my previous school, awareness of Asperger's could be found not only in staff, but also pupils – I recall one or two instances where fellow pupils might say, 'Are you Asperger's? 'Cos I am, too!' plus one other instance where an older pupil spontaneously called out 'Asperger's!' thus indicating that I was unable to hide my disability – or just be written off as a 'freak' – for much longer.

As for life after school, awareness of Asperger's among ordinary adults was quite slow to become widespread – in between leaving school and later graduating from university, certain other people would hint at the disability I had, by asking, 'Are you autistic?' to which an answer of 'yes and no' would be sufficient. The turning point in awareness would have to be the success of the fictional book *The Curious Incident of the Dog in the Night-Time*, by Mark Haddon – after this, awareness really was enormous, and somebody who has Asperger's only mildly (of which I am an example) would definitely be sussed out, in a short space of time.

As to whether or not staff at Farleigh understood Asperger's, this was not always clear, except within one-to-one or group therapy sessions in the daytime. What is definite is that being a member of care staff requires so much more training and hard work than simply being a teacher or Headteacher!

How the bullying was dealt with, varied – and not just as to whether the cases themselves were verbal or physical. If it was dealt with, it involved a severe ticking off by a member of staff (whether it be evening care staff, a member of staff who was around during the day such as the Deputy Headteacher or Head of Care, or a classroom teacher) – apprehending, perhaps, but never any prodding or classroom detention.

Certain physical situations that were ignored (or, more politely, listened to but did not result in any type of punishment) include being cornered, though life at Farleigh did become much easier. One way to cope with the situations was to tell someone immediately, even if it came to nothing. Another way was…simply to take deep breaths, stay calm, and try as much as possible to let it go, and ignore any torment when back among pupils and staff.

I am not sure if I learnt anything from these situations…but as time went on, life at Farleigh became easier and more enjoyable, and I became less vulnerable and/or likely to react. Come the end, I was so sorry to leave!

Well, more than one person really helped me actually! Those who initially came across as 'ignoring' certain situations became more approachable and helpful as time went on. But above all, those who gave the most advice and encouragement were the one teacher I had non-stop, and my separate out-of-hours tutor, and a member of the care staff by whom I was looked after for two-and-a-half years – they helped by giving advice, and being gentle or tough depending on how I reacted or whatever the situation was. As time went by, and I settled in, my confidence grew, and my relating towards other people (staff and pupils alike) improved a great deal.

A good staff member would need perception as an ideal start – being able to understand the level of trauma or frustration in a young person, when talking to them, is helpful, and at no point must the level in a young person be underestimated or undermined by a person who is trying to help. Secondly, much patience is required, so that whoever is helping can keep calm at all times, and offer solutions without needing to convey any aggression that could be alarming.

Some specific examples would be: always listening to whoever is seeking help, and never ignoring their pleas, even if what has upset them is trivial. While certain school pupils are more in need of help than others (with or without disability), they must learn to be selective of what they complain about, and what they can just ignore and let go – if a pupil seeks help for every little thing that upsets them, the patience of whoever hears the pleas can start to wear thin, and the pupil themselff will not exactly improve their own well-being.

Since Farleigh, finding the right sort of job has been tough – to date, I have had various gaps of unemployment between separate jobs, all of which have been temporary as opposed to permanent. And meeting the right kind of woman (in other words, a suitable girlfriend) is a never-ending struggle.

Finding work is difficult, partly because no matter what sort of job you aim to land yourself in, and whether or not you get short-listed for an interview, you are still competing with many other people, only one of whom will be hired. Plus, compared to most people I know, I have been to very many schools, am in some ways under-qualified (despite eventually graduating from university with a BA degree, level 2:2), and more to the point, am under-skilled (I have failed to land certain jobs, or even get short-listed for interviews, due to my computer skills, which are intermediate, rather than advanced).

As for the difficulty in finding the right sort of girlfriend (or wife), either it all comes down to what we have in common, or somehow the feeling of being on the same wave-length is just not there. I also do not get out as much as other people would, do not know very many people, and have had little success with dating sites (which can be breeding grounds for people looking for someone to scam, financially). Plus, of course, I have AS which may be far better known today than it was in the early '90s...but is still a barrier as it limits how easily a man relates to a woman, disability or no disability.

Well, I live with my parents, and so it is them I turn to mostly for tips on getting back into employment (be it interviews or applications), how to be more employable, and how to meet the right woman in the right place.

There is little support from outside agencies; once again I am held back by my being independent and not particularly partial to wide open environments. I have tried to join one or two AS-specific social groups online (leading possibly to genuine meet-ups in pubs or clubs), and either nothing came out of it, or my application succeeded and I was invited to a few outings, but I just could not motivate myself to get out and meet people, even if I had nothing else to do.

The only option now...is to keep calm, keep focused, do what is easiest (and of significance) and jump at any life-changing opportunity where possible – especially if it leads to change for the better, and improves sociability.

Student B

This student was undiagnosed but certainly saw the world from his own perspective and had a distinctive style to everything he did, as is demonstrated below. He related everything in my Geography examination group to differing forms of cheese. It was a challenge to describe 'coastal erosion' using different types of cheese, yet we managed it and he gained an admirable grade!

Hello Mr Bradshaw sir! We find it interesting and quite involving that you wish to write a full book on our past events at the school we resided at! I am more than willing to cooperate with that as that school gave me a strong sense of independence above all else for (me anyway) I was never the academic genius of class (there's life Jim but not as we know it) to coin a phrase. Remember that, sir?! Now I know you'd say not to call you sir any longer but I couldn't get used to (Steven) after so many years! I'm taking a look at the questionnaire you so kindly sent to start me off sir. I'm going to work through it bit by bit as they say! Thank ye kindly for thou remembrance tiss a nice thing to know thou hast not been so readily forgotten!

Till next message take care sir.

A few months later I then received this:

Hi Mr Bradshaw,

Sorry this has taken me a long time but not really computer literate! I am also sorry if what I have written doesn't sound very happy but I have a number of ongoing issues so just being honest about how things are really for me. Let me know if you need anything else sir!

I reside in a flat with my long-term girlfriend.

When I left school I worked for a hospital for a short time and after that it was decided that I should go to college. I studied there for six months but it became clear that working in an office was not going to be suitable for me. The college got me contact with a Trust to help me explore other work possibilities. I then discovered that Horticulture was the way forward for me. Later I became a green keeper at a golf course.

I really enjoyed working on the golf course but unfortunately I left it due to not feeling my own worth so sadly I have been unemployed since 2006. Currently I have no work support since the Trust are no longer in my area. I have no support to help me but I am hopeful.

Having Asperger's syndrome is like a curse, as the Asperger's amplifies my unstable personality. So interacting with others is very difficult as I don't have any friends to socialise with so I feel isolated.

I have never achieved getting over my difficulties, as I have never had the help I needed so I have a lot of difficulties right now. My own self-loathing amplified by my parents, aggression, the way I think, my isolation, hopelessness. Amplified by a temper – when I make a mistake I just get angry with myself so I hit an object. Things tend to disintegrate through my anger.

However, my latest breakthrough is the control my girlfriend has over me when I get angry through frustration and confusion and isolation.

Being at Farleigh taught me independence and self-motivation but I didn't study so I didn't get anywhere with the education side.

Being at Farleigh left me feeling isolated from home and other pupils taking the mick when I was calling home but the Geography teacher showed compassion and the Catering staff was very friendly, so I spoke to them quite a lot.

The best qualities in staff I found were: compassion, patience and understanding

In my current life I still have many difficulties, which I struggle to cope with: my parents splitting up, hating my parents' new partners – causing confusion, frustration and anger. Not having any friends to socialise with so feel very isolated and alone, depressed, feel hopeless. No job opportunities as I don't have any kind of support or interaction other than with my girlfriend. No life opportunities and I have now been told I have a balance problem as I keep falling over and having accidents at home. The balance section of my brain has shrunk so having physio and lots of tests to find out why this happened.

Only my girlfriend supports me, which isn't enough and it's not fair on her. She finds it hard to cope with it at times.

Student C

This student was a very feisty young lady – she knew what she wanted and she always wanted it yesterday. She found it very difficult to build relationships with other students, preferring to concentrate all her efforts on college work or, more usually, working out at the gym. She dealt with many major obstacles during her time at Farleigh – sometimes she won, sometimes she lost, but one thing that never changed was her determination to succeed.

When I left FFEC I studied music production, at Access to Music, and then when I moved to London I also did music production. But now I'm going to college to study Access to Medicine in the hope of going to Med School next year. However, I did not do this immediately as straight after Farleigh I moved back into my mum's house and then had to go into hospital with anorexia nervosa. But when I got out I moved into my own place and shortly after that moved to London and have been here ever since.

I work voluntarily at a Jewish care home with elderly people, some of whom have dementia. However, I have not had a job; whilst at Farleigh I did work in a café for a period and also at a Trust head office. I also went on Camp America as a camp counsellor for two months.

OCD is the biggest difficulty I have overcome. This hideous condition, it is fair to say, has ruined a huge portion of my life and at times made me wonder whether I even wanted to carry on. OCD was literally a long nightmare, it made me angry, volatile and above all else I was terrified of my own thoughts and of being in my body, but there was no way I could escape it. So I had to learn to live within my mind and body and be at peace and stop trying to run away. It's a fight for my life, but now I've started to beat it and the good days are beginning to outnumber the bad, that is what makes it all worthwhile. When the world comes alive and you again begin to experience all the things you've been missing, life can be amazing, truly.

I now believe there are no difficulties too big to be overcome. I believe you can achieve anything. These days my AS is different to how it used to be, but this is because I understand it and am living life differently to how I used to.

AS used to be a self-perpetuating problem. I didn't want to see anyone, speak to or be around anyone, I had no friends and was cruelly and brutally bullied, this just pushed me deeper into isolation. But it was depressing and miserable and now I thrive in other people's company. Isolation and loneliness was once a gift, but now I wouldn't wish it on my worst enemy. We all need other people and other people are a pleasure to be around.

I also still struggle tremendously with OCD, but now I am so busy with my life it takes a back seat and I fully believe that one day very soon it shall be no more. The anger and volatility, which used to be all-consuming, is also pretty much gone and I am no longer bullied by anyone. Perhaps my mum would argue that one place I still have issues is with tact. I do say things that are often offensive, without meaning to and can get people's backs up, but I just tell people how it is and if they don't like it they don't have to agree. I'd never ever intentionally offend or upset someone.

AS used to make me lack emotion, rather like a robot. But very recently I have managed to get back in touch with my emotions again and it is magical, like living in a world which is so vivid and alive once more. Living without emotions in all honesty was a half life, I missed out on everything, anything remotely enjoyable. Absence of emotions protects you from being hurt as well, but at what cost? I'd rather be hurt a million times than exist without emotions.

Meditating is the best strategy I have found to date. By this I mean observing, embracing, opening, letting be, accepting and non-judging. Before learning how to meditate, I spent my entire life running away from scary thoughts, which I couldn't control, but meditating enables me to live right now with whatever thoughts and feelings I have and not having to worry about them and living in constant fear.

Hiking as well has been a tremendous relief for me. It enables me to tune into the world around me and truly be present instead of living in fear inside my head. It is a marvellous distraction.

Although the bullying turned me into a complete hermit, what I have also found priceless is the touch and love of others, throughout all of this. Being amongst people who love me always calms me down; hugs, kisses and affection are magic.

Massage as well, it allows you to connect to and really feel your body, and these connections between the brain and the body, I believe, are vital for body functioning and can alleviate stress, constipation and all other conditions brought on by poor brain/ body connection.

Before Farleigh I was totally isolated. I had no friends at all, I had no life and I had no self-confidence or self-esteem. At Farleigh I met and made friends with the most incredible people I have ever come across. They showed me genuine care and love and affection and brought me back into the real world. Before Farleigh I'd given up any hope of ever fitting in, but the wonderful staff gave me the secure environment I needed to begin to start trusting and loving other people again. The opportunity to go to Farleigh for me was a gift. For those three years I felt truly loved and accepted, just as I am.

Farleigh did nothing for my OCD, nor did it help with the perpetual terror I lived my life in, 24/7. I know there is a lot more Farleigh could have done to help me, but this is with hindsight and back then, even I didn't know what I needed so I wouldn't expect Farleigh to know, but I would hope that Farleigh can learn from me and help others.

I tried everything external to solve my problems, but there was no way of avoiding the fact that I was the main cause of all of them. It took me to learn and love myself inside and out in order to begin to move forward with my life.

Love and absolute acceptance of oneself and all other people, patience, optimism, dedication.

I still suffer from constant fear of my own thoughts and body, and I have severe OCD. But every day it gets a little better and these problems are very rapidly becoming history. I do wish my family and friends lived much closer, I am very lonely and miss them all so dearly.

But one thing I must add is that I could have all the support in the world and still never get over my problems. The support we all need more than anything is the support and love within us, and that's not meant to be a cliché.

Something I must add which I forgot to put in my questionnaire is that in some ways the diagnosis of Asperger's Syndrome was a blessing, but in other ways it is a curse. Because it makes you think there's nothing can be done to change any of the problems it causes. But this is wrong. No matter what the problem is I believe it is always possible to change, regardless of any diagnosis.

Student D

This student had probably the most negative view of everything at school age, so I was pleasantly surprised that there was any aspect of his response that was positive. He feels now that he can cope so well he doesn't want anyone to know he has Asperger's Syndrome.

1. What were life and education experiences like before coming to North Hill?

At the time of my transfer to North Hill House I was ten years old and being educated at a Special School. My time at that school did nothing except worsen my behaviour and mental state. The school was primarily intended for individuals with autism, as opposed to my disorder of Asperger's Syndrome. If being schooled there provided me with anything long-lasting it was the capacity to survive in social isolation, with no peers to speak of. I was very much on my own all the time. Hence I was unusually enthusiastic toward the prospect of moving over a hundred miles, from London, to Frome in Somerset where NHH was based.

2. What was life like at North Hill for you?

At the time of my arrival I was the youngest pupil at the school, not surprising perhaps, as I was also the sixth to join the institution. Joining the school at this early stage gave me the opportunity to see it develop.

The original building and its grounds were superb, as was almost everything else about the institution. There was a genuine feeling that the staff wanted to help and that there was, with the odd exception of incident or individual, a mutual respect between the staff and students. This respect might almost have been said to border on friendship or the feeling of an extended family. This high level of quality continued to be maintained, despite the continued expansion of the school, until the Priory Group came into control of the Farleigh education group in October of 2002. The buyout initially only seemed to affect marginal issues regarding policy, reflected in the way we were treated as pupils of the school. Even at this stage, where and when a pupil had an opinion regarding the Priory's takeover, it was generally a negative one. This negativity continued to grow exponentially after the move to the new building.

The school moved from its original site in September 2003, to the universal dismay of all students I spoke to on the subject. The old building had been aesthetically pleasing, at least to me, and had grounds that backed onto the Millennium garden. In contrast, the new 'purpose built site' was exactly that, not an ounce of beauty and not an inch of grass save an area of muddy bracken, at best 10m^2 was all there was. Even at the time when I left, the recreational facilities did not even come close to those of the original building. More than this, the way in which the school was run was also changing drastically. The senior management team (SMT), or 'smut' as they became affectionately known by many of the pupils, became gradually more separate as an entity; rarely getting to see what happened on the pastoral or academic side of things. The rift that this separation caused was most visible in new students and staff, who rarely developed much of the mutual respect I spoke of earlier. Some staff toward the end of my time at NHH mentioned worries that the school was moving toward becoming something akin to 'a secure unit'. Considering the near utopian location when NHH first crossed my path, it seems to have come a long way.

It should be said that by no means were the staff always on side with the things they were instructed to do. Seeing staff on the edge of tears due to NHH requests was evidence enough of this for myself. These were usually the staff I sided with, or who sided with me, when something particularly unjust was on the cards. The issues with NHH were not usually caused by staff on the ground level, but due to the divorced nature of those at the top of the tree and the regulations binding SMT.

3. What has life been for you after North Hill in terms of how prepared it made you?

After my GCSEs, with which I miraculously gained entrance to a sixth form, I was given a chance to be part of a new project at NHH. This was to consist of two houses dubbed 'the sixth-form provision' in which I would reside most of my year for various reasons. Here they would continue to be watched over by the NHH staff, the difference between there and the school being, as I understood it at the point of sale, to promote more freedom and independence for the students involved. Unfortunately rather than being liberating and 'hands-off' the project became progressively more authoritarian; from what I saw and heard of the main school during this time this theme was mirrored there, leading even to incidents where some staff believed certain students' human rights were in question. The sixth-form provision was, in short, not a place you would want to bring friends after school. My survival was at least in part down to being able to deal with social isolation.

On leaving the sixth-form provision I was accepted on interview to university; from whence I write this piece. At the end of this month I begin a Master's degree in Music on scholarship. More than a decade has passed since I first stepped into the grandeur (not that the word does it justice) of NHH's original reception. There is little doubt that spending nine years of my life under the authority of NHH has shaped both my thinking and my personality, the key theme being self-reliance, not reached through positive reinforcement, but as a mechanism to defend myself from the onslaught of challenges NHH put in my way. One last thing NHH taught me was the value of having friends, a word which encompasses both peers and staff (though by no means all those at NHH), when under fire. Other than the genuine beauty of the west-country, I think that is all.

Student E

This student had Asperger's Syndrome and dyslexia. He joined Farleigh College very early in the school's development, moved into further education and into adult services. He always related to people on the same adult level, regarding himself as a member of staff with special privileges. He had an acute sense of fairness and injustice and found it difficult to see other people's points of view. He related to adults well and learnt which social skills would enhance his outlook.

Hi Stephen
    I don't really know what to say, tho' I will probably get there in the end.

I still remember the second time I met you (first being my visit with my parents to, at that time, your school, when on our way home I said to them, 'THIS IS THE SCHOOL I WANT TO GO TO'). I was sitting in my class at my previous school in London.

I think I had some of the best times of my life at Farleigh and you had some of the best teachers and care staff.

The day you gave me the laptop I still remember expecting one of the shitty Tandy ones my previous school had, but no, you gave me one that had Windows95 on it which at the time was state of the art.

Other things I remember, me telling you that you being acquired by the Priory was going to mean that forever after, and still now, when I tell people that I went to Priory Rookery Hove in Brighton they ask me things like, 'What rehab?' and, 'Do you know Amy Winehouse or Pete Doherty?'

You driving me from building to building in your Audi when it was raining cats and dogs and every time just for me you had the roof down. One time we took another boy and put him in the back seats on a freezing cold day and to this day he still says his arm was frozen solid.

Then there was the day when I was at the FE College and I came running over the road to talk to you because a member of staff had told me I was going to be expelled, basically for being a nuisance and doing nothing that they could expel me for. And because of you I was only sent home for a week, which was still wrong. I laugh at what happened that day as it was so stupid the way I was treated.

Before I left Farleigh, I became a level two trained car mechanic, not got a job yet sadly.

Since I left over two years ago I have moved back to London and am living in my own flat. Semi-supported by people that help me with things twice a week, e.g. living skills, cooking, cleaning, that kind of thing.

In 2007 I jumped out of a plane to save wildlife, raised $1898 (AUS) for Steve Irwin's charity Wildlife Warriors Worldwide. My dad and I have made videos. I tried to join the London Met police and failed the interview. Going to try again in six months and that's about it.

Student F

This student began at Farleigh College at Newbury before moving on to the further education college. She struggled to cope with any change, causing her OCD to go into overdrive. However, her love of cornflakes kept Kellogg's in business. Over her time with Farleigh her kindness stands out the most, although she would not be able to see this herself as her self-confidence was possibly the lowest amongst her peers. She also has great difficulty putting any thoughts down, as her responses here show.

I don't think that AS is noticeable in me but when I was about 12 it probably was then.

My OCD has been a very big problem for me. A few years ago I used to have really bad OCD, but now I can hardly notice it.

I'm glad to say there has not been anything that I haven't been able to overcome.

Farleigh helped me because it helped me become more independent and not rely on my mum so much. I was able to make new friends and I became more sociable.

However, being at Farleigh also detached me from my local area. I lost friends I had in school because I was always away.

My mum has been my biggest help. She has always been there for me, trying to do what's best for me.

The best qualities in a member of staff would be someone you can relate to and someone who is easy to talk to.

Since leaving Farleigh the normal things such as settling in to an area and a new college have been hard for me.

At the moment I live at home but I keep my independence by doing everything for myself.

Student G

This student took most things literally, was truthful to the point of bluntness and was obsessed with computers, wanting to spend his every waking minute engaged on them. Mathematically he was extremely able, which alarmed those who taught him – he saw no point in showing his working or to practise once he felt he had understood a mathematical process.

Hi Stephen,

Apologies for not getting back sooner, really struggling with house hunting at the moment. I'm entering my final year of study on a BSc Computer Science in London, went to work and ran a business selling trading cards until the calling to study came back and I decided to get the degree.

I feel that being at NHH really helped me understand what AS was, and improved my social skills. I enjoyed the activities and overall my impressions were positive.

Main issues were the poor Internet controls, lack of Internet to the bedroom. In this day and age, all people need access to these technologies 24/7 and I was in the pre-smartphone era where I couldn't use it on demand.

Planning to move abroad after I graduate with my partner, probably to Switzerland.

Student H

This student was unique in many ways, as well as being headstrong. He longed, however, to build sustainable friendships both with his peers and the staff, but of course these things are never easy with these students. Music was always a great love, especially those karaoke nights – he loved to tell everyone he could sing 'in perfect pitch'!

Hi Steve,

I'm really sorry for not replying sooner, been a really busy month with my band's first gig and a death in the family.

It was actually Psychology I achieved the B in, but thanks anyway for your compliments!

Answers to your questions are as follows:

Life and education was not easy before coming to Farleigh. In all of my schools and my family life as well, I struggled to gain acceptance and understanding from other people, had much difficulty developing and maintaining friendships and was often bullied. As a result, my education suffered and I didn't leave school with anything like the results or memories I would've liked.

Farleigh life was also a struggle at times, but more due to my emotional difficulties – I battled with depression for much of it – it was the best thing that could've happened to me in many ways though; at 16, as previously mentioned, I wanted nothing more than to start afresh, remove myself from all the bad memories and spend some time apart from my family. I had a lot of fun at Farleigh; regular trips bowling, swimming and shopping will remain long in the memory, and I made a lot of friends that I'm delighted to say I'm still in touch with today.

I feel since leaving Farleigh that I've become much more independent. Although I always admired the ethos of wanting to help students develop the social and independent living skills to be adequately prepared for the real world, considering it's a small and enclosed environment, not realistic to the outside world, it's difficult to learn about it until you're actually out there. Me and three other students got our own house together and we all realised, although our independent living skills were improving, we still had a lot to learn. I eventually went back to college to study Music Practice (five years ago now) and then onto university where I achieved a degree in Music Industry. I am now currently volunteering for three charities and in a band.

I'm sure things have changed in the last seven years (there have been many changes in the education system since then) and I hope that these days, students are properly assessed in advance or on arrival to Farleigh to establish what their difficulties are to ensure they are supported appropriately in the right areas. Because many people with Asperger's are entitled to free bus travel, there should be more expectations of independent travel for students – would be saving the company a lot of money in bus fares. I also think if they haven't already, all but one (for emergencies only) of the cars should be sold; it's important in these financially austere times that Farleigh is not wasting money where unnecessary. I also think students should be expected to budget for themselves when it comes to shopping, activities and essentials (bills, rent, etc.).

Answers to the questionnaire:

Asperger's Syndrome makes it more difficult for me to find work, feel comfortable in social situations, and make relationships with the opposite sex.

Bullying and discrimination are the hardest things I have managed to overcome. I feel that there's nothing I can't overcome.

I've never really been given any strategies to work with, but I always find keeping busy and doing everything I can to achieve what I want is the best way.

Going to Farleigh got me away from my family life and home area and bad memories which, at the time, were of little help to me and holding me back. I also became more independent, met a lot of new people and was able to do a lot of things (mainly social activities) that I couldn't previously.

As mentioned earlier, being at Farleigh isn't very realistic to the outside world. I don't think that's any individual or professional's specific fault, as such. However, there could have been much more onus on students being expected to do things for themselves; I actually feel that, since leaving Farleigh, I get much greater pleasure about being in control of what I do (and when) and being able to do it all independently.

Being able to listen and talk in the right measures, being able to accept criticism and being thick-skinned, being realistic to the job and telling students what they need to hear that will benefit them both in the immediate, supported environment and for later life in the big, bad world, not humouring or patronising them.

I'm still finding it quite hard to manage my negative emotions (anxiety, depression, anger, disappointment) – although nowadays I keep them bottled up much more, they still make it difficult for me to cope at times. The main difficulty, however, like many of us in the current economic climate, is being able to find paid work.

I have had no specific professional support. However, my friends and family are always available and willing to support me (not financially unless necessary) but with areas of difficulty, wherever possible and necessary. Sometimes, I feel a support worker would be helpful, but at a time when public services are being drastically reduced, I don't feel like I need one enough for the council to justify paying them.

Student I

This student was desperate to be 'fixed' and it took the entirety of her time at Farleigh to understand that she could not be fixed, nor should she want to be. She gradually learnt to love her faults and was able to learn numerous strategies to help her in all aspects of her life, in particular those issues with her family and with the astonishing amount of noise she could make just in general chat, as loud does not even begin to describe her when she first joined the college.

Now I feel that Asperger's Syndrome is just part of my personality. However, that wasn't always the case. When I first received my diagnosis, I was distraught and it took me a long time to realise my mistakes socially – I thought that it was just because I was a horrible person that no one liked me. Now I feel that my autistic traits have positive aspects to them – it allows me to have more empathy, which is key within the nursing field.

I think the best thing I have learnt has been learning to think before I open my mouth, thinking about how the other person will react to what I'm about to say, and also realising that not everyone sees situations in the same way I do, not everyone shares my opinion about things, or would make the same choices as I have.

I feel now I've been left Farleigh for a while and have done so many scary but wonderful things like travelling around Australia by myself and starting university, that there isn't anything I haven't improved on, if not overcome. I still get anxious about things, but I think I'll always feel anxious about certain things. I am able to deal with my anxiety now, better than I ever have before.

Well, I've changed A LOT over the last three years. I guess my traits haven't gone away, just lessened slightly now I know how to deal with them. I'm super loud and it used to be the more anxious I got, the more loud I would become. I'm not quite as bad anymore, but when I'm excited about something I get louder. I'd often say things without thinking about the consequences; some might say that I was rude, when genuinely it was just my sense of humour. What else? Ah yes! I had a total phobia of using the phone, something to do with not being able to see the other person's face, I think.

I guess I should put the trait that I'm most ashamed of... Before, when I had an issue I had to talk about it again and again and again and again and again and again until I got the answer I wanted from someone. Thankfully, I have been cured of that trait – maybe it's called growing up? Maybe I've just seen bigger and better things, that all the stuff I used to get in a total state about doesn't matter anymore.

I'm a compulsive list maker, so I don't forget things and it's useful to write things down. It all seems to make a bit more sense then.

I am also totally open about my diagnosis, asking people to tell me when I overstep the mark, so I can learn from my mistakes. I have found that if people know, they are much more...tolerant.

I used to write a little list of things I wanted to say when I was on the phone, so I wouldn't forget anything because of my anxiousness.

Farleigh changed me. It helped me become the person I always wanted to be. It's no secret to anyone that I found it hard to adapt to having a label, and then for being 'picked up' on each social mistake I made. My mummy was good, but because she knows me, my sense of humour and was used to me, it wasn't the same. After I realised that I needed to change, I was dedicated to the cause and would ask people to tell me when I overstepped the mark, figuring that if I knew then I could change it. I had trouble with my personal tutor in the first year because I was so used to my mother telling me directly what I was doing wrong, and she wasn't direct enough with me so I really struggled to see what I was doing wrong. In my second year, I had the best personal tutor in the world ever and although the last year was my hardest for so many reasons, it was also the one in which I grew up most, thanks to her, and I developed an understanding on how I wanted to learn from my mistakes. All the independence things I could already do, but I struggled with the social interaction, especially other members of the house and their own manifestations of AS. Overall though, despite the ups and downs (and there were many!) I had such a good time and met some absolutely amazing people.

I don't feel there was anything that did 'not help', as everything in life is a learning curve. There were things that frustrated me though and that from a health and social care perspective I think are wrong. Firstly, the very idea that I wasn't allowed to work drove me insane. I'd been working since I was 14 so not having my own money was awful. After all, the purpose of the college is to promote independence, and getting a job is a big part of being able to become independent. I'm not sure that encouraging or allowing people to live on disability benefit is quite the way forward. Also, I totally disagree with washing powder/washing up liquid/other household products being available, because in reality they are EXPENSIVE. Although I was only in one house, it frustrated me that the standards of discipline were different. You could do something in one house and get away with it, and practically get kicked out of the college for doing the same thing in another.

My personal tutor was a genius, they should replicate her over and over and over again, she should run all the houses in Farleigh simultaneously.

I had really good support from my support workers who went with me to college, both years, and also really good support from the learning centre staff.

I think a support worker needs to be dynamic, understanding and have the patience of a saint! I also think that they need to be able to give a little of themselves. I always found I got on the best with those support workers that I knew a bit about. I think it's important to establish firm boundaries, but to be open as well. I think it's important the support workers understand that no one person with AS is the same and to treat them all the same would be wrong.

Now, when things happen to me, I just get on with it and have learnt to deal with things as they come as opposed to worrying about things before they have even happened. Everyone knows of my diagnosis, in my student nurse placements, in university and my friends. It's more of a just in case measure really, but so far, I haven't done anything terribly AS. I'm quite self-aware and try to keep myself stable most of the time so I don't make silly mistakes.

Student J

This student had many learning blockages and a rigidity of thought. He would harbour grudges about individual members of staff or even schools who he felt had treated him unfairly. He took some two to three years before he developed sufficient trust in relationships to start to make progress. Then he actually flew and achieved tremendous levels academically and socially. A star pupil if there ever was one. When he came with his mother to look around the school, he had visited many other schools: none were impressive in his view so far. He had with him a clip board. When I enquired what it was for, he said there were eight categories and he was marking each category out of ten. When he returned I asked him what the scores had been. He refused to tell me but said that I had scored highly on a few.

So he was assessing us as we were assessing him, as it should be on every interview.

I first started at Farleigh Collage exactly one a week after my tenth birthday, and remember my mum being very upset with leaving her son at boarding school 3½ hours drive away. I settled in to the school quickly, and after about a year when asked by someone whether I was enjoying my time there I said, 'Yes, from Friday to Monday.' For many reasons, I didn't apply myself at school, picking which classes I would attend based primarily on my respect for the teacher, and on my interest in the subject. I had a great deal of 'hang-ups' with school work, and with socially interacting with the other students, which prompted me (occasionally with the help of one-to-one support) to develop a range of coping strategies. My 'reformation' came when I was around 14/15, and started working on GCSEs. By then I had developed enough coping strategies to be able to work around most of the major problems that had previously prevented me from applying myself to academic work – helped by the fact that I was now working towards permanent qualifications which I decided to start collecting, and the very free rein I was given. I remember disagreeing with a teacher about being given a detention that I felt was unjustified, and giving the teacher a detention for the duration of the lunch hour instead, although I did let the person out ten minutes before the end of lunch to let them have a toilet break before their next lesson.

Conversely, I don't believe that any other students voluntarily gave themselves an 'activity ban' as punishment for misbehaviour...

I did well in a range of GCSEs, which enabled me to go on to study A-levels at a mainstream college supported by FFEC. The first year at college was extremely challenging socially, with the academic help of a support worker countered by the major challenges of trying to make friends with other students whilst being accompanied by an adult. I only made some progress with getting to know people in classes where I elected to be unsupported by a scribe, due to the practical nature of the class. Over time I developed a balance of hanging out with friends, pursuing frequent and regular sporting activities, cooking for my housemates often, and working hard. Because of my focus, capacity to work hard, and good memory, I achieved the top mark nationally in Photography, one of the top five marks in the country in Geography and over 95 per cent in Environmental Science.

I've always enjoyed travelling, and decided that I wanted to take a gap year. I worked five part-time jobs for up to 80 hours a week to save up, and then went travelling for about 17 weeks, visiting eight countries around the world. My family joined me for a few weeks, but for the most part I travelled alone, making new friends, although I did plan the trip in a lot of detail beforehand.

When I was 16 I told my mother that she '...was just going to have to get it into her head that I'm not going to university.' However, my achievements at A-level were hard to ignore and I had enjoyed the studying. My parents once received a school report from a teacher, recommending that there was little point in me attempting GCSE Geography because I had no interest in the wider world. I think they were a little surprised by this, because I had always shown such a strong interest in the natural and built environment. Over the years there were many people at Farleigh who helped me a great deal, too many to mention but I believe they probably know how they are. When I got a geography teacher who I liked, respected (based on my own assessment of his competency to teach) and was innovative, I had begun to take an interest in academic geography, attaining an A* at GCSE, one of the top five marks in the country at A-level, studying Physical Geography at university from which I graduated Summa Cum Laude (top student) with two out of three departmental prizes, and was awarded a scholarship to undertake a Master's in river science and management. In a few months I'll be starting a PhD studentship looking at changes in soil carbon in desert soils in New Mexico.

I still have special subject(s), but I can now limit the time I spend on these, and generally discuss them at an 'audience-appropriate level'. My biggest passion over the last eight years has been kayaking. Starting initially at a youth club as something to do during the long summer holidays, I was disappointed when the youth club closed down at the end of the following summer. (Prompted by my mother) I asked at the watersports centre whether I could come along and help out on their instructional courses, doing all the menial jobs in return for being allowed to paddle. The manager agreed, and I had a very enjoyable summer. I resolved to undertake my instructor training to allow me to get paid to do the same thing next summer. I've now worked eight summer seasons at the same centre, instructing outdoor activities (principally paddlesports) to mainly young people but also adults and disabled people, through school, college and university although I won't be going back. I quickly progressed from a junior instructor, supported still by my desire to gain qualifications, and for the last three years I've effectively been the seasonal head of paddlesport, supervising and mentoring a team of staff to delivering a range of programmes to up to 60 8 to 16-year-olds each day.

Since starting at university, I've greatly progressed with my kayaking. While I'm not interested in the competitive disciplines, I've pursued recreational paddling on white water. Aside from housemates, all of my friends at university are paddlers (including converted coursemates), and I love the challenge. Over the last four years, I've been able to go paddling in Scotland, Slovenia, France and Canada. My parents think I like kayaking because it's an individual sport – I'm in charge of my own boat – which has some truth in it, but I'm happiest on continuous grade 4 rivers. It's very important if you make mistakes on serious rivers to be with mates who you can trust to do something clever in the few seconds they might have to resolve a situation before things go wrong. I tend not to have difficulties on rivers myself, and very often am the person sorting them out when people need technical coaching, swim (capsize their boat), or get pinned in the middle of alpine rivers, but I'm still not keen on paddling alone. I think that anticipation, the never-ending 'what-if' scenarios, is key to reacting quickly.

I'm still AS, but not many people would be able to tell and I've gotten much better at understanding other people's points of view. I've mellowed with time and don't brandish it about – perhaps ten of my close friends know. My support now is limited to the standard allowances for dyslexia. Farleigh (secondary) was a fantastic environment and I greatly value my education there (most definitely not mainstream). I would not have managed in those years without the one-to-one support from a number of teaching assistants – some of my strongest memories are:

• The flexibility of the school to accommodate me and the other students.

• Designing and building a four-storey den by reassembling the adventure playground and creating walkways between trees with scaffolding poles, and the underground bunker complex accessed via a tunnel inside a tree.☺

• Cooking for 12 people four nights a week when I was 14 because the school food was so bad (and I still love cooking, though a student budget means I'm less adventurous).

• Exceptional staff were S (who I was delighted to see advancing from an unkempt youth arriving as a care worker on Top Floor up to Principal of another establishment). And T – the teacher who rapidly earned my respect and enabled me to study geography. I've been in touch with him to let him know and to thank him for this.

• I still feel that being made to share rooms is a bad move for AS people, and that the benefits of social interaction were more than outweighed by the disadvantages of pressure on people of shared space and lack of personal space…

• I have a lot of time for many of the staff because I had respect for them as professionals and felt they did the right thing for the most part.

I've instructed outdoor pursuits to a number of boys with AS. Sometimes this is disclosed on the parental consent forms, sometimes not. Once when collecting my group of eight 9–11-year-old children for a five-day paddlesport course, three separate mums wanted to speak to the course instructor on the first morning. When the first one said her son had AS, the other two looked very surprised and quickly said that they each had an AS son on my course. After a minute of them trying to explain to me what AS meant, I said that I was fairly familiar with AS having spent eight years with AS children and decided to save time and explain that I was myself AS. Flabbergasted is probably the best description of their reactions. After confirming there was nothing specific they might want to let me know, I collected my group, who at the end of the week all claimed to have had a great time. There was definitely some anxiety amongst the mothers regarding my suitability to be in charge of their children on the river, but the manager was able to reassure them that I was extremely capable at my job. (I believe some parents are concerned about 'labelling' children, but when I skim the parental consents what I read DOES change my coaching style – extra clear instructions and longer than normal briefings on areas, behaviour and hazards). Last summer I coached a group for a week which included an 11-year-old who appeared to have severe AS. When I asked the mother at the end of the week, she said that no one else at school had noticed anything and that she'd never heard of AS. Either that child had fallen through a disappointingly large loophole in the education system, or she was deliberately withholding information (why she would want to do that at the end of the week I have no idea). I briefly explained what it was, explained my background, and suggested that she sought professional advice. She seemed to take the news relatively well but I've no idea whether she's taken the matter further – I hope for the child's sake she did.

Student K

This student was initially misdiagnosed and placed in a completely inappropriate institution. He was light sensitive and was taken to discos. He stopped talking as he saw very little point in conversation. He wasn't able to watch TV programmes apart from the news as he couldn't understand what was the beginning, middle and ending to the story. He grew in confidence and took his A-levels at a local mainstream school eventually without support. He developed a skill for lecturing about the difficulties of having Asperger's Syndrome and when he left was employed by the Local Authority Adult Services. He was able to talk about Asperger's Syndrome and how it affected him yet still have difficulty in coping with it. I have seen him address mainstream school assemblies, holding their attention for over an hour, yet struggled with the time boundaries imposed if they suddenly changed.

I believe I have fairly severe Asperger's Syndrome, which has caused me to experience difficulties in relating to other people and processing information, as well as causing high anxiety levels.

Before coming to Farleigh, I was really struggling in mainstream schooling, for the following reasons:

1. Lack of understanding among staff, which meant my learning wasn't personalised in the way that Farleigh could teach me. Consequently, many of my worries and concerns (which were significant to me) were not taken seriously.

2. The sheer size of the school and hence the noise and crowds I had to put up with every day.

3. Being bullied.

I was also experiencing huge problems at home, where I was very frustrated (mainly through not understanding what was happening around me and why people behaved the way they did) and very unhappy.

Being able to live independently and maintain a job is currently the biggest difficulty in my life which I have been able to overcome. However, I am unable to overcome my high anxiety levels and over-analysing of things. These high anxiety levels and difficulty communicating in social situations are usually how my Asperger's Syndrome manifests itself.

I use strategies to help with these difficulties, for example, structuring my time, talking through issues at length with those I trust (namely my parents and sister), and plenty of exercise.

Being a student at Farleigh made me feel less isolated with having Asperger's Syndrome, and it was helpful to have staff with an understanding.

Through the 24-hour curriculum, I was able to gain the life-skills which I believe have now enabled me to be independent. This is especially true of the sixth form, where I was able to further develop my social and life skills through integrating into the wider community. However, I really found that too much unstructured time (with a number of activities that were not ability-appropriate) did not help me at Farleigh. Also, until Farleigh sixth form, having to be so dependent on care staff and not being able to integrate into the wider community.

I also found at Farleigh College that there was a general lack of expectation to do well academically. I found this difficult, as I had always been very determined to achieve academically. However, this was very different at the sixth form, where staff worked really hard to support me to achieve my aspiration of succeeding in my A-levels and going to university.

Care staff should have:

- Knowledge and understanding of the condition.

- Empathy.

- Ability to listen without judging, to give the right length of time of silence after the young person expresses anxiety.

- Ability to focus on the young person's strengths and empower them to achieve.

The difficulties I still currently have are: socialising, loud noise, processing, transferring skills from one situation to another in social situations, loneliness (due to fear of rejection/getting things wrong).

Student L

This student came to Ravenscourt school, which was the precursor of Farleigh College and was a school for students with SpLD (dyslexia), and he remained when it changed to Farleigh College. He had dyslexia and Asperger's Syndrome, saw the world in his own way and was rigid in thought. He was larger than life both in physical stature and character and developed some very strong relationships whilst at the school. His family ties were very strong and supportive and as you can see from the response still are. When the Director of Education from his home county came to look round the school he did the tour. I introduced her as Dr so-and-so, and his retort was, 'I thought you were called Margaret.' When they both returned from the tour, I asked if she had seen everything. 'Oh yes,' she replied. 'The gym three times, the pig sty twice and the electric fence once – all those things that he thought were important.'

A brief history of my time in education

The early years

I went to a local Catholic primary school. I think my parents sent me there primarily because it was located quite literally 50 metres from my home but it was also a very nice and quite small school. My general experience of early learning was that I struggled to pick up handwriting and reading, although my science and maths were better. I certainly was never short of enthusiasm for a wide range of topics, e.g. History and Science, and once the school got its first PC (saying this now makes me feel quite old) I enjoyed making use of this. It did not take long for suspicions (especially from my parents who knew my older sister had dyslexia) that the difficulties I was having went beyond just being a little slower to pick things up and around the age of seven I was diagnosed as having dyslexia. This allowed me extra support and my dad took me every weekend to the Dyslexia Workshop for extra lessons. I believe it was two years later when I was diagnosed with Asperger's Syndrome.

I did have some difficult times in my second from last year when I had a teacher who did not fully understand me and a teacher doing her training who I hope never managed to qualify as a teacher because of the way she treated me.

One the whole I would say that my time at this school was pleasant even though I did not quite feel I fitted in.

Moving on

The time came for me to move on to secondary school and most of the students at this primary school would be moving on to the local Catholic secondary school. As mentioned neither I nor my parents were Catholics but they felt I should try this school out as I would have friends who I knew there. However, it became clear very quickly that I would find it very hard to learn in such a large school with many hundreds (possibly over 1000) students. My parents then searched for a school that I might be able to attend and I remember a visit to another school (although it was more of a care home for people with very complex difficulties) which to this day for not knowing its true name I still call doctor Tin Tin's clinic (although I am sure this was not its name). I didn't like the place at all. Looking back, I could say my memory of it was more of a mental ward than a school. I then remember having some home schooling which I did not take to well. Then my parents took me to look round a school then called Ravenscroft (which was the predecessor of Farleigh College, an independent school for students with dyslexia on the same site). I think I instantly liked the place. The old building with large grounds and long driveway must have seemed very grand and I expect at the time, being a fan of the Famous Five adventures, I thought that this would seem a very good place to have such adventures myself. I think to my parents it was very clear that this school was the place for me to be. With small class sizes of around eight the teachers had the time to spend with individual people in the right way. However, finding the right school was only half the battle – my parents still had to secure the LEA funding that would allow me to attend. But with perseverance, for which I will be eternally grateful (especially from my mum), I was eventually able to attend.

Ravenscroft

Starting at a boarding school for any 11-year-old child (regardless of their individual needs) is difficult and I was no exception. It was hard not seeing my parents and I was very homesick. During the first months my parents would come down every weekend to be with me and I would like to thank both P and M (my care staff at the time) for all they did for me to help me through those times. After a while I began to enjoy my time at Ravenscroft. Although my reading and writing had not really improved much during this first year I left Ravenscroft for the summer holidays happy. However, during those summer holidays there was an upheaval which to this day I do not quite understand. When I returned, the name was changed to Farleigh and some new staff had come in. The school now had a new computer suite which at the time was top of the range.

I think when we talk about anything in the abstract, such as educating children with learning disabilities, it's easy to think about institutions like the Dyslexia Association or Farleigh College. But when you ask the individual it comes down to people. I enjoyed Farleigh and Ravenscroft because I did not feel out of place: everyone had problems, so they in turn became less of a problem when dealing with each other. But that wasn't going to help me learn to read or write or motivate me to do more with my life. If you asked me to name some of the staff from Farleigh I could maybe name 10 people or 15 even, but if asked the same question in 50 years time I could probably only give you one, Andrew Chiffers.

Andrew Chiffers probably had the most profound effect on my life that any person has outside of my family. He brought learning to life for me and through sheer dedication that at times must have been pure stubbornness he was able to teach me to read and write. And more than that, he taught me to succeed, to set a goal and to achieve it, and then to set a new goal. He never gave up on me although at times he must have wanted to and in the end I like to think that did achieve things. When I finished with six GCSEs I like to think part of that achievement was his.

Farleigh Sixth Form College (Four Winds)

I finished Farleigh in 2000, the year before the school moved on to a new site. I, however, wanted to go on to college in order to obtain qualifications. Fortunately at this time Andrew Chiffers along with Stephen Bradshaw decided to open a sixth form college to help students not so much with their education – which would be taken care of by Trowbridge College (the college itself was excellent with many fine teachers, especially in ICT) – but with their extra-curricular lives.

Once again it was individuals who made the most impact on my life here: two support workers in particular, MW and TM, along with of course Andrew Chiffers who continued to have a profound influence on my life including being my training partner at quite a heavy duty gym run by a former Mr Universe body builder. Life at Four Winds seemed to go quite quickly but here I learnt to cook and to do my washing (although the lessons on 'hoovering' and tidying my room never quite sunk in) and other vital skills which many people take for granted – like how to go out for a night and how to do a weekly shop. Four Winds was about giving people the skills to go on in life without the need for support, and to this day I believe under Andrew Chiffers' leadership and with other personalities, it did that with flying colours.

Life after Farleigh

I won't go into this in great detail but to say that I graduated from uni and after a difficult period looking for work I found employment and I am an independent member of society. However, but for Farleigh, that could have been a very different story.

Closing statement

I think a lot has been said over the years about inclusion versus exclusion when it comes to people with learning difficulties. I think both policies have their merits but I do not think they are what most would make out.

I am going to try and summarise how I see the two systems, starting with inclusion – that is to say, keeping those children in mainstream education and supporting them. I think this system can be useful in a number of ways. Firstly it mixes people with learning disabilities with those without from an early age, and just like an end to segregation based on ethnicity has led to less racism I believe this has and will continue (as those children grow up to take on greater roles within society) to lead to less prejudice towards those with learning disabilities. Inclusion allows for the support of the family, who are often the best placed to help their child as within this environment the child should feel their safest.

However, I do not go along with the bean counters who say this is a cheaper system; in fact I believe it is more expensive because in the long run inclusion does not push the child to become independent but to become less independent, and that in turn will lead to a continued cost, be it low-level care such as supported living or more intensive care. If I had gone down the inclusive route I have little doubt I would not now be sitting here in my own house writing this. At best I would be with my parents, or more probably in a supported environment, and that would be for life, the cost of which far outweighs the cost of an exclusion approach such as Farleigh.

Exclusion benefits the child by giving them two things: adversity and the tools to overcome it. The tools are of course the staff who with a wide range of skills can help the child in a range of ways to overcome the adversity of an exclusive environment and to become more independent minded. Ultimately with AS it is the person's desire to be independent or not that will dictate how they turn out in life and I believe that my time at Farleigh gave me the desire to be more independent and therefore in the long run, despite the cost to the taxpayer, it will cost less than the other route. Of course that is not to say that inclusion does not have its place. Many difficulties can be overcome by support within mainstream education, such as dyslexia, but there will always remain those cases where what is in the best interest of the child will not always be the easiest or more obvious choice and it's our job to know what that is and to act upon it, always.

Student M

This student was very rigid in mind and struggled with some of the routines. He saw the world from his own perspective and was very talented in a few fields. He would struggle with some of the behaviour of the other students, regarding it as immature, and regarded himself as on a much higher cognitive level than many of the staff who worked with him.

1. What were life and education experiences like before coming to Farleigh?

I'm not going to go into too much detail about this. In a nutshell I finished middle school in 1998 and then ended up being out of school for a year and a half while my mother battled the education system to try and get me Statemented and sent to Farleigh. That year and a half was pure hell and hopefully will be the lowest point of my life – unfathomable boredom and loneliness, huge personal anxiety, panic attacks, awful.

2. What was life like at Farleigh for you?

This is going to take a bit longer! Ultimately my mother took the LEA to tribunal and succeeded in getting me Statemented. This done, a ridiculous amount of time was taken up by the necessity for her to visit/contact pretty much every school they suggested and explain to the LEA why they were totally unsuitable. She was convinced Farleigh was the right place for me but the LEA were very against the idea. Eventually we won through and I started Farleigh.

For the first year we were based at the 'old' site in Farleigh Hungerford. Initially it was a time of great anxiety and also great fun. To be learning again was wonderful. The other pupils were a little harder to adjust to. Part of the problem was that, whilst the idea of mixing children with Asperger's Syndrome and dyslexia is a great idea on paper and, to your credit, something of a vision, in practice by the time I joined, a rather high proportion of the kids who didn't have Asperger's Syndrome had dyslexia but also had EBD. Rather than mix and learn things from each other there was very much a sense of 'them and us', and this vision simply did not work in practice during my time at Farleigh. The other problem was that Asperger's Syndrome does rather produce 'characters' and putting a group of children with the condition together can and did lead to some quite major personality clashes. I think it was a combination of this and the fact that, having been away from other children for so long I was even less tolerant of their childishness than I had been, that led me to kicking one of the other pupils in the privates on my first night at the school.

The evening activities were a little taxing at first until I discovered just how much I enjoyed going to the swimming pool in Bath. At one point during the second year I was doing this at least four times a week and became rather thin and fit, a state I am frantically trying to return to now!

Mostly that first year was quite good: learning in the day, activities in the evening and trips into Bath/Trowbridge/etc. on the weekends. Occasionally we had film nights which were quite fun, and I got on well enough with my room-mates. A few helpful allowances were made for my maturity, not least being excused the mindless 'floor meetings' that took place after lessons each day.

It wasn't all sweetness and light though. Many things which may appear quite small on the surface bug me a great deal even now and this was very true when I was at Farleigh. Washing up is a key example – we had a rota which meant that once a week we ended up on washing-up duty for the whole floor after the evening meal. I felt it would have been so much better if everyone took responsibility for their own mess and washed their own damn dishes but it was not an optional chore and I hadn't the guts to flatly refuse.

Then there was the local music centre. I loved that place and being part of the Concert Band which met at the music centre within their grounds. This was pretty much the highlight of my week for two years. What soured an otherwise superb experience greatly was the tremendous inefficiency of the transportation system at times at Farleigh.

Two incidents occurred a fair way into that first year, though, that I think marked where things really started to go wrong. As I'm sure you're aware, the 'old' Farleigh site wasn't exactly in the best condition as a building. There were simple little things, though, that were easy to fix but had been left in a state – certain toilet cubicles without locks, massive limescale build-up on the showers, cupboards with faulty catches, etc. There were so many little things that I made a list and drew up a petition to get them fixed, and practically the whole floor signed it including many of the staff. I presented this to the Headteacher and to his credit and that of the caretakers the vast majority were fixed very promptly.

By and large though the first year was quite tolerable. Most of the staff, care and teaching, were nice although one had the sense, particularly with some of the care staff, that the tact and non-confrontation best suited to children with Asperger's Syndrome was decidedly absent from their personality and had not been at all compensated for by any training they had received. The summer holidays came and with it came the news that the 'old' site was no longer to be our main base.

And so it all started to go wrong. The Newbury site was really somewhat smaller than the previous one, and, although I was delighted to move in with a chap who's still now and always will be my best friend, there was quite a sense of living under each other's feet.

There were plenty of small annoyances again, new teachers to get used to, new pupils, new classmates. One thing that really annoyed me and I tried my damnedest to do something about without any luck was that my class was the ONLY one that never had lessons in the new building. This meant travelling to the 'old' site and back every single day of the week, something no other class had to do. So while those that did have classes exclusively at the new site could enjoy an extra hour for breakfast and relaxation, we were up and out on the bus, returning in the evening to our fellow pupils who'd been enjoying time to relax and do their own thing whilst we were making the return journey.

There were one or two members of staff willing to try and make things more manageable. One of the greatest heroes to all of us pupils was one of the members of staff. He was very enthusiastic, extremely easy to get along with and keen to engage with us. The décor at the new site was hardly spectacular and he was keen to get us in painting overalls and learning some practical new skills like decorating. Sadly, his huge enthusiasm didn't seem to be shared by the management and he disappeared quickly and quietly.

Indeed, all the staff in the second year seemed far more stressed that they had in the first, understandably so considering the difficulty of the move and the new situation. But some of them weren't exactly shy of letting their stress creep into their dealings with the pupils, and members of staff that in the first year had been easy enough to get along with soon became crotchety and unapproachable. Even the once outwardly jocular Headteacher was not immune!

True we were also feeling the stress and weren't exactly the easiest bunch of kids to handle, but people with Asperger's Syndrome are rather more prone to disliking change than the average person and can be slower to adapt as a result. For my part I found the move unsettling, and the daily transport between the two sites tiring. I saw the efficiency and approachability of the staff decrease drastically, the whole atmosphere seemed to have changed and as a result I began, for the first time in my life, not to care about learning. I soon regained my passion once I went on to college the next year but I largely gave up trying in the second year. The stress of GCSEs wasn't exactly helped by the circumstances and I found myself clashing in quite some style with a couple of the teachers. As a result I gave up caring and decided that I could at least have some fun messing around in lessons. This might have made me clash even more with the teachers in question but it was a lot more satisfying to annoy them than struggling on trying to learn in such an unconducive environment. As a result I left Farleigh with slightly poorer grades than I anticipated but they were still quite adequate to get me into college. I insist that much of this was more to do with my own abilities and knowledge, though, than as a result of the teaching I received at Farleigh.

3. What has life been for you after Farleigh in terms of how it prepared you?

Farleigh helped teach me some very basic universal truths. My experiences there and subsequently have taught me that inefficiency and lack of communication and 'joined up thinking' is pretty much a constant in practically every such institution of learning, be it school, college or university. The staff taught me that not just children but many adults can be right gits too. If I look back on my time at Farleigh with any annoyance and disdain, it is that it promised so much and could have delivered it all if only the original concept of the place held true during my time there and if the move between sites hadn't put such a huge spanner in the works. I also think, from the point of view of being on the receiving end, although I admit I may do you a slight injustice here as I don't know quite how this worked in practice, that staff training on Asperger's Syndrome and children with the condition could have been better. I do no injustice though to state the truth that, training or not, some members of staff certainly lacked understanding and any depth of knowledge on it.

All this said, Farleigh did ultimately do me more good than not. It provided me with my best friend and for that alone I will be eternally grateful. It was also during my time at Farleigh that I 'opened up' as a person. I had been a very regimented and overly serious person when I started. With the help of some of my friends there I 'loosened up' considerably and Farleigh provided a nice, self-contained little world that enabled me to explore my 'new' personality and define its limits, to see how far I could push certain behaviours before they became completely unacceptable. I am a much better and more rounded individual as a result and whilst some of the staff may have driven me completely nuts I do owe them my thanks for being on the receiving end! On the subject of staff I would not have survived Farleigh had it not been for some very sympathetic staff, many of whom really went above and beyond the call of duty in helping me with their kind words and actions – my most heartfelt gratitude for all that you did for me.

I suppose I must also extend my thanks to you also, Mr Bradshaw. I may have detested you at the time with your faceless bureaucracy but it was you who founded the place, you who provided the framework of the self-contained little world we found ourselves in; and although it would have been nice had I not had to deal with so much stress from living and learning at Farleigh College on a daily basis, it was ultimately of major benefit to my personal development and was instrumental in making me the person I am today. Since Farleigh I have gone on to achieve two Master's degrees and although university was again hardly the easiest of times for me I dread to think how much worse it could have been had it not been for the personal developments I underwent as a result of Farleigh College. In these ways Farleigh has had and will continue to have an important, lasting and positive effect on me for the rest of my life and for this I am most truly grateful and offer you my sincerest thanks.

Student N

This student was one who always wanted to ask questions and was given the target of limiting his number of questions per day. He also asked if the number of questions he was asked could be limited. He was a charming young man who was very vulnerable and could easily become a victim. When he first arrived at the school I asked what his interests were. He replied that he was interested in Manchester United. I felt at least we could have a conversation about a common interest, but when asking him what he thought about last week's game he replied that he knew where every player lived and their date of birth but didn't watch the matches. Once again I struggled to continue the conversation.

I'm very good and clever at some things that others aren't, like my memory. Some things I'm less good at than others, like communication skills.

I find understanding that things in life aren't perfect, and why, and accepting shades of grey, the most difficult.

My biggest difficulty, however, is feeling anxious. But I have found that social stories, setting targets, star charts to earn me rewards and talking to people useful strategies to overcome some of my difficulties.

Being at Farleigh helped me with my social skills, my anxiety, understanding shades of grey and my under-confidence and confidence. Not to ask so many questions.

Lots of the staff at the school were very helpful, care staff, teachers, Head of Care, the Headteacher and Stephen Bradshaw.

Staff need to be patient, have good listening skills, be someone who treats all according to what they need. Someone who is nice to them. Someone who helps build their confidence and independence. Someone that has a laugh with them and is fun to them but in a nice way, and helps them to think why they are firm and only if they need it.

Currently my problem is in understanding the world. I have a LSAs supporting me at college and a befriended who takes me out to do things like bars and days out.

10.2 Review of the responses

As you can see from the student responses, many felt that the experience was an extremely positive one and they have been able to go onto further and higher education and some of them obtain suitable employment. They are very personal and individual accounts of a crucial time of their lives. I have tried to keep track of all the students through Farleigh and North Hill House and would have liked a larger representative response but inevitably many students have gone onto better things and do not want to associated with a school that would be described as a special school.

There were many things that I would have done differently, some things I would not have done at all, and some things could have been managed better. But I do believe that more things were positive than negative and did make a difference to many student's lives, and these were the lucky ones who were able to have a flexible, understanding curriculum and staff that were prepared to listen and share experiences. If I started today with the same vision there are things I would not reproduce. At the time it was an innovation to put two groups of students together, with the frustrations that students with severe dyslexia brought to those with Asperger's Syndrome. So you ended up with students who were terrified if someone crept up behind them and shouted 'Boo!!' and others who wanted to creep up behind students and say 'Boo!!' just to see what would happen. Also, having a class or living area within a school that was for a different group made that group even more 'different'. Students with Asperger's Syndrome do not fit easily into a cohesive group as they all have different needs and their difficulties manifest themselves differently.

I certainly would have managed the changes a lot better and explained all of the changes to the students and where possible not made these changes. In hindsight it would have been easier to start 'new' establishments than try to move the schools. However, this would have required a capital input that just was not available at that time. I was forced to find a new site for Farleigh College at the end of five years, as I was unable to extend the lease or buy the property; this move was unfortunate as it meant that the school had to operate on a split site. Split-site schools do not work, and certainly not for students with Asperger's Syndrome.

Many of the students also preferred the smaller intimate environment that was North Parade, where North Hill House started, rather than the larger building of Stoneleigh despite all the bedrooms being purpose-built single ensuite ones on the Stoneleigh site.

There were also many positive things that happened. Not calling the schools 'special schools' certainly helped with the transition for students and parents. Taking GCSEs early when the students were capable and ready to do so was a real success, enabling the pace of work and external accreditation be at the student's pace rather than the traditional school pace and milestones. High expectations academically and a clear focus on strengths allowed students to achieve self-confidence where before they had regarded themselves as failures in the education system. Employing specialist teachers to work with small groups or one-to-one was also another strength that I would continue in future.

The amount and quality of the training I thought was excellent, and I was fortunate to have Prof. Francesca Happé and the steering committee to assist in that field. However, I did assume that all staff would understand how to work with these youngsters and I should have been more selective and ruthless with those staff that 'just didn't get it'.

The links that were developed with mainstream schools and further education colleges were good but I think it is important to realise that these students were still extremely vulnerable and at times the support was removed too soon.

I think the focus on the young people was good. Not to give up on students and to see the positive in every youngster was a strength. This focus could have been extended by asking their own views of their education and school systems more often. There was a school council but the depth of perception shown in the replies for this chapter has made me think it would have been useful for this to have met more often. I did feel that students were listened to and the majority of the staff understood how to work with these youngsters. Training should always be ongoing and I feel you can never assume that you know it and start to relax. There are different challenges daily and these constantly require new ways of working. All too often staff will join the school thinking they have experience and therefore know how to work with this group, yet all the youngsters are totally different.

The care pathways and transition into other services was also a strength that I would duplicate in future. This allowed the young people to continue their education and social care without the anxiety of changing services. Apart from the further education provision in Frome and Swindon, there are very few other educational facilities that will meet the needs of these students. Furthermore, there are almost no facilities for young people following on from the colleges. This is an area of need that certainly should be addressed or the work that has been started will be totally undermined.

The staffing issue is a crucial one and there are many people who worked at the school that I need to thank and I will do that at a later point. It is important to realise that for any school to be a success it needs to have dedicated passionate staff and I have been heartened that throughout these responses two names kept reoccurring: Andrew Chiffers and Des Walsh. Des came to Farleigh from a Local Authority school for behavioural difficulties and I am sure he will admit that it was a culture shock to suddenly work with students with Asperger's Syndrome. He was a quick learner and as many parents have said, 'they taught him well'. They all were impressed, as I was, with his skill, passion and dedication in making the switch and I thank him for his contribution. Andrew is one of life's real 'gentlemen'. He is still working with me as a board member with the Options Group (another group for students with autism) and will always have a place in my heart for all he contributed and achieved with Farleigh College and setting up the further education college. He also lectures about Asperger's Syndrome and is one of those rare individuals who has the ability to understand and inspire children with Asperger's Syndrome to believe in themselves. That is indeed a rare and exceptional talent. To both Andy and Des, I salute you and acknowledge your contribution to this project.

When I first started to receive the students' and parents' views my first reaction was to become defensive and want to explain why I did certain things and that I did everything for the benefit of the students. Then I started to understand that this was their perception of their experience and it would obviously be different from my own. I thought an explanation of what events happened through a time line and the reason for those decisions would assist the reader. For example, my first school site at Farleigh Hungerford was a very large country house that had previously had up to 95 residential dyslexic students. The site was 30 acres in total with access to another 200 acres including a lake and a wood. This was ideal for students who wanted the feeling of space and to be on their own at any time. However, the building dated back to the eighteenth century and was built out of crumbling Bath stone that required a lot of maintenance. The lease was for only five years and I would have liked to remain on that site and improve the building and classrooms. However, this wasn't an option as the owner had different plans. I thus spent the last two years of the lease looking for an alternative site. This meant that the school would have to move, and for the students and staff that was a major change that many didn't or couldn't understand.

Also when the Priory Group acquired the schools in 2002 they soon became the focus for anything that just wasn't the same or correct in the student's eyes. I have therefore listed the events from 1996 on a time line at the beginning of this book, which may help to clarify some of the students' and parents' comments.

Chapter 11

Parents' Views

These are the parents' personal accounts of their journey when their son or daughter went to Farleigh or North Hill House. They are very personal accounts and the comments and the chronology at the beginning of this book are equally relevant to this chapter. (Some are written in response to a questionnaire, whilst others wrote their story in the way they felt best.)

I think, as a parent, you strive for the best chance for your child in life. They only have one attempt at school and you are extremely protective of everything they do, no matter what anyone else tells you. As a parent it is very difficult to hand over the responsibility of your child to someone else, even if they are a professional in that field. You have to trust them and want to keep checking they are all right. This is heightened when your child also has a recognised difficulty. All these parents had to fight to get their child's needs recognised and then met at a time when the profession was slow to recognise Asperger's Syndrome, never mind doing something about meeting those needs.

Once they found a school, and maybe Farleigh or North Hill was that school, they then had to hand over their child to someone else to educate and look after for long periods of time, which must have been extremely difficult. How they ever trusted a system which many of them felt had let them down was at times amazing. It is not surprising that many of them were distrusting of everything and everybody, and wanted to be kept informed of every aspect of their child's life.

I talked about 'cutting the umbilical cord' and 'letting go', but that is very difficult when your child is so vulnerable. This was a major part of the work with parents, and I and the schools didn't always get it right. Parents were the school's biggest supporters and the biggest critics and they were very reluctant to let go of anything. When they did let go and the child started to wobble without the scaffolding they previously had, progress was often hampered or there was a dip in performance, parents would want to immediately protect the child against all comers. It was a process of give and take and developing full independence for the child, something we want for all our children but more difficult to achieve when the child is not understood or doesn't understand the rules of the game. The parent's anxieties were often as great as their children's and needed to be managed. Here are their accounts of what it was like.

Parent 1

As a family we were in the independent sector, not state 'Statementing', it was a lengthy process, potentially stressful and humiliating. It was not in the ethos of private schools to diagnose. His first two 'normal' schools failed by having no extra support, and his specialist school (Graded A*) failed for different reasons. We tried some schools that were for aspirational parents to get children through common entrance examination – but they failed to deliver specialist teaching as promised. (He attended three different schools from 9 to 13 years of age.)

Life at Farleigh was like a lifeboat in a stormy sea, knowing that your child was safe. Although boarding was always going to be difficult – there were no day schools in our area providing specialist help.

The qualities that were required in the staff were, obviously, sainthood – such a difficult job – but MOST important I think it is crucial that adults working with vulnerable children have a high level of emotional intelligence… They need to be in control of their own emotions at all times whatever the provocation. One member of staff failed this criteria and I believe was dismissed. Very few AS children lie successfully – they leg pull – but must be believed if they tell of abuse, theft or bullying.

Life since Farleigh has been a rollercoaster. Bereavement has taken its greatest toll on the child (now adult). Anger is still often present and potentially dangerous (to mother, not others).

Parent 2

1. What were life and education experiences like before coming to North Hill? How difficult was it to find a school and what battles did you have?

He was Statemented from a very young age so there was always the acknowledgement that he would require additional help. Back then there was pressure to send him to the local generic special school, although we fought this as he would have been the most able by far and we didn't feel he'd get the right stimulation. Luckily our local village school was happy to take him, with help, and provided him with a secure family-like environment. His helper was fantastic and was brilliant with him for several years.

Challenges arose when he was due to move to the middle school system in Frome. Both we and the schools didn't think they could cope with him and his needs. After much research and many visits an independent prep school agreed to offer him a place for a couple of years and his Statement was changed eventually.

The next battle came when he was due to leave that school at 13. He should have gone to the local high school, which clearly to us wasn't the right place for him. They did not at that time have the support and specialist help available to cope with his needs. It was then that North Hill House was due to open and after much letter writing and a few meetings eventually Somerset agreed to send him as a day pupil to NHH. Fortunately for us we never had to go to appeal but the whole process over the years was always a struggle, and we had to be very determined to win over the schools and the professionals involved.

2. What was life like once they got to North Hill?

Once he was there life settled down somewhat. He was one of the first pupils in a small school with great facilities and staff who understood his needs. I think the only thing he missed out on was the boarding aspect, which would have helped with his independence. But we were fortunate enough to secure a year of boarding once he was at the sixth form. He was academically quite able and was the first pupil to attend a local high school in a neighbouring town to study for his A-levels. His key workers were always very helpful and probably because we saw them regularly became friends. He was allowed to stay on some evenings to help him learn new skills outside the classroom and the school and staff were always very flexible. He thrived at NHH and we didn't have any concerns.

3. What has life been for you and them after North Hill in terms of how it prepared them for life and the challenges they met?

I think without the extra time in the sixth form he would have struggled with independent living. I think without the experience of

NHH he would have been ill-prepared for much. Because of the more personal help and guidance given by staff who understood his needs he was given the right support to learn new skills, etc. He certainly grew in confidence although through the teenage years things were sometimes a bit fraught for him. He was determined to find employment after school and despite several setbacks managed to gain full-time employment, albeit of a manual nature. Despite having Asperger's Syndrome he wants to socialise and is well known around Frome by many people. He knows more people around town than I do!

Parent 3

From the age of two I knew something wasn't right. He displayed very odd behaviours – everyone in the family said, 'He's your second child and a boy. What do you expect?' It was tough on his sister. No-one could quite work out what was going on – there seemed to be lots of uncertainty.

At primary/infants school he had no friends. The teachers knew something wasn't right. But mainly everyone told me he was just 'misunderstood'.

However, once we received the diagnosis we felt that we were all 'on the same page'. Something to work from – read up on. It was also utter relief – we could now move forward putting strategies in place – even though some of the family were in denial.

Before he attended Farleigh, he was a frightened person, who had almost lost his ability to speak. At Farleigh he was gently nurtured with understanding – again utter relief despite the distance from home. He had also been consistently bullied at his previous school.

Farleigh was great in every respect but the later mainstream college experience (sixth form college) aged 16–19 with many staff involved in all aspects of his care/education led to a lot of misunderstandings for him.

He moved to supported living 24/7 after Farleigh. It was good to hand the day-to-day care to someone else – to take some pressure off – and further encourage independent skills.

Sadly in 2008 my husband became ill and I have stopped being my son's carer. I am now my husband's carer. He has an awful illness – it is terminal. My son is coping well at present.

On a positive note he is very proud of his independent travelling skills – learned during his time at the sixth form.

Parent 4

The mainstream school was slow to recognise problems he had, and slow to instigate the Statementing process. However, once the application was made we had strong support from all of the professionals involved with us.

When we decided that a specialist school may be the answer we viewed 29 different schools in search of the right place for him. The LEA were not able to give us any direction in this procedure.

From before the age of two he was unable to cooperate in group situations. He was happiest playing to his own agenda. He dominated situations, conversations and our attention. We realised that he commanded close to 75 per cent of our time with his two sisters having to split the difference. He was unable to share or take turns, except on his own terms. We commented on our SEN Statement application that 'the intense input with regard to A has in fact masked the severity of the communication problems he has as our concerns with regard his behaviour were underestimated'.

The diagnosis was an enlightening and uplifting experience for us as parents. At last real recognition that the multitude of difficulties that this boy presents are real and that there is a reason for it all. The diagnosis enabled us to learn a great deal about the Syndrome and the learning curve was immense (Tony Attwood book). With that came better understanding so we were able to approach his needs in a different way. His sisters too were better informed, understood more and showed a mature approach to their brother.

Having a diagnosis helped him to fit in better with the family routine. The school experience was, however, completely different and despite best efforts the understanding and modification of approach was not forthcoming in the mainstream school environment.

Farleigh was residential. We missed A like mad and of course were left with a terrible void. We felt reassured that at last he was in an environment where specialised staff understood the AS Spectrum. It took Farleigh and him four years to reach the point where he wanted to access education. Once that hurdle was overcome there was no stopping him. He is now reaching his potential. One of the first things we did was to take the girls on holiday to Italy. It was spontaneous, unstructured, no specific routines and accommodation. We all enjoyed it.

He had a few incidents with specific members of staff where he feels he was unjustly and inappropriately managed (or mismanaged). However, he agrees that the senior management were always able to find some resolution. The only criticism we had is that perhaps there could have been more inclusivity with parents. However, we did get weekly academic reports and weekly telephone contact with care staff. We were also informed of specific incidents.

It is important that the staff have:

- Good training
- Clear understanding of AS
- Good communication skills, including listening skills
- Ability to develop a rapport
- Sense of humour
- Positive outlook
- Patience/tolerance/understanding
- Reliability/consistency
- Good organisation.

Since leaving Farleigh he copes so well that his sisters reckon he no longer has AS. His answer to that is they do not know the half of it. He has learnt coping strategies and knows when to walk away. He still gets enormously frustrated at lack of organisation/changes to routine or proposals. His AS traits now are often advantageous in that he himself is incredibly organised. He has very good communication skills. He is very methodical and reliable.

He has developed a few close personal friendships and some of these have been lasting and meaningful.

We are aware that he still likes to know plans ahead of time and needs space and time to prepare himself accordingly. His close friends also recognise this.

Parent 5

Our son was diagnosed with severe dyslexia when he was nine, after many years of being told, 'He's a boy, he will catch up, boys develop late.' Although the infant and junior schools knew he had problems they did nothing. We therefore decided to have him tested privately for dyslexia. When we told the Head of the junior school of the findings of the Dyslexia Institute and that we wanted to have him Statemented with appropriate support written in, he said, 'Of course they would say that, that's what you paid for.' We did achieve this, but our son continued to have problems at the junior school. One of the several times we were called to the school was when he had apparently made a bomb – out of an old calculator, Blu-Tack and batteries – I must say we thought it looked quite real! He had connected it up in the classroom, and the teacher panicked and called in the Head. The Head informed us that our son had no respect for him, nor some of the staff. We tried to explain that, for him, respect did not come automatically and he could not understand the idea of hierarchy. He ended by saying, and I have never forgotten this, 'He will never amount to much in life, probably ending up in trouble or in prison.' It had not helped that his sister previously attended this school and all the staff, including the Head, had thought she could do no wrong.

We hoped that things would change when he moved to secondary school.

About this time we were asked to get his hearing checked as the school thought he might have a hearing problem. This we did and discovered that he had no problem except for acute hearing and he was referred to another consultant. This was the turning point for us. He diagnosed that as well as the dyslexia he also had Asperger's Syndrome but with mute tendencies. He also told us that in the way we had brought him up, he had managed to mask his AS and this was why it had taken so long for the diagnosis. (At that time little was known about AS.) This has caused him many problems over the years and, to this day, people forget or do not realise his needs until something goes wrong and he goes into a massive decline. I still feel guilty for not recognising this earlier. At last, although we were not after a label, we could now start to understand some of our son's difficulties.

We obtained a secondary school place not far away with a specialist dyslexia cluster. Our son started quite positively, but within a few days problems started. He could not manage the classroom changing and especially the dinner hall. So we took him home for lunch and then returned him. This became difficult as he did not want to return to school. It became even worse when we had to catch him and try to get him dressed, retrieve him from the garage roof, or stop him climbing out of the bedroom window. On a good day he just locked himself in the bathroom! When we turned into the school road, he would be crying, asking not to go. We then started getting calls to the school because he had frozen and would not move or talk. We then had to go and physically pick him up to take him home. Eventually the school suspended him (wrongly) due to the fact that they could not cope. A meeting with the school and LEA followed when it was at last decided that our son needed a specialist type of schooling and meanwhile he was to be schooled at home. The person they sent was not a specialist in AS and tried to teach him whilst he was under the table or jumping up and down on his trampoline (his obsession at that time).

The LEA sent us several schools to look at: a school for dyslexia students which we had asked for before we had the AS diagnosis, but they would not take him as they did not feel they could cope with AS (by this time he had taken to rocking and banging his head against the wall). We also looked at LEA-run schools for autism, but neither felt they could meet his educational needs.

Eventually, and because our son had been excluded wrongly and against the law, the LEA agreed that they would pay if we could find a private school that could meet the needs of our son. We found very few schools for sufferers of AS, and it became apparent that this might mean his going away from home. This was hard for me as I had not had children to send them away, but knew it was in his best interests to do so. The first two schools we visited looked right on paper, and on arrival looked hopeful. However, after discussions with the staff and a tour of the school, we decided they would not suit him. All the doors to the classrooms were kept locked so the students could not escape and outside they were surrounded with locked gates. This was not the environment we felt our son would be happy in or respond to, and rightly or wrongly we did not feel we could leave him to be locked away.

Running out of options, our next school was Farleigh. Although on arrival we thought the building would be overpowering for our son, the open land in which it stood with no sign of fencing or locked gates gave us hope. When we entered it was like a breath of fresh air. Whilst we were waiting to see the Head, students were milling around going to the library, etc. There was laughter, smiles and noise, none of which we had seen at the other schools. One of the students showed us in to meet the Head (Stephen Bradshaw) who, after discussions, seemed to completely understand our son's needs and added that the school was not only for AS but also for dyslexia. Stephen gave us great hope for our son's future and we left feeling elated and hoping that the LEA would approve funding and that Farleigh would accept him. The induction process was very good: we had a visit from a senior member of the Care Staff to carry out an assessment in the home environment, and our son then had an overnight stay at Farleigh before a final decision was made. Our son coped well and liked the idea of staying somewhere that looked like a castle! The LEA agreed funding and we were offered a place at Farleigh to start after Easter. We were told that initially our son would have to remain at Farleigh for three weeks before coming home for a weekend, because they found that it was in a student's best interests to do this to form a good routine and help with behavioural patterns. We had been told that he could bring as little or as much as he wished to make him feel at home (they could even bring pets, which after a few weeks we did) and he decided on the latter. With our car bursting at the seams we set off for his new start.

The first week was difficult for us all. We were getting phone calls, when he cried and asked us to take him home. We consulted the staff who were very understanding and we decided we would take him away for the weekend, but not home. This was the best thing we could have done as after that he returned to Farleigh and, apart from the odd phone call when he was feeling sad, he settled in. Our son's obsession at that time was trampolining, and after several home visits and discussions with the school, it was agreed that he could take his trampoline to school. The school helped with this and I felt that it helped to make the students calmer and keener to learn when in class. There was also so much land where students could take themselves off when feeling stressed.

The Care Staff assigned to our son were great. They soon began to understand him and initially would telephone us every night to let us know how his day went, what he had eaten and how they thought he was feeling; the contact between school and home was extremely good. As time went on such daily contact was unnecessary and the calls were usually reduced to 2/3 times a week. The first term our son shared a room with a student with just dyslexia. This worked well and they struck up a good relationship, sharing similar interests such as skate-boarding. The school allowed them to build their own ramps in the woodwork lessons and in their spare time helped by the staff.

Over the first term we saw a vast improvement in our son's behaviour and his attitude to work, thanks to the patience of Stephen and his staff. The end of the first term is one that I still remember: we went to collect our son for the summer break and I was so excited at the prospect of having him home for longer than a weekend. We entered the main hall to see a couple of students sitting on the stairs crying. There was no laughter and students were quiet. A member of staff told us that a number of students did not want to go home as some felt they were not wanted and were a nuisance, and some were going into care for the summer as their parents did not feel they could cope. I was almost in tears myself, not understanding why they were not wanted or loved. I don't think I will ever forget the scene as I wanted to take them all home with me!

Our son returned to Farleigh in September, again with the contents of his bedroom. His room-mate had moved to another part of the school as part of his progression into independence. Our son, who had never set himself a goal, wanted to follow him (he did manage this the following term). His new room-mate moved in and has turned into a long-lasting friend. He has AS but was very verbal whereas our son was on the mute side, so they complemented each other well. Progress over the term was very slow and was hard work for the teaching staff. Our son's dyslexia was severe, but slowly there was an improvement. They also started teaching him negotiation skills, which I use to this day, and managed to get him to do things I never thought he would.

One of the great things about Farleigh was the policy that if a student needed to leave class, for example, because they were getting anxious, he was given permission to do this and could escape into the grounds. Our son used this on many occasions and this allowed him to calm down and then return. The ethos of the whole school at this time suited him and he became quite close to his English teacher which gave him, for the first time, some confidence in English. The after-school activities were very good and our son got a great deal from them, if not more than he did from school. These included horse-riding and caving. One of his favourites was fishing on the lake and perhaps, best of all in the summer months, swinging on a tyre over the river and just messing about there. These are the only two activities he still speaks about.

It was unfortunate that the following year the English teacher left and joined Stephen to start up a sixth form college for students with AS. As with most people with AS, our son did not cope well with the change, and we do not feel he progressed as well after that with the new teacher. He was then offered the option of taking photography, and which he really enjoyed. He took a GCSE in IT a year early and gained an A, of which we were proud. Unfortunately, with all the changes that took place at Farleigh, he never picked up a camera again until this year, when he re-kindled his love, albeit in underwater photography.

After two good years at Farleigh, great changes were ahead, as it was going to move to a new site, Newbury, which would be for students with only AS.

The move to Newbury was a nightmare, though things did get better and settled down – the new site did not have the grounds or the freedom of old Farleigh (which was one of the reasons we had chosen it).

With a new school and a new Head came new rules and boundaries. Most of the staff were brilliant with our son. The Care Staff were great and were fond of our son, but he soon learnt that because of this he could get away with murder! Being a mute AS our son would get in touch with us if he had a complaint and let us sort it out (he still does this even today), so the Head and I got to know one another very well over this period, and he did prove to be excellent with AS students. Like everywhere these days, health and safety became the 'in' thing, bringing more restrictions. His friend and room-mate could not cope with this and left.

Towards the end of the first year of GCSEs our son was struggling with all the changes and not maturing as much as he should, becoming more and more fragile, and his mental state was deteriorating. We tried moving him to the parallel school, North Hill, but there were even more restrictions and as he was becoming increasingly vulnerable, he moved back to Newbury. We agreed with the school's suggestion that it was in his best interests to repeat the last year giving him time to repair and grow. Stephen and the educational psychologist were brilliant and, with the school's backing, our education department agreed. This proved to be the right decision and with great support from the teaching and care staff our son began to thrive again. Had our son not attended old Farleigh, but had attended Newbury after it opened, I feel things may have been better for him, but he had been caught up in too many changes for someone with AS.

What to do with our son after Newbury? He had his GCSEs, and one of the positives from all the changes was the opening of the sixth form, the Head being our son's favourite English teacher from Farleigh. We met a few times to discuss this option, which would mean going to a mainstream college, and although heavily supported and with its own base camp, he felt our son might still be too fragile and vulnerable for this type of environment. It would also mean living in a large bungalow and having to learn more life skills such as doing his own laundry, cooking, shopping and managing money, etc. The final decision was left to us. Knowing this would either make or break him we decided to take a chance and we were so pleased we did. He had to obtain a place first and he decided to try for the computer maintenance course. I will never forget this interview as it took place in our car with our son under a blanket and the mainstream college Head trying to interview him through the car window, but thanks to his patience, our son was offered a place and he moved into the sixth form. It was a year's course and he excelled in the practical side of it, learning to build and maintain computers which he still does, and all the computers in our house have been built by him. He really enjoyed his first year, although not learning many life skills, for why cook for yourself when the college has a cook! He wanted to stay on (thank you) and take a 3D art course.

The sixth form college was beginning to become known, and as there was definitely a lack of this type of place in the country, it started to expand and again our son was caught up in the big change. However, he did continue, completing the course and gaining a BTEC National Diploma in 3D Design.

Whilst in sixth form our son applied, and was accepted, for a place at university to do a BA Honours degree. This was near to our home and so he was ready to move on thanks to all the staff and their hard work over the years. He now has a BA Honours degree, although this has not been without many ups and downs. This year he has also been offered a place on an MA course. We are so proud of our son (although he still does not see it), but we are still working on the life skills which can leave him vulnerable and open to abuse. My husband and I, and all our family and friends, feel that without Stephen and Farleigh, our son would not be where he is today. Thank you.

Parent 6

Our experiences of Farleigh – and what happened beforehand.

Our son (born 1981) was not diagnosed with Asperger's Syndrome until he was nearly ten, but we sought help for him from a much earlier age because of language delay, unusual use of language, echolalia and sometimes obsessive behaviour. Getting professionals to accept that there was a real problem, possibly relating to autism, wasn't always easy because he was very friendly and could read well. However, he couldn't cope in a group at school or in the playground and got very agitated over trivial issues. It became clear that he needed a lot of one-to-one attention even at primary school as he was easily distracted and would fly into a rage when frustrated.

Before he came to Farleigh at the age of 15, he had been to several schools and had had particularly disastrous experiences in two of them, caused by failure of the staff to understand his needs because of their lack of knowledge of his condition. (In both cases, we had been assured – wrongly – that the staff were familiar with AS.) He had to leave one of the boarding schools after two terms when the staff there could no longer guarantee his safety; such was the savagery of the bullying. We had had to push to get him Statemented but at last had a helpful educational psychologist who was trying to find an appropriate school placement. He had already been out of school for four months and we were all getting very despondent at the fruitless searches. The EP then went off on holiday, suggesting that we continue the search for a school in her absence as she hadn't managed to find anything.

We saw Farleigh College listed in a guide to special schools and it actually mentioned Asperger's Syndrome, which was very encouraging. Not feeling too hopeful after all the previous failures, we sent a letter of enquiry to Stephen Bradshaw, enclosing a copy of my son's Statement. To our amazement, Stephen phoned immediately to say that he thought he could help and invited us down for interview. Although it took a little while, our local LEA eventually agreed the funding after further pushing from us and the EP and he started at Farleigh in the autumn of 1996.

While life was not without some difficulties and hiccups, our son took to the calm and friendly atmosphere at school and, especially, to the very small classes and the continuity of staff. He began to relax as he gradually felt safer. He loved coming home at the weekend (often with something he'd cooked at school) – but also liked going back to Farleigh on a Sunday with the prospect of roast dinner waiting for him. He enjoyed the cinema outings and travelling to and from school each weekend by train with just a few other children greatly increased his confidence. He soon got used to travelling alone on the underground from Paddington.

By the time he left Farleigh at the age of 18, his self-confidence, sense of achievement and his social skills had developed considerably. He was also less rigid in his thinking and behaviour and had begun to appreciate surprises. He often looked back to how he had been as a much younger child and said he was now a different person. After Farleigh, he enrolled on a one-year skills for life course at a local FE college in London, making the transition seemingly effortlessly from a sheltered community of about 75 students to a busy and sometimes rowdy one of several thousand. He also found himself face to face with one of his most feared tormentors from a previous school. Both were able to shake hands on meeting and there were no further problems.

He went on to do a BTEC in Media Production at the college and one of his tutors, to his and our surprise, suggested he apply to university. His entry conditions at Southampton Solent were a merit for his BTEC and a B in AS Film Studies, both of which he achieved, as well as a college prize. He completed an honours degree in Culture and Media Studies there and enjoyed living away from home in a hall of residence, cooking and cleaning for himself. He opted to repeat his first year because he hadn't managed to finish all the assignments as it had taken a while for his Disabled Student's Allowance to be processed, which meant that he hadn't had any study support in the first term. Although he still found it hard to integrate into a group, he did join in some student activities and even went to two balls.

Since graduating in 2006, he has had various temporary library jobs (including one lengthy contract), as well as working on short contracts for the Royal Bank of Scotland, Colindale Newspaper Library and currently Southwark Council. While he is still hoping for permanent work, he now has a varied and quite impressive CV and also volunteers on a regular basis at the Canal Museum in London. It was during his time at Farleigh that his aptitude for library work was discovered and a work experience placement at Trowbridge library was found for him. This too helped to boost his confidence.

From learning to travel to and from Paddington and then on to Bath while he was at Farleigh, he has become a seasoned and competent world traveller.

His time at Farleigh gave him a sense of confidence, self-worth and helped to repair some of the damage done by previous attendance at totally inappropriate schools. It taught him to become independent, to cope with the unexpected and to think and plan ahead. He himself is aware how much he changed as a result of his time there, learning to become more flexible in his behaviour and to cope far better with setbacks, disappointment and frustration. And, most importantly, he has also learnt to laugh at himself...

Parent 7

Life before the diagnosis was puzzling – we kept exploring different avenues of healthcare – she was very difficult at home – she was very demanding and manipulative of my time.

My daughter didn't leave much space. When she went to Farleigh the other two children could be naughty! No ability to do so with her here. Once, she expressed to her social worker that she wished we would get divorced so she could be adopted by someone else – her real parents. She has made us feel totally inadequate – useless.

The diagnosis helped us to begin to understand what direction she was coming from. Didn't make it much easier – just able to explain to others what was wrong – they still didn't understand! The diagnosis went hand-in-hand with her attending Farleigh. We could all breathe again.

When she came to Farleigh – found her tribe – had friends she didn't have to work at. People who understood her. Once there, it took a long time to heal wounds. It allowed our other children to blossom. I had to remember my husband's name!! (We are still together.)

No panacea – my daughter was horrid to me when we came to pick her up for holidays – emotional turmoil as I was desperate to see her. I often drove home in tears.

The process of leaving Farleigh and what to do next was awful. We really could have done with much more help. One area that is still difficult is that she has not really been able to develop a relationship with men. After Farleigh we have used the psychologist from time to time as she is local. Listen to one of the other girls talk about the therapist.

Life since Farleigh is still as confusing as it was before she moved to Farleigh – but we are all still alive – I'm sure someone would have been murdered if she had been left to live with us – not joking...

Attached letter:

Dear Stephen

Oh such accurate timing! Your letter arrived on the doorstep as I am knee deep in further negotiations for my daughter's continuing care.

She has been 'looked after' by the local authority and has done nothing but sit on a settee for the last two years. This has resulted in her now being diagnosed as a borderline personality disorder. So more arguments.

One thing this highlights to me is the expertise of your staff. Constantly being trained and exposed to various displays of autism/Asperger's behaviour in all its manifestations, having a multi-disciplinary approach so the training comes from every angle, leads to a great resource, your staff.

You were the first person who knew what I wanted to say about my daughter before I had opened my mouth. Even 24 years ago, you just knew... That gave me the confidence to leave her with your organisation, not an easy task. There were only two schools who took girls at that time, and the other was much less friendly.

Her relationship with me has always been difficult. She substitutes other people into my spot in her affections very often. Still does.

B (a member of staff) recognised what was going on and helped me through some very difficult times with her when I'm not sure whose needs were being met by me coming to visit Farleigh, or indeed when she needed to come home for a holiday. Perhaps holidays are my only criticism, too long and disruptive.

As I have mentioned on the form, we still see one of the other girls. And I am still in touch with another parent after meeting the family at Farleigh and sharing lifts from their home in Kingston.

Thanks for all that, it is very good to hear from you and I wish you well with the book.

Parent 8

His early period at primary school was rather eventful. He never seemed to fit in with the rest of the children in his class. His reading and writing skills were well behind the rest of the class. We had a few discussions with his teacher and the Headmaster. Some of teachers did not have any experience of children with special needs and treated him badly. We eventually paid a visit to see a private educational psychologist, who diagnosed him as being dyslexic. Having obtained a report on his dyslexia we approached the Dyslexia Association for help. They ran special workshops on a Saturday with only two pupils per teacher. All of the teachers were qualified to teach children with special needs. He did benefit a lot from this one-to-one interaction.

We then approached the LEA for a Statement of his educational needs. The LEA appointed their own educational psychologist to test him and he came to the same conclusion as the private psychologist, but rather than providing a Statement for him they offered additional classroom support on a one-to-one basis. This additional help was also beneficial but T was still displaying some strange behaviour.

By now we were both getting really frustrated with the lack of progress and my wife went to see our GP for further advice and help. Our GP recommended that T be assessed by the specialist unit. The psychologist at the clinic diagnosed his Asperger's Syndrome. The LEA then decided that in the future they would only provide help for Statemented children, so we insisted that they should provide a Statement for him. The LEA educational psychologist, who was working on his case, suggested that he would benefit from attending a school with smaller class sizes and specializing in teaching pupils with dyslexia and Asperger's Syndrome. After visiting the school, he strongly recommended it and persuaded the LEA to fund a place for him.

When we first visited, we were very impressed. The buildings and school grounds were very impressive. The welcome we received from the staff was very warm and friendly. The accommodation comfortable. He also liked the place but was a bit apprehensive about being left on his own. I explained to him that if he stayed during the week I would take him home every weekend. This arrangement stood for about four weeks before he suddenly decided that he no longer wanted to come home at weekends as there were too many interesting activities, which took place at the weekend, that he wanted to join in.

He settled down well at the school and was happy with his teacher. She at least understood his problems and had strategies to help him overcome them. We were very apprehensive about leaving him at a boarding school – we both felt that we had in some way let him down. However, we came to terms with our worries, especially when we were no longer being contacted about every minor behavioural problem as the teachers and care staff took full responsibility and resolved the problems. We had regular weekly reports on his progress, which included his academic and behaviour progress. Later that academic year he said to his mother, 'Don't worry about sending me to Farleigh as it was the best thing that has happened to me, I really like it there.' This was a welcome relief to both of us and it vindicated our decision.

Following on from Farleigh College, he went to the local college but was still supported by Farleigh sixth form college. The sixth form college really helped him to establish his independence. He learnt about preparing a weekly budget, how to cook, wash his own clothes and how to live independently.

His success at the college enabled him to gain a place at university to study for a degree in Computer Games Development.

His independent living skill really came to the fore as he was in a self-catering hall of residence.

Overall he has benefited a lot from his time at Farleigh and we would recommend the school to any parents with children with Asperger's Syndrome.

Parent 9

1. What were life and education experiences like before coming to Farleigh?

As a baby he didn't require much sleep, he was always up and awake by 5.30ish. He would cry and cry and cry until he was fed and had my attention. I carried him around in one of those baby slings until he was far too big and heavy as that was the only thing that seemed to give him any comfort. Everything else seemed to be OK with him; he met some of his milestones early and continued to grow.

Although, I had known from a young age that he was not quite the same as other children. He ran around as if he were constantly on rocket fuel – no matter how long the walk or how far he would run, he never seemed to tire. Nor did he have any sense of coordination – it took forever to teach him how to ride a bike, he preferred a tricycle and played on that until he outgrew it. He also never saw hazards such as door frames and doors, he has had so many huge bumps to his head. I'm sure the GP and hospital thought I was a dreadful parent. He constantly dribbled and ran around on his toes. Life was one fast dash. Nevertheless, he was loving and I loved him as every mum loves her child.

2. How difficult was it to find a school and what battles did you have?

When he attended primary school he was thrilled and excited, he loved being with the other children. But this is when professionals became involved. The teaching staff were lovely and told me they had concerns over his behaviour. He couldn't colour within the lines of any pictures...ever, had difficulty sitting in one place for any amount of time, and so the list went on. They therefore referred him to an educational psychologist who diagnosed him with clumsy child syndrome and hyperactivity; later to become ADHD and dyspraxia. The school did all they could to help and left me to it.

Thankfully my parents were able to see what was happening and helped me move back closer to my family. My son was able to start a new school and I hoped for the same level of support as he'd been fortunate to access in his previous school. Sadly this was not the case, as the headmistress was very old school and would not accept that he had any learning issues. She didn't really want to have these people in to see him, or have it known that there were children with special needs at her school. So no real support was there; that is unless I wanted to place him in a special facility where there were children with Down's Syndrome and severe autism. It wasn't suitable at all, so I accepted the place in the local school and did the best I could at home…life seemed good. We did lots of simple play at home, cooking, drawing, trying to learn the times tables, with little success, but it didn't seem to matter. We were all safe and well.

One day I saw a cutting in a local paper about ADHD, and attended a talk. This is where it all fell into place and I knew that was him they were describing. I met a health visitor who supported us in seeing a paediatric specialist and he was prescribed Ritalin. This calmed him down no end and it was lovely to see him sit and colour in – actually to see him just sit was quite something. The down side to this was the emergence of other behaviours which were worrying, always locking the front door and checking it frequently, as well as other behaviours. During a routine visit to the hospital I had flagged up all the symptoms and after a few tests R was diagnosed with Asperger's Syndrome. I was upset and relieved, for now we could have him Statemented and hopefully access some real support.

He was now 12 and moving on to a Welsh comprehensive school in the village where we lived. I thought things would get better as it was local and he could make more friends. Wrong again! The bullying started again, things were wrought at home as he and his step-dad weren't getting on and he (my husband) suffered from severe depression and got very angry and frustrated with my son. This tore me apart to see them both very upset, but I did what I could to keep the harmony at home. As the bullying got worse it was decided to look at specialist provision, as the links with a support group had provided me with much information on this process, plus this would also be a safe haven for him away from a bullying environment.

The LEA didn't want this provision to go ahead so they offered him a placement in a specialist provision in a town about 25 miles away. We were invited to visit before we made our mind up. I was horrified and it has haunted me ever since. It was an institute of the very worst kind; like something out of the 1970s where youngsters were locked up in rooms, treated like animals and left to fend for themselves against carers who were nothing more than wardens and bullies. We saw and heard far too much to ever consider such a place.

Obviously I turned it down in favour of the local school, where they had a small unit for children with autism. This was not ideal as they had no idea of the learning style and support young people with AS needed, although they did reassure me the women working in the unit had degrees!! How lovely, shame they didn't have an idea of what AS was, as no degree of theirs was ever going to help my son learn.

Things went from bad to worse – he was once again bullied, had his rugby togs stolen, was called names and generally abused. This made him very unhappy and troublesome in school. It became so bad that on two separate occasions I caught him trying to hang himself in the bedroom with his dressing gown belt. He was often taken out of class for his poor behaviour and left to sit for hours outside the Headmaster's room and generally left unsupported.

I would be at the school every couple of weeks arguing a case for him to be in a specialist provision; but until I could give valid reasons why, it wasn't going to happen. I therefore looked for reasons to prove the school was unsuitable. So I found out that all children from this unit had to sit at separate tables from other school children, had to have separate breaks, earlier leaving times for school transport, and no formally qualified staff in AS, etc.

I then kept details of all the things that were going wrong and brought them up in a meeting of professionals and accused the school of apartheid-type behaviour to children with learning disabilities and proceeded to produce the evidence collated. They then accused me of not understanding as I was not qualified in any way to comment...this enraged me even more.

The final straw came when he was in a technology class and some one had a go at him, so he picked up a hammer and hit the guy over the head. That was the end of his placement, he was then home tutored.

During this time I was looking at out-of-county provision and looked at two main options.

I decided on Farleigh and decided to arrange a visit and brought my son along too. What a place...calm, friendly staff and pupils...JOY! We were reassured by the Headmaster that my son would get a good education and be very safe. Having a tour of the school and meeting the youngsters made a big difference as well as not being seen as some sort of dreadful parent.

This is where the next battle started…to get the placement.

So we applied for a placement, the LEA of course said no, so we asked for reasons why, it was of course down to funding. This wasn't going to stop me as I knew we could access funding from the Welsh Government. So we had to go to a tribunal, where the case was discussed. Fortunately, I had built a good relationship with Mr Bradshaw who attended to give a full overview of the school, the benefits to a child attending and how a youngster such as my son needs such support to progress into a well-adjusted adult.

This of course fell on deaf ears; the panel were so uncooperative and not really willing to take such an idea on board. Although they were meant to be impartial, this was never the case. I have never forgotten this day as it was one of the most awful days. This was due to the fact a professional said it would be better for him to be mad and bad at home rather than mad and bad out of county…this was the most devastating thing I had heard as my son was neither mad nor bad, and it was this contempt that drove me on to get the placement.

The whole panel were hostile and out to make out that we were the worst of parents. At one point I was also accused of having Munchausen by proxy, social workers were sent to my parents' house to investigate me, my son was also put on the 'at-risk register' (I didn't know this until some years later). Fortunately, I had made a good friend that took minutes during the panel hearing (much to their disgruntlement); this turned out to the best thing we ever did as I was able to use these minutes at an appeal hearing. You cannot usually have an appeal hearing unless you have a minimum of four points of law (I think that's what it was). After much reviewing and typing up, we had 12 points of law to appeal on, so we could take the LEA and the Tribunal to court. Great…or so we thought. This meant having to find a barrister. We had been using a specialist solicitor and we found a first class barrister who specialises in this field.

We were successful in our appeal and ended up going to the High Court in London. We did have to stand in front of the judge and tell him who we were and why we didn't have a social worker, and read a statement out from R, saying that he wanted to be happy in school and have friends just like other children and to have the opportunity to learn. I think I was in tears at this point and the judge believed in him and us as parents...so the case was successful and the placement granted. The good news is that this outcome has been used to place many other children at Farleigh and many other schools.

3. What was life like once they got to Farleigh?

We were all very excited and pleased at the outcome. However, I did get some very cruel comments, especially from one member of my family who said I was putting my son into care, and this hurt more than anything. I think the rest of my family felt the same but didn't say.

Anyway dates were set and my son packed. One thing happened that I didn't expect – C, my other son, packed too as he thought he was going with him and he too was very excited at going to a new school. C was devastated to find out he wasn't going; the two boys hadn't been apart before and this was very traumatic for C. This too was hard to overcome initially as C missed his brother very much.

Once he went off to Farleigh things settled at home, although I missed him immensely and worried every day as you hear so much about child abuse and I wasn't there to look after him anymore. I felt like an awful mum, sending him away.

He was thriving, though, and doing so well. He was coming home every other weekend, putting on weight and seemingly happy. He did say on a few occasions he was homesick, but this was to be expected.

During his time at school we built up a great relationship with the administrator at the school. She was my lifeline when I needed to speak to someone, or info had to come back to me. This was the best point of contact, and a lady whom I will never forget for her kindness.

In the early years things were great. I had good communication and I think I built up a bit of trust with the staff, although I don't think they were able to tell me all the things I wanted to hear – what he had been doing, how he was, all the things you take for granted when you see your child every day...I missed that. I missed out on some very important times of his life, and he missed out on a family life. Sadly, things weren't always good when he came home. People objected to him coming home so there were rows all the time. He was beginning to grow and realise he had a voice and the strength to have an opinion and he shared it. This made life grim again and he was encouraged to stay in school... again, that was me being a coward and not standing up for him.

What I did like was the fact he had other boys like himself to mix with, people who would understand him, he was safe, and had structure and the opportunity to do things he would never have at home.

What I didn't like was staff not understanding how much info I needed, missing him grow and not having as much input as a full-time mum would have.

The transition into independent travel was a real trauma for me...and the school. This was because I was terrified in case anything happened to him...and again I wasn't there to protect him. What if he got on the wrong train, off at the wrong stations or even worse...abducted!! I was manic and in hindsight I'm sure everything was well planned and risk assessed, but I was a completely neurotic mum and worried constantly. I think I was a nightmare. Of course nothing happened and he always arrived safely and happy.

Moving from Farleigh to North Hill House and sixth form college was a big move. I felt he was making the wrong decision in his choice of learning, but felt there was little support to guide him into other options...he chose childcare over computing!?? A decision I think he has regretted ever since. The decision I feel was made on the fact there were lots of girls on the course.

His second year was the right choice of computing as he realised that childcare wasn't for him after all. This is where things got really challenging for him as he wouldn't accept learning support and didn't get the grades he needed. I don't know what could have been done differently, I just know it didn't work well for him. Making it very obvious that he had some sort of learning difficulty made it hard for him to accept support when with his peers in class, and I know if he had accessed this it would have made a world of difference with his learning and the outcomes.

Life after Farleigh has been tough for him as he had to adjust to being part of the family again, no friends his age, no contact with the local environment for over five years, it was hard coming back. Some members of his family didn't like it and there was a constant row going on. The good thing is I couldn't take it any more and decided to divorce; my son came first, and about time too. His relationship with his brother was never the same either, they had grown apart, and this was one of the biggest regrets. In hindsight I would do things so very differently.

Going to Farleigh gave him so much but also denied him a family life.

He hasn't done too well since leaving Farleigh. He's managed to keep a job, but only just. He has worked as a carer in a couple of nursing homes, and now works as a carer in a centre for adults with brain injury. He hates it and wants to work somewhere else, such as in computing. He's obsessed with computers, phones and all sorts of technology. I wish we (me and Farleigh) could have been there to show him how to socialise more, make friends and how to self-regulate when on the computer. He still does spend days and days on the computer...jeopardising work and girlfriends.

He has no idea how to manage money and has had to be bailed out several times. I have now stopped helping him and he's now in £5,500 pounds worth of debt. He's in the process of dealing with this. He's now living independently in a flat, which he is managing, working one day a week and planning to join the Army. I think he's finally realised that things can be good when you take responsibility and apply yourself. He sees he has a future, a flat, a job and a lovely girlfriend. For the last few years we have been able to say 'I love you' at the end of phone calls and he is maturing into a fine young man. Would I change much, Oh yes. Can I, No. But that's OK, because he is a fine young man who's going to get there eventually, now he knows he can...and I will be there to support him. And he's not a spaz, gay or a twat...all the things the bullies and members of his family called him.

Parent 10

Our son was ten years old when he was diagnosed with AS. At the time this was quite young as most children were not getting a diagnosis till 13. Our son's words on hearing the diagnosis were, 'I am not stupid then, I have a reason to be like this.' Whilst he was pleased he had answers, we knew we needed to get him out of a mainstream environment and into a school that not only understood his needs, but could meet his academic ability too.

We knew primary school was a very frightening place for him and over a period of time it was having a severe effect on his mental health. According to his psychiatrist, going through the school gate was like giving him an electric shock every day!! He was bullied by both staff and pupils; we changed his school once and were told by the new Head she could cure him – that just showed us her lack of understanding of our son.

Our son became a 'school refuser' in Year 3 and it would take 2–3 adults to get him dressed and in the car. Thinking back I feel this was a form of abuse and we should have had some support from the LEA. This was an extremely upsetting time, not helped when his class teacher told me it was my fault he was like this. Eventually, due to truancy, the LEA sent in an educational welfare worker to take our son to school. (We knew this would not work but wanted them to see for themselves the problems we were experiencing.) She arrived at our house, took one look at him screaming and being violent and said, 'I cannot deal with THAT.' At this stage I gave up work and decided to home-school him, because even if I got him to school he ran away.

Being at home together was awful and not a positive experience for either of us. One of his obsessions was not being away from me, so I never got a break. His behaviour became more challenging and was having a major impact on all our lives, especially his two sisters. It was suggested to us that we look for a school with a 24 hour curriculum. This was not something we had considered as we did not want him to be away from home. However, for the sake of the girls and the fact that all the non-mainstream schools locally would not meet his academic ability, we decided it was in his best interest to research this area.

We knew we would need to get an Educational Statement, but having tried twice before, we knew this would not be easy. We initiated the process ourselves, which gave us more rights regarding the time limits. This was a very difficult and challenging time and was not good for my mental health. I spent all my free time in the library researching the Education Act. The LEA tried to block us at every turn; there was no support anywhere. Eventually we did get a Statement which needed a lot of changes to stop it being woolly. When it came to naming a school we knew we would have big problems as we wanted an out-of-county placement. Eventually we hired an educational lawyer to support us.

Whilst all this was happening we needed to find a school. We looked at one well-known school that was recommended by our paediatrician; however, this was not a suitable environment for our son as the children were more HFA than AS. We eventually found Farleigh College and, more importantly, Stephen. We loved the school and especially Stephen – for the first time we felt we had found someone who would understand our son. We also liked the fact that the school took dyslexic children as well as AS. We felt this was important as he would be mixing with pupils who have social skills as well as AS pupils. We thought the hardest part would be persuading him to leave home and go; however, as usual, he surprised us and said he 'wanted to go to a school that looked like a castle!'

Our son started Farleigh College in Sept 1998. The induction process was very good and he felt that he already knew some of the staff. He arrived with all the contents of his bedroom, as he was told he could bring anything he needed from home!! He was one of the youngest pupils and they did have reservations because of his challenging behaviour. His AS was very subtle a lot of the time and then when he got anxious and became aggressive staff often found him hard to understand. He took a while to settle and often asked to come home, which was very distressing for us.

The staff were very good at talking to him and teaching him negotiation skills (which he uses to his advantage today...thanks guys!!). If he wanted to run, due to the extensive grounds he was left to calm down in a safe environment. This was much better than trying to confront him. Our son became very close to a new member of staff and they learnt from each other. Without this person I do not think he would have settled so well. In his first year he made a friend, something he had never done before; they shared a room and became inseparable.

Academically two teachers had a really positive impact on our son. One was an English teacher who taught him that reading was not just words but that the words could tell a story. The first book he read and understood was *Lord of the Rings*. He now reads all the time. The second teacher was a photography teacher and he inspired our son in photography which he still enjoys today.

Academically he was extremely able and Farleigh built on this and gave him confidence in his own ability. He achieved a GCSE Grade A in Photography at the end of Year 8.

Farleigh was a progressive school and did not have silly health and safety policies. Whilst it was safe, the pupils were able to explore new opportunities. Our son learnt caving and this built on his self-esteem. He loved caving and still does as an adult. At the end of Year 8 everything changed as the school was moving to a new site. To us it was the end of the school we chose for our son.

After a term at Newbury our son asked to come home and try mainstream again. We agreed to this and he left Farleigh at the end of Year 9.

Year 10 was a disaster in mainstream and resulted in him having a nervous breakdown. I phoned the Head of Farleigh and asked if he could come back for Year 11 and he agreed. Farleigh was like an extended family and they always tried to do what was best for the child. Our son went back in January and thrived for two terms and took his GCSEs. It was a good six months and he was pleased to be back with people he knew and who cared about him. There was only one problem – one teacher who had been promoted still did not understand our complex son even after three years.

He went on to Farleigh sixth form college which in principle was great, but our son felt he had been boarding away from home most of his adolescent years and after one severe incident he decided to leave in the March. It was a sad end to what overall was a great experience for him which now he can appreciate.

He came home and did nothing for four years except gaming all night. He then had another nervous breakdown, quite severe this time, and we enlisted the support of the adult mental health services. This was nearly as hard as getting a Statement and again I spent a lot of my time in the library researching the Mental Health Act and the Disability Act. Eventually after a long fight we secured direct payment and were able to employ a PA to work with him. During this time we taught him to drive and he passed his test first time. Eventually he had CBT and this has had a major positive impact on his life.

He joined a fishing syndicate and met a guy who told him about a mainstream college near Winchester that does fishery courses. We went along and he got a place on a National Diploma in fisheries management. This required him to board again, but in a mainstream setting. Our son found the boarding easy as he had had the experience at Farleigh. He has excelled on this course and has made friends for the first time in a mainstream setting. After a year he was given a senior residency looking after 16–18-year-olds alongside his studies. We do not think he would have been able to do this if he had not been able to use his experiences from the great care he received at Farleigh College.

Our son passed his course with distinctions, and has found a career path that encompasses one of his AS interests. This interest in fishing comes from learning to fish at Old Farleigh on the lake in the grounds. Next year he starts a degree in aquaculture and hopes to secure a job at CEFAS (Centre for Environment, Fisheries and Aquaculture Science) when he has finished his degree.

Farleigh gave our son hopes and aspirations. It taught him that a disability should not stop you achieving what you want. Our son has very fond memories of Farleigh and we still talk and laugh about his experiences, both good and bad. Farleigh has given him and us life-long friends.

Thank God we found Farleigh and especially Stephen. Without our extended 'Farleigh family' our lives would have been very different. Our son would not be a functioning adult in a mainstream society; he probably would not be living at all.

Parent 11

My son was diagnosed at two years four months with a learning disability. At the age of three, he was diagnosed as being *not* autistic by a Child Psychiatrist. Neither of these diagnoses really seemed to fit the pattern of his difficulties and so I asked the GP for a referral to a specialist centre, where the assessment was significantly more comprehensive than either previous assessment. He was then diagnosed with autism.

At the time, I queried ADHD, because he had been markedly over-active since birth. However, I was told that the behaviours that I was reporting were the outcome of his autism and not a distinct condition. His activity levels and impulsivity – and just his sheer speed! – remained a real challenge. By the age of ten, they were adding significantly to the difficulties that arose from his autism and, in particular, contributing to real problems at school, so I sought a referral to a psychiatrist working in a local specialist service. As a result of their assessment he was trialled on Ritalin and has been taking it ever since. He has found it very helpful.

He was Statemented before he started nursery but we felt that the infant school options that he was offered were unsuitable, largely because of the large class sizes and his extreme distractibility and over-activity. He was accepted by a small private school, who accepted him on the basis that we employed and paid additional support for him every morning, which we did. He moved to a Church state primary school, and received additional support through his Statement. I don't think it was ever quite enough but the school had a real commitment to helping him and found ways to do so. I think they also genuinely liked him. Hearing the stories of others, I think we were extremely lucky to have found a school with such a kind and positive ethos. I wasn't working at the time and did as much as I could to 'back-fill' what they were doing for him through some unpaid classroom assistant work and other things. In his final year at primary school, the pressure increased and school became much harder. He was assessed by an educational psychologist from the LEA who recommended a special school.

I continued to look at local mainstream options. Although the SENCOs were very kind and willing to try to mainstream him, I didn't feel confident that they had fully taken on board the challenges and complexities of his particular pattern of skills and difficulties.

The local MLD school said that they could accommodate him and counselled against an ASC-specific school because they said he would not learn social skills from other children with ASCs. However, I did not feel confident that they could either challenge him to develop the skills that he clearly had or provide the sort of structured support that he needed to address his social difficulties.

Before he was diagnosed, life was terrifying, incomprehensible. There was no road map and no instruction manual. I felt that I must be doing something horribly wrong. Somehow, in the teeth of all that confusion, fear and guilt, you have to find the strength to seek answers and go on seeking them, however much people tell you that You Are Being Neurotic or They Just Need a Firm Hand.

He is our eldest. We just couldn't seem to get a toe-hold on normality. Some things that should have been easy were impossibly complicated – but other things, that we might have expected to be challenging, weren't. We couldn't make sense of it at all. And relatives couldn't accept that there was a real problem, their attitude being: if he can do all these complicated things, he is clearly just wilful and choosing not to do the other things – so, you need to make him. Dreadful!

Once we had that diagnosis, though, it was an enormous help, to know what we were dealing with – although I can't say that we took it in all at once and, back then, the information and resources for parents were more limited than they are now.

It also raised some fears. I was concerned that the label autism would overshadow all the things that he *could* do and that people would write him off. So, for a long time, I avoided naming it and, instead, described him as having 'a social communication disorder', which told people what was going on but avoided a label that I saw as wholly negative. In hindsight, I think that standpoint made life harder, in some ways. But, as I say, the whole cultural meaning of autism at that time was very different. I would like to think that it is now a diagnosis of inclusion and acceptance. Twenty years ago, I don't think it was.

One grandfather flatly refused to believe that there was anything wrong with him and kept asking when the speech and language therapist was going to teach him to speak! The other took the view that it was modern, new-fangled nonsense and that there was nothing wrong with him that proper discipline couldn't sort out! They were both very kind and well intentioned and I can laugh about it now – but, at the time, it didn't help much! The grandmothers were either more tactful or more understanding: not sure which!

We then found NHH. It was a long way from home and suggested by the educational psychologist more or less as a last option. From the moment that we set foot in the door, my son was treated with respect, compassion, appreciation and humour. I felt we had come home.

From the outset, it was evident that his difficulties were recognised and taken extremely seriously at NHH and that the staff had the knowledge base to understand them and to help him. But, at the same time, the senior staff had a wonderful lightness of touch and humour and seemed to celebrate the very particular world view of their AS pupils. There was a real feeling of warmth and respect in the school.

As a parent, it felt like there was a really good, working partnership with the school. The school staff gave regular feedback by phone and there was a weekly, written report. Each pupil had a tutor, usually a member of the care staff. I always felt able to ring up with any concerns but, in practice, rarely had to. He had two tutors over the seven years and both listened to my views, tried out my suggestions (if they agreed with them!) and reported back. I felt that I learnt an immense amount from them but also that they were perfectly willing to learn from me, too. The emotional impact for me of knowing that he was happy and cared for was enormous.

For him, all the building blocks were there that would help him learn. In the early days, the school day always began with exercise to lower emotional arousal levels. The classrooms were equipped to minimise distractions. The food was particularly good and healthy. The social relations of the boys were supported as much as possible. I remember being told that, initially, the bedrooms were all single, because it was assumed that they would find relationships difficult, but, when some boys wanted to share, partitions were taken down so that they could. However, difficulties arose in the sharing so, nothing daunted, the staff thought again and came up with the idea of having sliding doors between some rooms so that the incumbents could share space or opt for solitude on a daily – or even hourly – basis! Brilliant!

Looking back, I think his time out of the mainstream system, in a place where he felt safe and accepted, meant that he was relaxed enough to be able to absorb new learning: about himself and the social expectations of others, as much as about academic things. I had fought to keep him in mainstream up to secondary level, believing that he needed to have the example of neuro-typical children to learn from. In hindsight, I am not sure how much he is able to learn from that sort of observation. And the anxieties and stressors of being in a secondary mainstream setting that cannot realistically adapt much to the quirky needs of someone with an ASC would, I think, have generated anxiety at such a level as to inhibit what he was able to process and learn. I think we were extraordinarily lucky that he was placed at NHH.

Sometimes, when things are difficult for him, he asks if it is because of his ASC. At first, I feared that he might be upset if I said Yes. But, actually, that explanation seems to satisfy him and enable him to accept the particular difficulty. NHH gave him that vocabulary. But I also think it is important to make sure that conversations about difficulties also make reference to the very particular strengths of people with ASC, so that is what we do.

At the end of Year 11, with no obvious place for my son or his year group to progress on to, the school bought two adjacent houses and set them up as a sixth form, arranging for the pupils to attend the local FE college, with staff support. This was a huge relief.

However, the early days weren't good. The setting was very different and presented new challenges for the boys, who had much less space to get away from each other. Because there were fewer boys, the staff team on site was much smaller and I think the responsibilities of managing some quite challenging characters probably felt more onerous for them with fewer colleagues around to share thinking. The practical responsibilities were also different, in that the staff had to think about meals and laundry in an ordinary house, rather than being able to rely on the infrastructure of the school. Possibly, the idea was that the boys would become more autonomous in planning their leisure time but, in practice, it felt like there was insufficient structure and clarity. For the first time ever, I complained (about too many takeaways and not enough home cooked food) and felt I had to keep asking about activities and planning, because I could sense my son becoming anxious with too little to do. The FE college wasn't great, either – but I don't think that could be blamed on NHH, who did all they could to make it work.

But, throughout that period in the house, things got steadily better. And I remember all the staff involved with gratitude for their kindness and professionalism and perseverance. I don't think the difficulties were the fault of any one individual so much as systemic issues that arose out of a desire to be helpful without, perhaps, those driving the initiative having fully thought through how different the new model of working was going to prove for all concerned.

I think one of the best things that he has taken away from NHH is his insight into his ASC.

In the first five years at Farleigh, I honestly can't think of anything that could have been done differently. The regular exercise fell off a bit and that was a shame, so that's one thing that could have been improved, perhaps. But, otherwise, it was excellent.

The final two years weren't so good – and I feel unkind saying that because I think the school management were genuinely doing their best to help us and that some of the problems, that look so obvious now, would have been hard for anyone to predict in such a new venture.

It is imperative that the staff like people with ASC and understand that their role is to use their strengths to try and help them, with warmth and good humour. On no account must they interpret their role as one that involves a power struggle to make the person with ASC conform – not least, because they just won't win! People with ASC seem to be surprisingly astute in identifying people who like them and my experience has been that they respond best in those circumstances.

The support worker needs to have a good grasp of the logical, associative thinking style of the person with ASC. With that understanding, they will be able to recognise and appreciate the complete reasonableness of the person with ASC (mostly!) and not confuse extreme logical thinking with unreasonableness, manipulation or even psychosis. It also helps if they have good skills in planning and organising things, since people with ASC often don't.

They need good communication skills, including an understanding of the social communication style of people with ASC and an appreciation of how the support that they are given, and how it is given, can impact their comprehension and learning. In particular, they need to be able to be preternaturally thoughtful, calm, quiet and clear in circumstances that would normally lead to more spontaneous and combustible forms of emotional expression.

It helps if they can do some of the things that the person with ASC may struggle with, such as planning.

Since leaving Farleigh, surprisingly, life has been rather better than expected. I was very concerned about how he would fare in a generic LD setting and then (because he did so well) in a mainstream setting, albeit with support.

He says that he is happier now than he has ever been. Credit has to go to his current college for that but I also feel it has only been possible because we are still drawing on the learning and the confidence that he acquired at NHH.

This year has been more problematic than some others but he is now at a stage where the sorts of difficulties that have occurred provide a useful testing ground for strategies that will hopefully benefit him in later life. It is a bit chastening to realise that I didn't see some of them coming, when in hindsight they look quite obvious. But I think that is part of the business of parenting someone with ASC.

It's a bit like being the sweeper in a curling match: you dash on ahead, trying to keep everything as smooth as possible for them. But now and again you just don't manage it because, really, life isn't like that. At that point, it's important not to get sucked into the distress of the person with ASC; instead, your role becomes to help them to accept and tolerate the messy, unpredictable reality – using explanations, reassurance and endorsement.

The bottom line is that most people with ASC are utterly heroic and, along with all the other stuff that has to be said, it is important to let them know what they do right and how much they enhance our lives.

Since leaving Farleigh he has continued to grow and develop his interests. He plays for a local 'inclusive' football team. He has just joined the local gym, where they seem to be sympathetic to his AS and he is able to go on his own.

Every Friday, he goes with a paid carer to a local pub, where he meets up with other young men with developmental conditions and their PAs. He goes to a local AS club run by the NAS. He has maintained contact with three of his former primary school friends and invites one of them round to watch videos or play computer games every month or so.

He was given travel training by his local FE college and mastered the bus route quickly. There have been some social difficulties along the way but he generally manages well and we have developed strategies along the way to keep him safe and to help him to manage challenging situations (after the event, unfortunately!). He is beginning to venture further afield (albeit to familiar places) on the bus.

At home he likes cooking and is admirably systematic but needs someone around – or, at least, on the end of the phone – for urgent queries. There have been a few issues to do with him not seeing the bigger picture (e.g. he can be a bit rigid about cooking times, even if the food is underdone – or burnt to a crisp; he burnt out the frying pan three times before I realised that this was how he interpreted 'properly heated through'). He is developing skills in laundry and cleaning – but also dogged by the same literalness.

Information accompanying the responses to the questions sent by the parent:

I think one of the best things that NHH did for him was to give him an insight into his AS and enable him to accept it. We have been able to continue to build on that and, if he is finding something difficult, he often asks: 'Is this because of my AS?' If I say that it is, he seems content that there is a reason why some things are harder for him – and he is usually surprisingly accepting of it. I think it is also crucial, though, that we counterbalance that by talking as much about the things that he is good at 'because of his AS'. I try to frame it for him as a thinking style, rather than a deficit model. And there are plenty of things to praise!

He has had three good years at the local FE college, achieving a Grade C in Photography A2 last year. This year, we thought we would try something more vocational and he enrolled for a horticulture course. It all seemed promising because a local gardener also reckoned he could offer him some work experience. But, unexpectedly, there have been parts of the course that have been very, very difficult for him (knowing when paving flags are 'even enough'; understanding what it means when he is told to 'dig that bit'!). I should have seen it coming, shouldn't I?! And the work experience hasn't come through, either. So not such a great year. But I am resolved to try to sort things out for him in a more proactive and coherent way this New Year...

He plays in the same inclusive football team each Sunday, with one of the other students from NHH, so some old links persist!

CHAPTER 12

CONCLUSION

This book has been an attempt to explain the journey I and other staff took with young people with Asperger's Syndrome. I hope it highlights how passionate I feel about the plight of this particular group. It is not an explanation of what is the right way to work with this particular group, as there is no 'right' way. It is what we learnt on the way and has highlighted the things that didn't work as well as those that did work. It is true that at the beginning we were naïve, but we were willing to learn from our mistakes and wanted to 'get it right'. You never stop learning about a condition or syndrome and once you think that you know it all you realise how little you actually do know.

It is important to re-emphasise that it is an understanding of Asperger's Syndrome that is so important, and adopting an accepting and flexible culture that accepts the differences rather than having an education system that children must fit into. If professionals are willing to understand and adapt, then it will work.

The book has probably asked more questions than it has answered and it certainly does not explain everything. But if it has awoken or stimulated a desire to learn and understand more about the subject then it will have been a worthwhile project. There are many other areas that need to be explored: the co-morbidity with other difficulties, the transition from child to young person to adult, and the support that is offered for those different stages. Maybe another project will cover those areas.

There are many similarities between autism and Asperger's Syndrome: the levels of anxiety, the lack of understanding of the social rules, the inability to see another's point of view, a different cognitive style, a logical and orderly view, a desire for order and sameness in the world, a difficulty in communicational skills and an inability to form relationships easily. The main difference that one draws from working with these two distinct groups is that the individual with autism is happy with their own company and often develops strategies to cut out everything and everybody, building a virtual wall around themselves for protection against all invaders. The individual with Asperger's Syndrome, on the other hand, wants to be part of this social world we live in, wants to communicate with and relate to other people. They want to be a member of differing social groups and enjoy mainstream music, art and culture, but do not always have the skills and strategies to achieve those aims.

The main role of the school was to explain that if they really wanted to be part of society's social world then they had to learn the rules and play the game by those rules, not object or have a 'meltdown' when something changed or they didn't understand the rules. This often was a long and painful process but many achieved remarkable results and an admirable level of independence.

One of the main issues throughout the book has been that although there are different criteria for diagnosing Asperger's Syndrome, each individual will be unique. However, there are strands and characteristics that run through the majority of people with the Syndrome. This is where you should start when working with such students. The main one is probably anxiety, which may manifest itself in many ways and may be a result of not understanding the 'rules' or of something that has changed or of a feeling of injustice – whatever causes this it needs to be dealt with first, as nothing will be achieved without dealing with it and lowering the levels of anxiety. Obviously it is far better to avoid anything that would induce high levels of anxiety, and although it is possible to minimise this it is virtually impossible to avoid all anxiety-inducing situations. Life is just not the same every day; the unexpected does happen no matter how hard we plan. It is how we cope with the unexpected that allows us to live life without becoming too stressed.

There is the need for routine and sameness in all of us; we all have clear routines that we like to stick to every day. I, like most people, have a clear daily routine that I like to adhere to. I also have a colleague who makes his porridge for breakfast the night before and has to do this before he goes to bed. The difference is that if the routine is changed or something happens unexpectedly we can still function and the rest of the day will be all right. Although we may feel a little more anxious, it doesn't stop us functioning or make us go into 'meltdown' so that we cannot do anything. An individual with Asperger's Syndrome, however, may not be able to function at all as the level of anxiety will have become debilitating.

There are occasions when all of us behave in a similar way. If I change my routine when I go to watch my football team I feel I am then responsible for the poor performance of the team which I believe will inevitably follow.

Another strand that runs through Asperger's Syndrome is a difficulty with communication. This may be at many different levels, but is usually highlighted by an inability to read non-verbal cues or signals, which makes many social situations difficult. I discussed in Chapter 7 the importance of social frameworks and how to work within them. This will assist the individual with Asperger's Syndrome to try and make sense of this world we live in.

The final strand that I think runs through all individuals with Asperger's Syndrome is the varying difficulties with social interaction and the ability to form friendships. They seem to have a distinct lack of empathy, yet mean no harm. This often leads to them saying things that may be truthful but often cause offence without them meaning to. They lack the empathy to consider others' needs in any form of relationship, whether it is in the family, in school or in the wider world. This often will isolate them and create loneliness without them realising what they are doing wrong. It is important to teach these things and not criticise individuals for 'not getting it right'. Far too often I hear people using the word 'inappropriate' when describing someone's behaviour. What does 'inappropriate' mean, and inappropriate for whom? It is important that individuals with Asperger's Syndrome have explained to them in a non-critical way what is meant by 'inappropriate' behaviour or dress or speech, or they will never know.

It is important to remember that with guidance, support, coaching and good teaching there is nothing that an individual with Asperger's Syndrome cannot achieve. At its worst it is truly a 'curse' but it is also a 'gift' as Temple Grandin says:

> After all, the really social people did not invent the first stone spear. It was probably invented by an Aspie who chipped away at rocks while the other people socialized around the campfire.

Without autism traits we might still be living in caves. (Grandin 1996, p.57)

Hans Asperger stated:

This knowledge determines our attitude towards complicated individuals of this and other types. It also gives us the right and the duty to speak out for these children with the whole force of our personality. We believe that only the absolute dedicated and loving educator can achieve success with difficult individuals. (Asperger 1944, cited in Frith 1991, p.90)

The last word should be left to one of the students. This really encapsulates some part of everything:

In some ways the diagnosis Asperger's Syndrome was a blessing, but in other ways it is a curse. Because it makes you think there's nothing can be done to change any of the problems it causes. But this is wrong. No matter what the problem is I believe it is always possible to change, regardless of any diagnosis. (Student at Farleigh)

BIBLIOGRAPHY

Asperger, H. (1944) *Die Aunstisehen Psychopathen im Kindesalter (Autistic Psychopathy in Childhood)*. English translation in U. Frith (ed.) (1991) *Autism and Asperger's Syndrome*. Cambridge: Cambridge University Press.

Attwood, T. (1998) *Asperger's Syndrome*. London: Jessica Kingsley Publishers.

Baron-Cohen. S. (1989) 'Are autistic children behaviourists? An examination of their mental-physical and appearance-reality distinctions.' *Journal of Autism and Developmental Disorders 19*, 4, 579–600.

Baron-Cohen, S. (1993) *Autism: The Facts*. Oxford: Oxford University Press.

Baron Cohen, S. (1997) *Mindblindness: Essay on Autism and the Theory of Mind*. Cambridge, MA: MIT Press.

Baron-Cohen, S. (2011) *Zero Degrees of Empathy: A New Theory of Human Cruelty*. London: Allen Lane.

Bettelheim, B. (1967) *The Empty Fortress: Infantile Autism and the Birth of Self*. New York: Free Press.

Bilham, T. (2001) Department of Health. Bath: Bath University.

Bogdashina, O. (2003) *Sensory Perceptual Issues in Autism and Asperger Syndrome: Different Sensory Experiences, Different Perceptual Worlds*. London: Jessica Kingsley Publishers.

Cohen, S.L. and Payiatakis, D. (2002) 'E-Learning: Harnessing the Hype.' *Performance Improvement 41*, 2, 7–15.

Davis, L.J. (1997) 'The Encyclopaedia of Insanity – A Psychiatric Handbook Lists a Madness for Everyone' *Harpers Magazine*.

Deisinger, J.A., Burkhardt, S. and Wahlberg, Timothy J. (2012) *Autism Spectrum Disorders: Inclusive Community for the Twenty-First Century*. Milwaukee, WI: Information Age Publishing.

Delfos, A.F. (2005) *A Strange World: Autism, Asperger's Syndrome, and PDD-NOS: A Guide for Parents, Partners, Professional Careers, and People with ASDs*. London: Jessica Kingsley Publishers.

Ehlers, S., Gillberg, C. and Wing, L. (1999) 'A screening questionnaire for Asperger Syndrome and other high-functioning autism spectrum disorders in school age children.' *Journal of Autism and Developmental Disorders 29*, 2, 129–141.

Ehlers, S. and Gillberg, C. (1993) 'The epidemiology of Asperger's Syndrome – A total population study.' *Journal of the American Academy of Child and Adolescent Psychiatry 35*.

Eysenck, M. (1992) *Anxiety: The Cognitive Perspective; Essays in Cognitive Psychology*. Hove: Lawrence Erlbaum.

Frith, U. (ed.) (1991) *Autism and Asperger's Syndrome*. Cambridge: Cambridge University Press.

Gazella, K.A. (1994) 'Autism, journey out of darkness.' *Health Counselor Magazine 3*, 6, 34.

Ghaziuddin, M. and Butler, E. (1998) 'Clumsiness in Autism and Asperger syndrome: a further report.' *Journal of Intellectual Disability Research 42*, 1, 43–48.

Gillberg, C. (2002) *A Guide to Asperger Syndrome.* Cambridge: Cambridge University Press.

Gillberg, C. and Billstedt, E. (2000) 'Autism and Asperger syndrome: coexistence with other clinical disorders.' *Acta Psychiatrica Scandinavica 102*, 5, 321–330.

Grandin, T. (1992) *An Inside View of Autism.* New York: Plenum Press.

Grandin, T. (1996) *Thinking in Pictures and other reports from my life with Autism.* London: Vintage.

Gray, C. (1993) *The Original Social Story Book.* Arlington, TX: Future Horizons Publishing.

Haddon, M. (2003) *The Curious Incident of the Dog in the Night-Time.* London: Cape.

Happé, F. (1994) *Autism.* London: UCL Press.

Howlin, P. (2000) 'Assessment instruments for Asperger Syndrome.' *Child and Adolescent Mental Health 5*, 3, 120–129.

Howlin, P., Baron-Cohen, S. and Hadwin, J. (1999) *Teaching Children with Autism to Mind-Read: A Practical Guide for Parents and Teachers.* Chichester: Wiley.

Humphrey, N. (1976) 'The Social Function of the Intellect.' In P. Bateson and R. Hinde (eds) *Growing Points in Ethology.* Cambridge: Cambridge University Press, pp. 303–317.

Jordan, R. (1999) *Autistic Spectrum Disorders.* London: David Fulton.

Jordan, R. and Powell, S. (1995) *Understanding and Teaching Children with Autism.* Chichester: Wiley.

Kanner, L. (1943) 'Autistic disturbances of affective contact.' *Nerv. Child 2*, 2, 217–250.

Kimble, C., Hildreth, P. and Wright, P. (2001) 'Communities of Practice: Going Virtual.' In Malhotra, Y. (ed.), *Knowledge Management and Business Model Innovation.* Hershey (USA)/London (UK): Idea Group Publishing.

Lewis, N.J. and Orton, P. (2000) 'The five attributes of innovative e-learning.' *Training & Development 54*, 6, 47–51.

NAS Autism 99 Conference (1999) *Wing & Potter Prevalence of Asperger's Syndrome.* www.ncbi.nim.nih.gov/pubmed/12216059.

Newson, E. (1983) *Pathological Demand Avoidance syndrome: Diagnostic criteria and its relationship to autism and other developmental coding disorders.* Nottingham: PDA Contact Group Publishing.

Picoult, J. (2010) *House Rules.* New York: Atria.

Prior, M., Leekam, S., Ong, B., Eisenmajer, R., Wing, L., Gould, J. and Dowe, D. (1998) 'Are the subgroups within the Autistic Spectrum? A cluster analysis of a group of children with Autistic Spectrum Disorders.' *Journal of Child Psychology and Psychiatry and Allied Disciplines 39*, 6, 893–902.

Ramsay, J.R., Brodkin, E.S., Cohen, M.R., Listerud, J., Rostain, A.L., Ekman, E. (2005) '"Better strangers": Using the relationship in psychotherapy for adult patients with Asperger Syndrome.' *Psychotherapy, Theory, Research, Training 42*, 4, 483–493.

Rimland, B. (1964) *Infantile Autism: The Syndrome and its Implications for a Neural Theory of Behavior.* New York: Appleton-Century-Crofts.

Rogers, B. (2009) *How to Manage Children's Challenging Behaviour.* London: Sage Publications.

Ronson, J. (2011) *The Psychopath Test: A Journey Through the Madness Industry.* New York: Riverhead Books.

Rosenhan, D.L. (1973) 'On being sane in insane places.' *Science 179*, 250–258.

Salmon, G. (2002) *E-tivities: The Key to Active Online Learning*. London: Kogan Page.

Schopler, E., Mesibov, G.B., Kunce, L.J. (eds) (1998) *Asperger Syndrome or High-Functioning Autism?* New York: Plenum Press.

Shriver, L. (2010) *We need to talk about Kevin*. London: Serpent's Tail.

Smith Myles, B. and Southwick, J. (1999) *Asperger Syndrome*. Overland Park, KS: Autism Asperger Publishing Company.

Ssucharewa, G.E. (1926) 'Die Schizoiden Psychopathien im Kindesalter.' *Monatsschrift fur psychiatrie und neurologie*, 60.

Szatmari, P., Bryson, S.E., Boyle, M.H., Streiner, D.L. and Duku, E. (2003) 'Predictors of outcome among high functioning children with autism and Asperger syndrome.' *Journal of Child Psychology and Psychiatry and Allied Disciplines 44*, 4, 520–528.

The Special Education Needs and Disability Review (2010) www.ofsted.gov.uk.

Volkmar, F.R., Paul, R. Klin, A. and Cohen, D.J. (2005) *Handbook of Autism and Pervasive Developmental Disorders, Diagnosis*. New Jersey: John Wiley & Sons.

Wenger, E. (1998) *Communities of Practice. Learning Meaning and Identity*. Cambridge: Cambridge University Press.

Williams *et al.* (2008) American Psychological Association. www.apa.org/pub/magination

Williams, D. (1992) *Nobody Nowhere*. London: Jessica Kingsley Publishers.

Wing, L. (1981) 'Asperger's Syndrome: A clinical account.' *Psychol. Med. 11*, 1, 115–129.

Wing, L. (1996) *The Autistic Spectrum*. London: Constable.

Wing, L. and Gould, J. (1979) 'Severe impairments of social interaction and associated abnormalities in children: Epidemiology and classification.' *Journal of Autism and Developmental Disorders 9*, 1, 11–29.

Wolff, S. (1995) *Loners: The Life Path of Unusual Children*. London: Routledge.

Ziatas, K., Durkin, K. and Pratt, C. (1998) 'Belief term development in children with Autism, Asperger Syndrome, Specific Language Impairment, and normal development: Links to Theory of Mind development.' *Journal of Child Psychology and Psychiatry and Allied Disciplines 39*, 5, 755–763.

Websites

www.autism.org.uk

www.nas.org.uk The National Autistic Society website, go to page entitled 'What is Asperger Syndrome?'

www.who.int/classifications/apps/icd/icd10online/?gf80.htm+f840 World Health Organisation International Statistical Classification of Diseases and Related Health Problems (ICD-10)

http://cdc.gov/NCBDDD/Autism/overview_diagnostic_criteria.htm US National Centers for Disease Control

http://en.wikipedia.org/wiki/Hans_Asperger Biographic details of Hans Asperger

www.bestbehaviour.ca/briefhistory.htm Brief history of Autism

www.thegraycenter.org Carol Gray social stories

Glossary of Terms and Abbreviations

ABA — Applied Behavioural Analysis

ADD — Attention Deficit Disorder

ADHD — Attention Deficit Hyperactive Disorder

AS — Asperger's Syndrome

ASC — Autistic Spectrum Condition

ASD — Autistic Spectrum Disorder

BESD — Behavioural, Emotional and Social Difficulties

CBT — Cognitive Behavioural Therapy

DfE — Department for Education

DSM — Diagnostic Statistical Manual

EBD — Emotional and Behavioural Difficulty

FEFC — Further Education Funding Council

GP — General Practitioner (Doctor)

HFA — High Functioning autism

ICD — International Classification of Diseases

ICP — Individual Care Plan

IEP — Individual Education Plan

LA — Local Authority

LEA — Local Education Authority

LSC — Learning Skills Council

MLD — Moderate Learning Difficulties

MRI — Magnetic Resonance Imaging

NHS — National Health Service

OCD — Obsessive Compulsive Disorder

ODD	Oppositional Defiant Disorder
Ofsted	Office for Standards in Education
PAD	Pathological Avoidance Deficit
PCT	Primary Care Trust
PMLD	Profound and Multiple Learning Difficulties
PDD	Pervasive Development Disorder
PDD-NOS	Pervasive Development Disorder – Not Otherwise Specified
SEN	Special Educational Needs
SENCO	Special Educational Needs Coordinator
SLD	Severe Learning Difficulties
SpLD	Specific Learning Difficulties (dyslexia)
SSD	Social Services Department
SSRI	Selective Serotonin Reuptake Inhibitors
TEACCH	Treatment and Education of Autistic and Related Communication Handicapped Children
TS	Tourette's Syndrome
WHO	World Health Organisation
YPLA	Young Persons Learning Agency

Index